EMIGRATION FROM ITALY

Author and Publishers are
indebted to the trustees
of
THE TAIT FUND
for a contribution towards
the cost of publication

EMIGRATION FROM ITALY IN THE REPUBLICAN AGE OF ROME

by

A. J. N. WILSON

MANCHESTER UNIVERSITY PRESS
BARNES & NOBLE, INC., NEW YORK

First published
in the United States
1966
BARNES & NOBLE, INC.
105 Fifth Avenue, New York 3

Printed in Great Britain by Butler & Tanner Ltd, Frome and London

CONTENTS

MAPS

PREFACE

THE interest of various people has encouraged me in the composition of this book. They are salutary critics who recommend the writer 'male tornatos incudi reddere versus'; Professor A. H. M. Jones was generous of his time both in criticism of the work in draft and in positive advice. My hope is that it has profited to the full from discussion with him; the suspicion remains that, should he look at it again, 'mutanda notabit'. The advice of Professor F. W. Walbank was also helpful, and I much appreciate the ready assistance of several friends. T. J. Cadoux has answered questions with alacrity and precision; H. H. Huxley has given much time and care to purge the proofs of formal blemishes and inconsistencies; in cartographical matters W. Brice gladly answered calls for advice. My way towards publication was smoothed by Professors H. D. Westlake and W. H. Semple. There was much help with typing from Miss Joan Sutcliffe.

The main concern of the book, for reasons explained in the first pages, is with private emigration, not colonization by the state. The range of matters is, I trust, clear from the Contents and Introduction; but I may perhaps explain here what is excluded and why. Movement into Cisalpine Gaul has been omitted, as a subject which might better be treated in a study of migration and settlement within Italy and the part played by such movement in the unification of the peninsula. I have not gone on from the Republican period into the Principate, deterred by the prospect of difficulties, in some aspects of the subject, more severe than meet the student earlier. The eastern provinces only supplied adequate material for study of the provenance in Italy of the emigrants, and I have eschewed, here and in the West, retrospective argument from provincial inscriptions evidently belonging to the Principate; in too few cases can it be certain that a provincial family epigraphically attested in that period *must* go back to some emigrant of the Republican age. More splashes of colour can be introduced by the writer on provincial matters, if he draws eclectically on different ages. But I have refrained from using local colour from

ix

later times; a restraint that seems too severe when I consider the vigour of Dio Chrysostom's account of Phrygian Apamea in the bustle of the assizes, or the allusion of Pausanias to Patrae, where the young women make linen, have no rivals for beauty and charm, and outnumber the men by two to one. My documentation generally does not aim at absolute completeness, in the sense that it excludes scraps of material of marginal value. Whilst I have made it my normal practice to allude to the primary sources, I have been content to cite modern books or articles, where this enabled me to shorten the notes.

These will reveal my indebtedness to other scholars in particular matters. In a larger way, and more particularly as concerns the involvement of provincial Romans in the politics of the late Republic, it will be apparent that I have worked in the framework set by *The Roman Revolution* of Sir Ronald Syme; whether worthily, others will judge. In the half century from the arrival of Sertorius in Spain the western settlers played a considerable part in the marches, battles, and sieges of recurrent civil war; for these my guide was *The Roman Republic* of Rice Holmes, which treats clearly and fully the impact of the campaigns upon the regions where they were fought.

For the Eastern part of the Empire this work has a predecessor in the book published in 1919 by Jean Hatzfeld, *Les Trafiquants Italiens dans l'Orient Hellénique*; since I discuss this book later, here I need say only that its elegant French and imaginative touch made readable for me matters which, in another writer, I might have found unreadable. For the West no general study existed, but the student interested in the colonization of Caesar and Augustus had at his disposal *Die Kolonisation und Bürgerrechtspolitik* by Friederich Vittinghoff; my book, with its emphasis on private emigration, is complementary in theme to his.

The late Leo Teutsch travelled in Roman Africa, and *Das römische Städtewesen in Nordafrika* should be mentioned here, not only as a closely argued book, but because it enters (as I could not do) into considerable detail in local and topographical matters. In my treatment of Dalmatia I have not dealt very fully with such matters; they will receive elaborate and careful treatment in the study of the province to be published in Jugoslavia by J. J. Wilkes of the University of Birmingham. The work by Geza Alföldy, *Bevölkerung und Gesellschaft der römischen Provinz Dalmatien*, appeared too late for me to make use of it.

A. J. N. W.

1965

ABBREVIATIONS

A.J.A.	*American Journal of Archaeology*
A.J.P.	*American Journal of Philology*
A.M.	*Mitteilungen des deutschen archäologischen Instituts, Athenische Abteilung*
Ann. Ep.	*Année Epigraphique*
Appian	Appian, *Bella Civilia*
Appian *Mithridatica*	Appian, *Bella Mithridatica*
B. Afr.	*Liber incerti auctoris de Bello Africo*
B. Alex.	*Liber incerti auctoris de Bello Alexandrino*
B. Hisp.	*Liber incerti auctoris de Bello Hispaniensi*
B.H.	*Bulletin de Correspondance Hellénique*
Broughton	T. R. S. Broughton, *The Magistrates of the Roman Republic*
Bruns	*Fontes Iuris Romani Antiqui*, Ed. VII (C. G. Bruns)
B.S.A.	*Papers of the British School at Athens.*
Buckler and Robinson	W. H. Buckler and D. M. Robinson, *Sardis, Publications of the American Society for the Excavation of Sardis*, vol. VII
Caesar *B.C.*	Caesar, *Commentarii de Bello Civili*
Caesar *B.G.*	Caesar, *Commentarii de Bello Gallico*
C.I.G.	*Corpus Inscriptionum Graecarum*
C.I.L.	*Corpus Inscriptionum Latinarum*
Délos	Hatzfeld, 'Les Italiens résidant à Délos', *Bulletin de Correspondance Hellénique*, XXXVI (1912) 5 ff.
Durrbach	Durrbach, *Choix d'Inscriptions de Délos*
Ehrenberg and Jones	V. Ehrenberg and A. H. M. Jones, *Documents Illustrating the Reigns of Augustus and Tiberius*, second edition
Ephesos	*Forschungen in Ephesos* (inscriptions by R. Heberdey and J. Keil)
E.S.A.R.	*Economic Survey of Ancient Rome*, ed. Tenney Frank
F.G.H.	Jacoby, *Fragmente der griechischen Historiker*

xii

Gabba	E. Gabba, *Le Origini della Guerra Sociale*
Hatzfeld	J. Hatzfeld, *Les Trafiquants Italiens dans l'Orient Hellénique*
I.B.M.	*Ancient Greek Inscriptions in the British Museum* (C. T. Newton, E. L. Hicks, G. Hirschfeld)
I.G.	*Inscriptiones Graecae*
I.G.R.	*Inscriptiones Graecae ad Res Romanas pertinentes* (R. Cagnat)
I.L.S.	*Inscriptiones Latinae Selectae*
I. von Magn.	*Die Inschriften von Magnesia am Maeander* (O. Kern)
I. von P.	*Inschriften von Priene* (F. Hiller von Gaertringen)
I. von Perg.	*Inschriften von Pergamon* (M. Fränkel)
J.H.S.	*Journal of Hellenic Studies*
Jones	A. H. M. Jones, *The Cities of the Eastern Roman Provinces*
J.R.S.	*Journal of Roman Studies*
Laidlaw	W. A. Laidlaw, *A History of Delos*
Le Bas	Le Bas, Waddington, and Foucart, *Voyage Archéologique en Grèce et Asie Mineure.*
Livy *per.*	Livy, *periochae*
Magie	D. Magie, *Roman Rule in Asia Minor*
Milet	*Milet, Ergebnisse der Ausgrabungen und Untersuchungen seit dem Jahre 1899* (ed. Ch. Wiegand).
O.G.I.	*Orientis Graeci Inscriptiones Selectae* (W. Dittenberger)
Olympia	*Olympia: die Ergebnisse der von dem Deutschen Reich veranstalteten Ausgrabung* (E. Curtius and F. Adler)
P-W	*Real-Encyclopädie der classischen Altertumswissenschaft* (Pauly–Wissowa–Kroll)
R.E.G.	*Revue des études grecques*
Rostovzeff	M. Rostovzeff, *Social and Economic History of the Hellenistic World*

Rostovzeff *R.E.*	M. Rostovzeff, *Social and Economic History of the Roman Empire*
Roussel	P. Roussel, *Délos, Colonie Athénienne*
Sallust *Hist.*	Sallust, *Historiae* (ed. *Maurenbrecher*)
S.H.A.	*Scriptores Historiae Augustae*
S.I.G.	*Sylloge Inscriptionum Graecarum* (W. Dittenberger)
Smith	R. E. Smith, *Service in the Post-Marian Roman Army*
Syme	R. Syme, *The Roman Revolution*
Verrines	Cicero, *Verrine Orations*
Vittinghoff	F. Vittinghoff, *Die römische Kolonisation und Bürger rechtspolitik unter Caesar und Augustus*

UBICUNQUE VICIT ROMANUS HABITAT

Alios alia causa excivit domibus suis; illud utique mani-
festum est nihil eodem loco mansisse, quo genitum est. Cotidie
aliquid in magno orbe mutatur: nova urbium fundamenta
iaciuntur, nova gentium nomina, exstinctis prioribus aut in
accessionem validioris conversis, oriuntur.

Romanum imperium nempe auctorem exsulem respicit,
quem profugum, capta patria, exiguas reliquias trahentem,
necessitas et victoris metus longinqua quaerentem in Italiam
detulit. Hic deinde populus quot colonias in omnem provinciam
misit! Ubicunque vicit Romanus, habitat. Ad hanc commuta-
tionem locorum libentes nomina dabant et, relictis aris suis,
trans maria sequebatur colonos senex.

SENECA *ad Helviam* 7 (5 and 7)

CHAPTER I

INTRODUCTION

WRITING early in the reign of Claudius, the younger Seneca declared 'ubicunque vicit Romanus, habitat'. The claim, which concludes a swift and sweeping sketch of the great migrations about the Mediterranean, could have been uttered with justice already in the late Republican period; but the subject of settlement from Italy in the provinces is not treated, in a comprehensive historical way, in any surviving ancient work.

The subject has not been neglected by modern scholars, so far as concerns public colonization, the foundation by the state of chartered *coloniae civium Romanorum*; this has been studied both in its early role in Italy and as it was carried out later overseas.[1] Little colonization overseas took place before Caesar, but the few schemes that went through are discussed in the standard works, though more from the viewpoint of Italy and politics than as an aspect of settlement generally; the colonizing work of Caesar and of Augustus has been examined, most recently, in a very thorough and penetrating way, by Friederich Vittinghoff.[2] Yet movement to the provinces took other forms, which have not yet been included in a general review.[3] The survey here undertaken does not go beyond 30 B.C., and devotes more space to private settlement than to public colonization. Before the Dictatorship of Caesar, the few public colonists, together with settlers in the publicly organized, but not chartered communities,[4] had an importance beyond their numbers in the first

[1] Kornemann, *P-W* 'Coloniae', surveys Roman colonization both in its general characteristics and in detail, with documented lists of colonies by type and period; see this article 568 for the constitutional procedure for the foundation of a *colonia*. A. N. Sherwin-White in *The Roman Citizenship* gives thorough treatment to the importance of colonization in the political development of Rome, Italy, and the provinces.

[2] *Römische Kolonisation und Bürgerrechtspolitik unter Caesar und Augustus,* Akademie der Wissenschaften und der Literatur in Mainz, 1951.

[3] Only the eastern provinces are treated by J. Hatzfeld in *Les Trafiquants Italiens dans l'Orient Hellénique* (1919). For observations on this work see below chapter VII *ad init.*

[4] For this particular class of community see below chapter III.

stage of the Romanization of the West—and I have considered them in this light. On coming, however, to the Dictatorship of Caesar I have not resumed the work of Vittinghoff. Not only did I feel unable to add substantially, in this field, to his book, but the colonization of Caesar and the Triumviral period can be satisfactorily treated only if the writer also considers Augustus and his work in the establishment of *coloniae* and *municipia c. R.* in the Western provinces. This is partly because there is doubt, in the case of many colonies, between the claim of Caesar and that of Augustus to be the founder; more because a great new development can be properly seen only in a view embracing the early Principate. The groups of private settlers overseas, hitherto without recognized public status, and the indigenous communities within which they have sprung up, now tend more and more to be merged, sometimes through colonial foundations, often by the establishment of *municipia c. R.*, to form new chartered Roman cities;[1] a review of this subject extending only to the early years of Augustus' Principate would be purposeless.

People may emigrate to avoid starvation, to make a better living, to invest their capital to better advantage. Sometimes they are flying from persecution, indignity of life, or an atmosphere of despair. They may be seeking adventure, power, or glory. Motives such as these, which have taken millions in modern times from Europe to distant lands, existed for emigration from late Republican Italy. The conditions, therefore, obtaining in Italy, the evident attractions of many provinces, may appear irresistible circumstantial evidence for private emigration on a large scale.[2] But people do not always act as they seem to have motive to act. Here, since the persons involved are known, on the whole, only in a general and impersonal way, the circumstances of the age do not more than heighten the significance of the direct evidence, when it is assembled.

In the West we depend, since there are no substantial re-

---

[1] For this development see A. N. Sherwin-White, op. cit., 170 ff.

[2] The degree to which unemployment or underemployment is likely to have prevailed in rural Italy in the second and first centuries appears from convincing evidence set out by P. A. Brunt in 'The Army and the Land in the Roman Revolution', *J.R.S.* LII (1962) 69 ff. Brunt is not to be taken as thinking that the unemployed or underemployed often emigrated; in the first century, as he shows, and perhaps earlier many of them joined the legions.

mains from the cities to illuminate settlement, on some few inscriptions and numerous, but scattered, literary allusions. This material indicates, in a patchy way, the pattern of settlement. It suggests that many a provincial Roman family of the Augustan age may have been first established by a refugee from Italy, in earlier, more violent times, or by a soldier of some army driven from the country in civil war. In Spain, Africa, and Dalmatia it allows us to follow the fortunes of settlers and settlements when the struggles of the revolutionary period reached those provinces. But it provides only general information about their occupations and sources of income. There were bankers and moneylenders (*negotiatores*), traders, arable farmers, and graziers, and, in some number everywhere, representatives of the *societates publicanorum*, since these companies collected the *portoria* even in provinces where they did not collect the other taxes. But only in the case of the Romans in Sicily is there considerable detail about these various classes, and much of this relates only to the special circumstances of life under Verres. As for the part of economic motives in causing men, in the first place, to emigrate from Italy, little is said in the sources; the absence of such information could not be repaired by a general account of economic relations with the western Mediterranean lands (which would in any case be speculative) and I have not attempted such an account.

With the eastern lands the case is different. Early economic relations between Italy and those lands are not wholly obscure, and it seemed worthwhile, in my introduction to part II, to consider the bearing of these on settlement when it began in the second century. In other respects too the student of emigration eastwards is differently placed. The far more numerous inscriptions and useful literary material give a better picture of the pattern of settlement. Interesting details of the economic activities of the settlers emerge, and the story of their relations with the native communities can be followed, at least in the Anatolian provinces. But there is no indication of the effect on emigration of the upheavals in Italy, nor much of the part played by emigrants in the struggles fought out in the East. I shall confine myself, both in West and East, to matters for which there is some tangible evidence, alluding very briefly to those that permit speculation only.

Because less is known about the *negotiatores*, in the detail of
their activities, in the West than in the East, it is not to be
assumed that they were much less important in the western
provinces. The *negotiator*, who will appear frequently in these
pages, was clearly, as often as not, an independent banker-
moneylender, if 'moneylender-banker' is not more appropriate,
in respect of emphasis, for our period.[1] He might sometimes be a
financier, with wide-ranging activities, though perhaps few
negotiatores did business on the scale suggested to us by 'financier'.
Sometimes, when the business of an individual *negotiator* is unknown, he is simply the 'man of business' (for old fashioned
though that term is, it is better than 'business-man', with its
inappropriate ring); when, in a type of inscription common in
the provinces, the emigrants in a particular city pay honour, as
a body, to a patron or benefactor, designating themselves by
phrases such as 'Italici quei Argeis negotiantur', 'qui negotiantur' must indicate, comprehensively, men engaged in various
types of business. But in one passage of Cicero, where the context appears to define the word quite clearly, the *negotiatores* are
the traders in the province of Asia, and this usage, found again
in Sallust, became increasingly common, till, under the Principate 'negotiator(es)' is normal usage for 'trader(s)', with or
without indication of their particular branch of trade. In this
study, since the English terms 'man of business' and 'business-
man' are each, in a certain way, inconvenient, 'negotiator(es)'
will be used fairly often in its least specific sense.

Note: a comment on the word 'negotiator'

Since the observations of Ernesti ('de negotiatoribus Romanis'
in his *Opuscula Philologica et Critica* 3 f., and 'negotiator' in *Clavis
Ciceroniana = Opera Ciceronis* v.333 f.) it has been accepted that
the words 'negotiator', 'negotiari', 'negotium', were closely
associated, in the usage of Cicero, with banking as practised in
his age, when moneylending was important and very profitable,
but other sides of the business fairly rudimentary in their stage
of development. Ernesti brought the references in Cicero
together most thoroughly and discussed them acutely; but some
further observations may be offered here.

---

[1] For substantiating references for this whole paragraph see the note on
'negotiator' immediately below.

(1) There is no need to illustrate fully the use of 'negotiator', 'negotiari', 'negotium' by Cicero to convey moneylending operations, or the way in which these words are sometimes little more than euphemisms for 'faenerator', 'faenerari', 'faenus'; this sort of use is apparent in *ad Att.* vi.1.6, v.21.10, and *ad Fam.* xiii.56.

(2) In various passages, where Cicero has occasion to distinguish men by their occupations, the 'negotiator' is marked off from the 'mercator' (the trader buying from, or selling to, more or less distant places), though not in such a way as to suggest that the one could not, by definition, interest himself in the activity typical of the other (*pro Plancio* 64, *Verrines* ii.2.188 and ii.2.6, connecting the *mercator* explicitly with travel); in other passages the 'negotiator' and the 'publicanus' are distinguished (*pro Flacco* 38, *ad Q.f.*1.1.7).

(3) Those directing the *societates publicanorum* saw the profits possible through moneylending and banking, and the *societates* had money-lending and banking among their important operations, along with other activities not directly connected with their main business (see below chapter xi). The great *negotiator*, C. Rabirius Postumus, had shares in one or more *societates*, along with his other large interests (of which moneylending was the chief) and was, indeed, a full-blown financier (see Cicero *pro Rabirio Postumo* 4).

(4) It seems likely that moneylending was normally carried on in conjunction with banking as practised in Rome and by Romans and Italians overseas from the second century (see T. Frank, *E.S.A.R.*1.206 f., for banking at Rome, and below chapter viii for Italian/Roman bankers on Delos in the second century B.C.); thus the word 'negotiator' combines the fields separated by the words τραπεζίτης and δανειστής.

(5) Those who established themselves on Delos from Italy in the second century B.C., pursued various occupations; some traded in slaves, others in other commodities, and others again were banker-moneylenders (see below pp. 102 ff., 118 f.). It is clear that 'Italicei qui . . . negotiantur' (*C.I.L.* iii.7237) means all the various classes of *Italici* in business on the island; in the inscriptions from other parts of the East 'qui negotiantur' is applied to locally resident 'Italici'/'cives Romani' in the same comprehensive way (cf. *C.I.L.* iii.455 = 7160, from Mytilene, and iii.531, from Argos). The common description, in Greek

inscriptions, of local ʿΡωμαῖοι by the comprehensive term πραγματευομένοι confirms this.

(6) In Caesar and the Caesarian Corpus 'negotiator(es)' is used sometimes comprehensively (*B.Afr.* 36.2, 90.1, elucidated by *B.C.* II.36.1), sometimes vaguely (see Merguet *Lexicon zu den Sätzen Caesars und seiner Fortsetzer* s.v.), and perhaps the vague or comprehensive use of the word was already common earlier (Cicero *pro Fonteio* 46).

(7) But already in Cicero 'negotiatores' can signify, in a perticular context, 'traders and merchants' (see *ad Att.* II.16.4, with observations below p. 182); Sallust (*Jugurtha* 47.2.) uses the word for traders from Italy gathered at Vaga in Numidia at the time of the Jugurthine War. Perhaps common usage of the word was changing in the late Republic; for in the Principate 'negotiator(es)', in literary and epigraphic language, very commonly and perhaps usually, signifies 'trader(s)' or 'merchant(s)', with or without an adjective indicating the field of trade.

PART I

THE WEST

CHAPTER II

THE SCALE OF THE MOVEMENT

THE western evidence hardly extends beyond sporadic literary allusions to settlements and settlers. Epigraphic material survives from few of the places where the later stages of Romanization are documented by such material in abundance. But, since even in Italy private inscriptions of Republican date are rare, this epigraphic scarcity does not make it inconceivable that the scale of western settlement in the period was very considerable; and some of the literary material, properly considered, gives us, at the start, an idea of the magnitude of the movement.

We have in the East, what we do not have in the West, references to the total number of settlers in each of two regions early in the first century B.C.—and these figures suggest in what sort of terms it is reasonable to think about the West so far as number of settlers is concerned. In western Anatolia there were perhaps as many as eighty thousand settlers at the beginning of the century—men, women, and children, freemen and freedmen; if this figure—the traditional number of those killed by Mithridates in his victorious invasion of 88—is conceivably exaggerated, there is no reason to think it a wild multiplication of the truth.[1] At this same time there were perhaps twenty thousand settlers on Delos and the neighbouring islands.[2] Elsewhere, already before the end of the second century, there were small groups of immigrants scattered about Greece. Despite the massacres in 88 of the settlers in Anatolia and the traders on Delos, it seems likely that even more Romans settled in Asia after the final withdrawal of Mithridates; no decline of their numbers need be assumed in continental Greece and the neighbouring regions, and they begin to appear in new parts of the eastern Mediterranean. There is no ground for thinking that settlement was diverted from the East to the West in consequence of the Mithridatic wars. On the other hand, even were there less trace than exists of western settlers, it would be hard to

---

[1] See below p. 125 f.   [2] See below p. 101 f.

believe that these were insignificant in number or negligible in importance compared with the Romans in the East. The western provinces were not so very inferior in their attractions. Sicily, in the second century, despite the devastating wars of the previous era, had not lost its singular fertility; the Carthaginians had shown what wealth could be obtained in north Africa or from its ports; southern Gaul and southern and eastern Spain, where Punic or Greek business men and farmers had long been profitably at work, were far from being lands of primitive barbarism; Spain had the minerals in which Italy was poor. There is no bar to supposing that the western settlers, in the later second century and in the revolutionary age, came close to the eastern Romans in number and wide dispersion.

Turning to particular regions, we find more direct evidence for Spain, in and after the second century B.C. In 122 the Balearic islands were taken by Rome. 'Romans from Spain' were settled there by Q. Metellus Balearicus, who, as Strabo briefly states, εἰσήγαγε ἐποίκους τρισχιλίους τῶν ἐκ τῆς Ἰβηρίας Ῥωμαίων.[1] These men may have been mainly veterans discharged from Spanish service, with only a sprinkling of civilian immigrants. But the statement is sufficient evidence for a fairly large body of settlers in Spain by this period, since it cannot be supposed that the three thousand sent by Balearicus comprised the whole of the Roman/Italian population of Spain at the time.

But the best material bearing on numbers is from Spain in the middle of the first century; it relates to Romans resident there who fought against Caesar in the Pompeian army in Hispania Citerior in 49. The Pompeian generals had five legions, three belonging normally to Citerior, two to Ulterior: about twenty-five thousand men, if they were up to usual strength.[2] After the Pompeian defeat at Ilerda the survivors were allowed to choose, each man for himself, whether to march under orders with others to the boundary of Italy and there be discharged from service, or to receive discharge in Spain. About a third chose discharge in Spain. Some of these were men permanently settled and domiciled there, the others lived and had property

---

[1] Strabo 168.
[2] Caesar *B.C.* 1.39.1 (whence the restoration of the text in 38.1) and 1.83.1.

in one or other of the provinces, without being in law domiciled in Spain.[1] It is reasonable to suppose that among those killed in the fighting roughly a third likewise possessed some sort of base in Spain. The conclusion is that in a Pompeian army of some twenty-five thousand men about eight thousand had been recruited from Spanish cities, not brought to Spain from Italy. Some of these may have been raised from peregrine to citizen status before the war, or, conceivably, have been made citizens for form's sake on enlistment into the Pompeian army in the emergency of 50–49;[2] yet, in the circumstances of the age, it is fair to suppose that there was a considerable element drawn from immigrant or veteran families.[3]

Of the two legions kept in Ulterior by the Pompeian governor during the battle of Ilerda one was the 'vernacula legio'. This legion, as the name indicates, must have been composed chiefly of men born in the province, and, very probably, mainly of members of Roman provincial families, so that considerable addition may be made to the number of provincial Romans in the Spanish Pompeian armies, bringing it up, perhaps, to ten thousand.[4] That figure would still be far from the total of male residents. For those too old or too young for service must be added to the men of military age; and to those enlisted those who evaded conscription, either because they did not want to serve or because, at this stage, they did not want to serve on the Pompeian side.

In Narbonese Gaul, which did not become a province till the late second century, the multitude of settlers, already in the early first century, is attested by a well-known passage in Cicero. M. Fonteius, who governed Narbonensis for two years about 75 B.C. and squeezed it severely to get supplies needed by the

---

[1] Caesar *B.C.* 1.86.3, 'ei qui habeant domicilium aut possessionem in Hispania', with 87.4–5. The distinction between 'domicilium' and 'possessio' is pointed out by Smith 54.

[2] More provincials, as appears from Cicero *pro Balbo* 46 ff. (especially 50 f.), may have been given the citizenship individually in this period than are now known; and many of the soldiers of Afranius and Petreius may have been peregrine sons of legionaries by Spanish women. See the discussion in Smith 55 f.

[3] See below chapters IV and V, sections on Spain.

[4] For the 'vernacula legio' see Caesar *B.C.* II.20.4 (49 B.C.); *B. Alex.* 54.3; 53.5; and 57.1 (48 B.C.). The inference that it consisted largely of members of families settled in the province is from *B. Alex.* 53.5.

senatorial armies in Spain, was later accused of extortion and embezzlement by M. Plaetorius on behalf of Gallic chiefs. The prosecution alleged that Romans, as well as Gauls, had suffered. 'But', Cicero says for the defence, 'how is it that nothing is heard from the resident Romans, when they are so numerous?'

Referta Gallia negotiatorum est, plena civium Romanorum. Nemo Gallorum sine cive Romano quicquam negotii gerit, nummus in Gallia nullus sine civium Romanorum tabulis commovetur. . . . Unae tabulae proferantur, in quibus vestigium sit aliquod, quod significet pecuniam M. Fonteio datam, unum ex tanto negotiatorum, colonorum, publicanorum, aratorum, pecuariorum numero testem producant; vere accusatum esse concedam.[1]

The first two sentences are not to be taken literally; the rhetoric is obvious, nor can Romans have been living in every district of a region much of which was fit only for native peasants and shepherds. But the exaggeration would have been absurd, even before a sympathetic jury, had the Narbonensian Romans been confined to one or two places. It is reasonable to suppose that Romans were to be found, in the early first century B.C., not only in the capital and *colonia* Narbo (118 B.C.) and the unchartered military settlement of Aquae Sextiae (122 B.C.), but at Massilia and in most of the major towns of the province.

The known western settlements clearly belong to a greater number, not involved in events in a way of interest to ancient writers and so unmentioned. It is likewise clear, since Italians and Romans ventured well beyond the frontiers of the Empire for purposes of trade, that isolated settlers may have penetrated to places more out-of-the-way than those in which emigrants formed communities. But it is to these communities—'conventus civium Romanorum', as they are termed in speeches and writings of the revolutionary age—that most of the western material relates.

[1] *pro Fonteio* 11 f.

CHAPTER III

THE NATURE OF THE CONVENTUS CIVIUM ROMANORUM

WHEN circumstances produce a movement of private emigrants overseas, of the kind that took place in the late Republic, under no form of public guidance, and when lands relatively near offer the advantages of the homeland, without perhaps its disadvantages, the emigrants are not likely to look beyond these; it is hardly surprising that settlers are not found, in this period, further from the Mediterranean than the varying limit of its climatic influences. When the emigrants have had their homes, like most inhabitants of Italy, in towns or large villages (so that the farmers go out from these to work land or supervise its working), they are likely, on finding a similar pattern of life in the new land, to converge on the larger existing communities; negatively, at least, our material answers to this presumption, for if private settlers occasionally established themselves out in the countryside, there is one case only where this appears from the evidence.[1]

Not less naturally, if they have the Roman and Italian readiness for self-organization, they will form themselves locally into organized bodies, the better to confront their new neighbours, potentially, if not actually, hostile. In the East such bodies are mentioned once only before the Principate.[2] In the West they appear in the late Republic, first in Sicily in the *Verrines* of Cicero, then in Africa, Spain and Dalmatia, in

---

[1] Roman settlers seem to have lived for a time scattered in the district around Lissus in south Dalmatia (see below p. 17), but even these may have been in *townships*, smaller than Lissus. In 36 B.C. two Roman brothers appear in ownership of land in the country well out from Narona (central Dalmatian coast), but did not necessarily live there (see below p. 74 f).

[2] A passing allusion by Caesar *B.C.* III.32.6 to the exactions of Metellus Scipio in 48 from the *conventus* of Roman Asia generally. Inscriptions where local 'Italici' or Ῥωμαῖοι combine to honour a magistrate or one of their number are not sufficient evidence in themselves that the group had standing organization.

13

Caesar and the Caesarian *corpus*, and are described as 'conventus civium Romanorum'; some *conventus* may have existed from the second century B.C. The term 'conventus' suggests a gathering of people united by a common interest or characteristic, but not recognized as having public status; thus when the Senators were called together by Caesar in 49, they formed for Cicero, since the whole thing was unconstitutional, a mere 'conventus senatorum'.[1] Nothing suggests that the *conventus c. R.*, as they appear in the western provinces in the first century B.C., had public status, but literary and epigraphic material indicates that they had definite organization.

The traders from Italy resident at Cirta in Numidia at the outbreak of the Jugurthine war are not described in so many words as a *conventus c. R.*, but they held together as a body and were the backbone of the defence so long as the city held out against Jugurtha.[2] Later, during campaigns of the civil war of 49–45, the western *conventus* appear as sufficiently organized to take effective action in political or military emergency. In Hispania Ulterior, when Caesar advanced from his victory at Ilerda southwards, the *conventus* acted usefully to help him and against Varro, the Pompeian governor. Along the Dalmatian coast, in the next stage of the war and later, the *conventus* gave Caesar considerable aid in a way that indicates effective organization. In Africa in 46, the great *conventus* in the capital, Utica, gave most important support to the Pompeians—who were also helped by lesser *conventus*.[3] Though a few of these *conventus*, as will appear, were a-typical (in the manner of their formation), the *conventus* at Utica was typical of its class, and so, almost certainly, were most of the others.

Many *conventus* were no more than bodies, if sometimes very powerful bodies, within a provincial city. Such, strong though it appears to have been, was the *conventus* at Utica; the position was the same of the other *conventus* within the African cities in the fighting area of 46 (heavier fines were indeed imposed by Caesar in 46 on the *conventus* at Hadrumetum and Thapsus for aiding the Pompeians than on each city, but the *conventus*

---

[1] *ad Fam.* IV.I.I. Festus 29(41) defines one meaning of 'conventus' as 'multitudo ex compluribus generibus hominum contracta in unum locum'.

[2] Sallust *Jugurtha* 21.2 f., with 26.1; see also below p. 44.

[3] See below chapter V for Hispania Ulterior, Dalmatia, and Africa.

were perhaps the worse offenders[1]). Other *conventus* evidently achieved full control of the places in which they grew up; thus, at Salonae in Dalmatia, the *conventus* clearly 'was the place' at the outbreak of the civil war in 49, and the position seems to have been the same, by this time, at Hispalis in southern Spain.[2]

At Narona, south of Salonae, on the river Narenta close to its mouth, inscriptions attesting an organized Roman community, clearly a *conventus*, are probably to be dated about the period of the civil war. As is indicated by these inscriptions, the community had two *magistri* and two *quaestores*; these men were responsible for the walls of the town, and one of each pair was a freedman.[3] This suggests similar arrangements in other *conventus*; but no other relevant material exists for the Republican period, and inscriptions from the early Principate have little bearing, since the organization of social bodies of every kind tended to get changed in that period.[4]

Provincial Roman communities rather different, at least in origin, from those discussed were, on occasion, termed *conventus c. R.* This type of community was brought into being by an administrative act of state, but in such fashion that it was quite inferior in status to a *colonia c. R.*; a settlement, that is to say, was founded, without legislation, simply by decision of the representative of the state in the province. Its usual function was to provide for the future of time-expired troops already on the spot and to help the provincial garrison police and control the district;[5] it might be coupled with another foundation of the

[1] See below chapter v, section on Africa, for Utica and the other African *conventus*.

[2] For Salonae see below chapter v, section on Dalmatia; for Hispalis see chapter v, section on Spain.

[3] *C.I.L.* III.1820 = I²(2 fasc. 1).2291 = *I.L.S.* II(i).7166.

[4] The inscriptions adduced by Kornemann in *P-W* 'conventus' 1188 *ad fin.* ff. must be ruled out here, either on this score, as uncertain in date, or as merely attesting sacral *collegia* within settlements. Schulten in his very fully documented study *De Conventibus Civium Romanorum* is more conscious of the need to consider the periods separately, but not as rigorous in this as seems to me necessary; inscriptions relating to *collegia* are introduced which seem irrelevant.

[5] Provision for the future of the men: Appian *Iberica* 38 (foundation of Italica by Scipio in 206 B.C.). Military function: Strabo 180 (foundation of Aquae Sextiae in 122 north of Massilia in the land of the defeated Salluvii).

same kind not very far away, but it did not form part of any larger scheme of settlement, and lacked anything like the public dignity of the *colonia c. R.* To this class of foundation there belonged, in Spain, Italica (206 B.C., at Santiponce near Seville), Corduba (152 B.C., eighty miles further up the Baetis), Metellinum and Caecilius Vicus (founded on and north respectively of the Anas, in the Sertorian War), Palma and Pollentia (122 B.C., on Majorca); in southern Gaul, Aquae Sextiae (122 B.C., at Aix-en-Provence); on the Dalmatian coast, Lissus (*c.* 54 B.C., just within the present Albania).

Metellinum and Caecilius Vicus, Palma and Pollentia, and Aquae Sextiae will be noticed later;[1] Italica and Corduba call for brief notice here, with Lissus, which, though the settlers were civilian, belongs with the class by the manner of its foundation.

Italica, established by Scipio Africanus when he was about to leave Spain, as a place of settlement for his wounded,[2] took root satisfactorily; yet in 146 B.C. it was still only a *vicus*[3]—that is, it had no recognized status or chartered rights—and it appears to have remained in this position till it obtained municipal standing under Augustus.[4] Corduba received its first settlers through M. Claudius Marcellus, presumably when in 152/151 he concluded a short-lived peace with the Celtiberians;[5] his winter-quarters were there,[6] and the main body of settlers can only have been veterans, though 'picked natives' were included in the foundation.[7] Under what arrangements this was done is not known, but it is clear that the settlement did not receive colonial status; for in 49/48, when Corduba was the established provincial capital, the population are described as 'conventus Cordubae' by Caesar and by the *Bellum Alexandrinium.*[8] It is

---

In most other cases the function is clear from the date and the circumstances. 'Praesidium' has been taken to be the formal appellation for these settlements, but is not found for those attested.

[1] See the index s.v.   [2] Appian *Iberica* 38.

[3] *C.I.L.* ii.1119 = i²(2 fasc. 1).630. 'L. Mummius L. f. imp. dedit Corintho capta' (as restored).

[4] See below p. 38.

[5] Strabo 141 describes it as Μαρκέλλου κτίσμα, without specifying the Marcellus or the date; the truce, Polybius xxxv.2.

[6] Polybius xxxv.2.2.

[7] Strabo says only ᾤκησαν . . . ἐξ ἀρχῆς ῾Ρωμαίων τε καὶ τῶν ἐπιχωρίων ἄνδρες ἐπίλεκτοι.

[8] Caesar *B.C.* ii.19.3, with *B. Alex.* 58.4. It is impossible, given these references to Corduba as a *conventus*, to take as referring to 152/151 B.C.

not clear at what date subsequent to this Corduba became a *colonia c. R.*; the point here is that the community there in 49/48, because it lacked public status, is described by the same term as was used for the groups formed by private immigration; and that the importance and prosperity of the town had not availed, by the Dictatorship of Caesar, to secure it a publicly recognized position.

Lissus was an Illyrian township till about 54 B.C. Then Caesar, as governor of the province, handed it over to the local Romans (who had presumably been more scattered) and fortified it for them;[1] this implies that he made of them a compact community with some definite form of organization. Yet this community, when it appears in his account of the fighting of 49, is 'conventus civium Romanorum qui Lissum obtinebant', as the community at Salonae is 'conventus Salonis'.[2] Caesar, in concentrating the Romans at Lissus, may have had in mind to secure them from attack by the mountain Pirustae (whom he had occasion to check in 54[3]) or from hostile elements among the local natives—which protection would, in turn, assure him the help of the new community at Lissus in case of need;[4] he is unlikely to have been establishing a *forum* to be a market-centre and no more. That was presumably the intention when he established Forum Iulium (Fréjus) in southern Gaul, and when, much earlier, Domitius Ahenobarbus established the *Forum* known by his name in building his road through the region after the conquest. But it is not clear whether those *Fora* were primarily for immigrants or for natives, and thus they hardly belong to this study.[5]

As has been seen, the *conventus c. R.* was in some places a solid

Strabo's statement that the first *colonia* established in the province was there. The 'cohortes colonicae' of *B.C.* II.19.3 have no bearing here. In the first place, the passage suggests that they belonged, not to Corduba, but somewhere else; secondly, just as 'colonia' was used loosely on occasion in literature, so it may have been used, and 'colonicus' with it, in the language of Spain or other provincial regions, to refer to the kind of community discussed here. 'Quae colonicae *appellabantur*' confirms this (loc. cit.); there is comparable inaccuracy in the reference (*B. Alex.* 52.4) to a man of Italica as 'municeps'.

[1] Caesar *B.C.* III.29.1.   [2] Ibid. with III.9.2.   [3] Caesar *B.G.* v.1.5 f.
[4] Which did in fact arise in 49: *B.C.* III.29.1.
[5] Their origin is clear from their names, but nothing else is known about their foundation.

c

community such as could control its site and exact respect from local natives; but in many, perhaps most places, it was no more than a Roman community within a much larger native community. Since the *conventus c. R.* seems to have had no recognized place in the graded order of provincial communities, there seems no reason to introduce into our subject the 'oppidum civium Romanorum' of Pliny, as is done by the late Leo Teutsch in his closely reasoned and elaborately documented discussion of settlement and colonization in Africa.[1] That term first appears in the *Natural History* of the elder Pliny (published *c.* A.D. 80), in the geographical sections of which provincial communities are listed and classified by status. These lists present various difficulties, and it seems necessary to believe that Pliny, or whoever devilled for him in this part of the work, was dependent in large measure on an Augustan source.[2] If Pliny could allow his lists to depend on a source so out-of-date as Augustus, it is not inconceivable that his source was still earlier; but, in fact, to hold, as Teutsch does, that Pliny's source must belong to the Caesarian period creates more difficulties in Africa than it solves.[3] In general it seems a risky procedure to make one particular author the crucial source for a particular period, when his value can be maintained only by elaborate— and therefore highly vulnerable—argument.

[1] *Das römische Städtewesen in Nordafrika . . . von C. Gracchus bis zum Tode des Kaisers Augustus* 27 ff.
[2] See Detlefsen *Die Anordnung der geographischen Bücher des Plinius und ihre Quellen*, especially 26 ff.
[3] Utica appears in Pliny as 'Utica (oppidum) civium Romanorum' (*N.H.* v.24): as Teutsch sees it (57), because there was a *conventus* there under Caesar and this was listed as an *oppidum c. R.* in a Caesarian document. But why is there no mention of the much more important native community? Again, there were *conventus* within Hadrumetum and Thapsus; but these places are mentioned by Pliny only as *oppida libera* (*N.H.* v.25) and there is nothing about the *conventus c. R.*

CHAPTER IV

THE BEGINNINGS OF SETTLEMENT
IN THE SECOND CENTURY

SICILY

THE Oscan mercenaries—the famous Mamertini—who in 289 seized Messana on the Sicilian strait for their town and women of the place for their wives, do not belong to this study. This was an isolated exploit, and the first western settlers, in our sense, are the Romans and Italians who established themselves in Sicily and southern Spain at the end of the third century; in the earlier part of the second century there was already appreciable emigration to both regions.

The Greeks, when they first came to Sicily, had chosen places on or near the coast to establish their cities, and it is in these cities that Italians and Romans now begin to take up residence, in numbers by comparison minute. About half the island, its more western part, became provincial at the end of the first Punic war; the rest, Syracuse and her subject towns, in 211, when the city was taken by a Roman army after siege and storm. Immigrants into Syracuse or its territory appear in a passage of Livy relating to the years 211–205 B.C., the earliest in chronological reference of the three texts alluding to settlers in Sicily before 100 B.C.

Scipio Africanus, coming to the city in 205 for the invasion of Africa, found a local matter which he felt bound to set right. 'Graeci res', as Livy relates,[1]

a quibusdam Italici generis eadem vi, qua per bellum ceperant, retinentibus, concessas sibi ab senatu repetebant. Omnium primum ratus tueri publicam fidem, partim edicto, partim iudiciis etiam in pertinaces ad obtinendam iniuriam redditis, suas res Syracusanis restituit. Non ipsis tantum ea res sed omnibus Siciliae populis grata fuit eoque enixius ad bellum adiuverunt.

It is clear that it was civilians from Italy, not serving soldiers, who had to be called to book; the phrase 'quibusdam Italici

[1] xxix.1.16 f.

generis', the appeal, not to Scipio as commander, but to the Senate, Scipio's use first of an edict, then his resort, where this is not enough, to 'iudiciis . . . in pertinaces . . . redditis' show this. The guilty persons had been residents in or near Syracuse for some time, for they had acquired the property in 211, during the siege or the sack of the city; since Livy says 'quibusdam Italici generis', they were presumably mainly south Italians, but it is quite conceivable that Romans played some part in the business, lost in the tradition or ignored by Livy.

The 'Italicei', who honoured the provincial governor in 193 with a monument at Halaesa near the northern coast, were again presumably from southern Italy, though the use of 'Italicei' does not exclude Romans or Latins from the group.[1] They may well have been landed proprietors, since Halaesa does not appear as a commercial centre and many important landowners from Italy were residing in the eastern part of Sicily later in the second century; but the value of the inscription is to show that settlers had already reached beyond Syracuse and the eastern coast to a small town half way along the northern side of the island.

Diodorus Siculus, presumably writing from local tradition, mentions landowners from Italy, besides Sicilians, as responsible, by their treatment of their slaves, for the servile rising in 134 B.C. He calls them in one place Ἰταλιῶται,[2] elsewhere, however, Ἰταλικοί.[3] In Diodorus' time Ἰταλιώτης could mean specifically Italian-Greek,[4] whilst 'Italici'/Ἰταλικοί would normally be people of Italic origin, as distinct from Italiotes or Romans. But, since, in this connection, it is difficult to have two classes of immigrant landowner, he must be thinking of the landowners as simply coming from Italy, Romans not being necessarily excluded.

This scanty evidence hardly does more than bear out the

---

[1] *C.I.L.* 1².612 = *I.L.S.* 1.864, 'Italicei L. Cornelium Sc[ip]i[one]m honoris caussa'. L. Cornelius Scipio Asiaticus was praetor in Sicily in 193 (Livy xxxiv.54.2 with 55.6). The spelling 'Italicei' suggests an early date, though not necessarily as early as this; the usual attribution, then, seems likely, though not certain. V. M. Scramuzza, *E.S.A.R.* iii.336, speaks of this group as a 'trading association'; there is no evidence for this.

[2] xxxiv/xxxv.2.27.

[3] xxxiv/xxxv.2.27 and 32.

[4] Strabo 243: Cumae . . . πρεσβυτάτη τῶν τε Σικελικῶν καὶ τῶν Ἰταλιω-τίδων (πόλεων).

KEY:
LAND OVER 9000 FEET
3000-9000 FEET
LAND UNDER 3000 FEET

AETNA PLACES WHERE SETTLERS (OTHER THAN PUBLIC COLONISTS) ARE CERTAIN PRIOR TO 30 B.C. IN SICILY AND DALMATIA

0 — 100 MLS.

Athesis
Eridanus
IADER
ANCONA
SALONA
Tiber
ISSA
NARONA
Narona
LISSUS
Drilo
ROME
PRAENESTE
Liris
ANTIUM
TARRACINA
CAIETA
Volturnus
CAPUA
NOLA
CUMAE
NEAPOLIS
PUTEOLI
NUCERIA
BRUNDISIUM
TARENTUM
VELIA
HERACLEA
PETELIA
VIBO
MESSANA
PANORMUS
LOCRI EPIZEPHYRII
HALAESA
RHEGIUM
LILYBAEUM
TAUROMENIUM
AETNA
AGRIGENTUM
LEONTINI
SYRACUSE

Map 1. Sicily, Italy and Dalmatia

antecedent probabilities. It is clear, however, that the immigrants soon equalled the Siceliote landowners in social power, wealth, and pride. About that Diodorus is explicit and need not be doubted.

Hispania Citerior and Hispania Ulterior were established as provinces in 206 B.C., when the Carthaginian forces were driven from the land. Hispania Citerior then centred on the lower Ebro valley, but extended as a strip of territory from the Pyrenees to Carthago Nova and beyond on the south-eastern coast; Ulterior embraced most of the southern coastal region and the valley of the Baetis—the Guadalquivir. Both provinces —subject at first to dangerous revolts or invasions from unconquered territory—were still in the first century liable to raids or border wars, and their extension was piecemeal; but there is no evidence that settlement in the coastal regions or the great valleys was much retarded by the series of wars— motivated partly by the needs of defence, largely by individual Roman ambition—whereby the peninsula was conquered over a period of two centuries.[1] Ulterior has produced as good a view of settlement in the late Republican period as any other western province; from Citerior hardly any trace has survived of the presence of immigrants. It is not to be doubted that there was settlement in Citerior, perhaps as early as in Ulterior; but what follows will be mainly about the south of Spain.

Strabo, as has been noted, speaks of the dispatch of three thousand men of Roman/Italian extraction from Spain to the Balearics in 122 B.C.[2] This settlement, which established Palma and Pollentia as unchartered towns,[3] suggests that by this time the total number of Romans and Italians in Spain must have been much above that figure. The inference is confirmed by other information. Italica on the Baetis river, which had been

[1] The complicated wars which involved Ulterior are clearly described by R. Thouvenot, *Essai sur la Province Romaine de Bétique.* Viriathus' invasions in 147–141, which reached the southern coast, are well treated by Gundel in *P-W* 'Viriathus' 207 *ad fin.* ff. (see map on 209).

[2] Strabo 168.

[3] Palma and Pollentia appear in Pliny *N.H.* III.77 as *oppida c. R.* This rules out the possibility that they were founded as *coloniae* in 122 B.C.

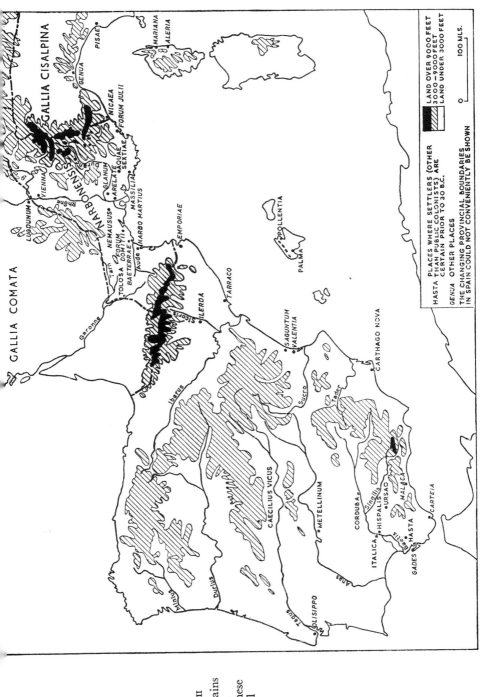

MAP II
The Spains
and
Narbonese
Gaul

GALLIA COMATA

GALLIA CISALPINA

PISAE

GENUA

MARIANA

ALERIA

NICAEA

FORUM JULII

AQUAE
SEXTIAE

GLANUM

ARELATE

VIENNA

LUGDUNUM

NEMAUSUS

NARBONENSIS

MASSILIA

FORUM
DOMITI

TOLOSA

NARBO MARTIUS

BAETERRE

Aude

Tarn

Garonne

EMPORIAE

POLLENTIA

TARRACO

PALMA

Sicoris

ILERDA

SAGUNTUM

VALENTIA

Iberus

Sucro

CARTHAGO NOVA

Tader

CAECILIUS VICUS

METELLINUM

CORDUBA

Singilis

URSAO

HISPALIS

MALACA

ITALICA

Gua...lis

HASTA

CARTEIA

GADES

Anas

Baetis

Durius

Minius

OLISIPPO

Tagus

PLACES WHERE SETTLERS (OTHER
THAN PUBLIC COLONISTS) ARE
CERTAIN PRIOR TO 30 B.C.

HASTA

GENUA OTHER PLACES

THE CHANGING PROVINCIAL BOUNDARIES
IN SPAIN COULD NOT CONVENIENTLY BE SHOWN

LAND OVER 9000 FEET
3000 – 9000 FEET
LAND UNDER 3000 FEET

0   100 MLS.

founded in 206 B.C. by Scipio Africanus as an unchartered settlement of ex-soldiers, was important enough by 146 B.C. to get a share in the spoils of Corinth, or their proceeds, from L. Mummius,[1] who had presumably stayed there in 153, in charge, as he was, of one of the long series of campaigns against the Lusitani of western Spain. In the year after Mummius' campaign Corduba, further up the Baetis, received what was probably a settlement of veterans—accompanied by chosen natives—after Claudius Marcellus had won successes against the Celtiberian peoples to the north and reached a short-lived settlement with them.[2] Meanwhile a host of private immigrants from Italy was pouring into southern Spain in a 'rush' after its metals, in which some made great fortunes; that term seems warranted (though the mineral wealth of Spain had long been known and exploited) by the consuming eagerness of the new-comers to get rich quick.[3]

The number of *hybridae*—sons of Romans by non-Roman women—in the early second century, and the position in Spain of these non-Roman children of Roman citizens, are also significant. In 171 four thousand *hybridae* sent representatives from Spain to the Senate, asking that they might be given a town for themselves to inhabit.[4] The Senate decided that they should have Carteia (close to Gibraltar) and the status of a Latin colony (and that existing Carteians, if they so wished, should belong to the colony). Such *hybridae*—if only because of their status in law—were clearly regarded in the province as a class by themselves, rather than as belonging with the Roman communities; hence their petition. On the other hand, they had fair influence collectively, as the success of their petition shows, and some substance individually, since a number had their own freed slaves as dependents; they were evidently not outcasts between the Roman and the Spanish world, the neglected off-spring of chance affairs, but rather the fairly prosperous sons of Roman soldiers (or veterans) who had been living in Spain in stable, if not legally recognized, unions with native women. Presumably, since Carteia was chosen for the settlement, these

---

[1] The foundation, Appian *Iberica* 38; Mummius, *C.I.L.* II.1119 = I²(2 fasc. 1).630.

[2] Strabo 141, with comments above p. 16.

[3] Diodorus v.36.3.

[4] Livy XLIII.3.1–4 is the only source for the foundation of Carteia.

families were mostly in Ulterior; as appears from the title given to the settlement at Carteia, 'colonia libertinorum', the women had been originally slaves, and had been freed, along with the children, so that the sons were *libertini*. Carteia is the only known colony founded in this way; but the number of *hybridae* in Spain must already have been considerable when the Carteian colonists, on their own, were a body four thousand strong.

From 184 there were always at least two legions in each Spanish province, and some troops were kept in Spain for long periods.[1] In the early second century soldiers in Spain agitated for return to Italy. But, as time went on, those who had acquired (as many obviously did) a new home in Spain and children by Spanish women or by wives from the new settlements, would naturally prefer to stay in Spain rather than return to an Italy the prospects offered by which they might find not particularly attractive.[2] Such men will have tended to establish themselves in the new Roman/Italian communities, so that these, whether or not veteran settlements in origin, acquired men of military experience, able to lead in emergency; such a man was C. Marcius of Italica, sent in 143 B.C. against Viriathus by the Roman commander in southern Spain, afraid to attack Viriathus himself.[3]

In this period both Spains were exposed to damaging raids and incursions, not altogether a thing of the past even in the middle first century B.C.[4] But it is still likely that settlement, in each province, was considerable in the second century, extending to places where no evidence now survives; for Italian and Roman communities grew up in other lands in conditions as or more difficult, and the troubled state of the country would hardly deter veterans who had endured long Spanish mountain wars—or the type of trader that ventured boldly into disturbed regions beyond the frontier of the Empire.

There is no epigraphic material certainly assignable to this period.[5] In the scarcity of evidence, it is something to know that

[1] See Smith 14 and 21.   [2] See above p. 2, n. 2

[3] Appian *Iberica* 66: ἄνδρα Ἴβηρα ἐκ πόλεως Ἰταλικῆς. At this date Marcius is more likely to have belonged to one of the Roman or Italian families of Italica than to have been a Spaniard raised to the citizenship.

[4] *B. Hisp.* 8.3.

[5] Some inscriptions of Carthago Nova, *C.I.L.* II(1)3408, 3433, 3434, 3439 (= *I.L.S.* II(2)8706), 3495 have been assigned to the second century B.C.;

Hadrian traced his paternal ancestry to the foundation of Italica and thence to Hadria in northern Italy.[1] The importance of the Aelii then is unknown, but there were not altogether insignificant Roman families in Spain in the late second century, members of which entered political life. Q. Varius, the author of the Varian commission of 91,[2] and the senator L. Fabius Hispaniensis, proscribed by Sulla in 81 for desertion in Spain to Sertorius,[3] now poorly documented figures, were probably born in one or other of the two provinces to immigrant parents. When Sertorius reached the country, the immigrant communities may not have been numerous or large; but a number had certainly struck firm roots.

It is clear enough in what fields the early settlers in Spain could make money: agriculture, especially in the fertile parts of the south and south-east, trade (since many of the coastal cities had a tradition of Mediterranean commerce), banking and moneylending[4] (perhaps from quite early days in the coastal cities), and exploitation of the mineral deposits in different parts of Ulterior. But no evidence shows the relative importance of these sources of income, and it is hardly to be inferred from Diodorus' reference to the early rush after the Spanish metals that prospectors and mining contractors were the most numerous among the settlers.[5] But at least there are Roman and Italian names to associate with this activity. In Hispania Citerior

---

but this is not certain. These inscriptions appear in *C.I.L.* I^2(2 fasc. 1) as 2269–71, 2397, and 2273. 3434 ($=I^2$.2271) appears to belong to about 70 B.C. (see Badian *Foreign Clientelae* 319, 'Pupii').

[1] *S.H.A. Hadrian* 1.1. Trajan also, on his father's side, had ancestors from Italica, but it is not known how far back he could trace his ancestry there. For genealogical detail in each case see R. Syme *Tacitus* 603 f.

[2] Varius was called 'Hispanus' by M. Aemilius Scaurus: Asconius ed. Clark 20 = p. 22 line 16. 'Hispanus' means strictly a Spaniard of native stock. Varius is unlikely to have been that, but rather Scaurus will have been 'smearing' him, making use of his birth in Spain to Roman parents domiciled there. Valerius Maximus' reference to him, VIII.6.4, 'Q.... Varius propter obscurum ius civitatis Hybrida cognominatus', suggests the same thing: enemies tried to prejudice his career by hinting slanderously that he had no right to the citizenship he claimed. See Gabba 85[3].

[3] Quaestor in 81 to the C. Annius whom Sulla sent against Sertorius (Broughton II.77), and deserted in Spain to Sertorius (Sallust *Hist.* III.83, Maurenbrecher). Spain was presumably his home, since his brief quaestorship would hardly explain the *cognomen*.

[4] The earliest evidence for moneylenders is Plutarch *Caesar* 12.2.

[5] v.36.3.

Carthago Nova was the economic centre and port for the important silver and lead mining district along the coast in its immediate neighbourhood, and ingots of lead of apparently early date found here are stamped with names of men who must have been lessees from the state of mines or connected with *societates publicanorum* engaged in mining.[1] According to Polybius, the mining area was extensive, employed forty thousand men, and produced twenty-five thousand *drachmae* daily for the Roman state;[2] it is clear enough that the mines, though owned by the state, were worked in his time mainly by *publicani*.[3] The director in chief of such a company need not have been permanently resident in the province, but a company exploiting mines would need Roman citizens (freemen or freedmen) in the senior positions on the spot, just as the *societates* collecting provincial taxes kept such men resident in the province for the most responsible work.[4]

[1] *E.S.A.R.* iii.139 *ad fin.* f. The *nomina* are Iuventius, Roscius, Ponticienus and Turvilius.

[2] Strabo 147 *ad fin.* f., reporting Polybius.

[3] At Sisapo (Almaden) north of Corduba a *societas publicanorum* conducted cinnabar mines under some arrangement with the state from the middle first century B.C., if not earlier: Cicero *Philippics* ii.48, with *C.I.L.* x.3964 = *I.L.S.* i.1875, and Pliny *N.H.* xxxiii.118 and 121. For the operation of mines in Paphlagonia by a *societas publicanorum* in Augustan times see Strabo 562.

[4] See below chapter x, section on the staff of the *societates* operating in the East.

CHAPTER V

THE SETTLERS IN THE AGE OF UPHEAVAL

(*c.* 130 B.C.–30 B.C.)

By 130 B.C. people from Italy had been settling for seventy years or more in Sicily and the two Spains. Settlement in Africa may have begun even before the destruction of Carthage and the establishment of the province in 146,[1] and certainly started soon after 146. These early settlers were almost unconscious, one may be sure, of the political life of Italy. But in the ascendancy of C. Gracchus and its aftermath they began to be affected by the politics of the capital: the issue of public colonization overseas, violently contested for years, could not but arouse, not merely colonists and prospective colonists, but other Romans abroad, especially in the provinces involved, Africa and Narbonensis. In the age of strife and upheavals which began with the Gracchi, the settlers overseas, growing in number, were increasingly caught up in the troubles of Italy. These troubles themselves are likely to have added to the number of provincial Romans. From the beginning, as has been contended, many of the soldiers sent to guard or extend western provinces ended up, if they survived their service, as settlers near the scenes of their military life; in the revolutionary age, when many armies went to the provinces for civil war, in pursuit of fellow Romans or in flight from them, veteran settlement probably became more important, since to the older type of veteran settler must be added the defeated survivors of civil war, afraid to return to Italy or, after a long absence, not attracted by return. Such people would probably have been glad, in the end, to forget politics and civil warfare; but such isolation was not allowed them by the great politicians of Rome, now busying themselves more and more to secure influence in the provinces, active in peace time to win supporters among the settlers, and, when it came to civil war, quick to use them for recruits, money and supplies.

[1] Appian *Punica* 92.

SPAIN

When Sertorius reached Spain in 83 he found at least the nucleus of the provincial Roman class that was flourishing there at the opening of the civil war of 49–45 B.C. The Sertorian movement plunged the Spanish Romans into embroilment in Roman political affairs. In three wars fighting in Spain involved, not only armies from Italy, but troops raised from the provincial Roman communities and from the Roman exiles and refugees. All this, since some refugees and disbanded soldiers must have survived war and stayed on in Spain, certainly added to the Roman population of the land.

In 88, when Sulla secured his temporary victory at Rome, M. Iunius Brutus, the Marian, took refuge in Spain and others with him;[1] but this group of exiles was apparently insignificant. In 83, however, Sertorius, dispatched to take charge of Citerior for the Marian government, led with him a larger force of men, presumably the army, or part of the army, which he had raised earlier in the year in pro-Marian Etruria.[2] Roman residents in Spain joined this force before he was driven out in 81.[3] When in 80 he recovered his foothold, he had two thousand six hundred men, probably in the main exiles, emigrants, or veterans,[4] the core of the Roman and Iberian army he soon created.

The Marian troops and exiles that left Italy later, in the defeat of the cause, are mentioned only incidentally by the ancient authors, who hardly attempt to bridge together the history of Italy and Spain. But their picture of the *Sullanum regnum* suggests that the exodus must have been on a great scale; what is known about Sertorius and Spain indicates that it must have been chiefly in that direction. Some people reached exile even from Samnium, where Sulla enslaved or massacred entire communities;[5] the punishment of the recalcitrant cities in

[1] Appian 1.60(271), with Granius Licinianus p. 16 (Teubner).
[2] Appian 1.108(506), with Exsuperantius 7 f. Exsuperantius here is thought to be based on Sallust: see 'Exsuperantius', *P-W* vi. 1695(2). A. Schulten, *Sertorius* 38 ff., illuminates the evidence for Sertorius in 83 B.C.
[3] Plutarch *Sertorius* 6.9.
[4] Plutarch *Sertorius* 12.2 says 'whom he called Romans'. Perhaps they were partly Italians, whose claim to the citizenship Sulla rejected, but Sertorius asserted.
[5] Strabo 249 *ad fin.*: προγραφὰς ποιούμενος οὐκ ἐπαύσατο πρὶν ἢ πάντας τοὺς ἐν ὀνόματι Σαυνιτῶν διέφθειρεν ἢ ἐκ τῆς Ἰταλίας ἐξέβαλεν.

Etruria and Campania by fines, disenfranchisement, or confiscation of land, left multitudes with their lives, but a dismal future at home;[1] among the enemies of Sulla individually proscribed many escaped the country, senators among them.[2]

Such senators, when they reached Spain, headed the council of three hundred—proclaimed as the true Senate—which supplied the magistrates and commanders of Sertorius' state.[3] The junior officers and soldiers of the Roman-Italian core of his army may be presumed to have come from devastated southern Italy or from those cities which lost land for Sullan veterans in Campania and Etruria. Etrurians joined Lepidus in 78;[4] after the defeat of this rising a large body of men followed him to Sardinia, and, when he died there, went under the Etrurian Perperna to Spain, where they joined Sertorius.[5]

Names typical of Etruria appear prominently in the higher entourage of Sertorius and of Perperna.[6] These confirm obvious presumptions about the movement and suggest a background for the settlers with such names caught up in events of 49–45 B.C. in Spain;[7] but it would be absurd to conclude, from this sort of evidence, that there was a microcosm of the Etrurian region anywhere in Spain.

Some of the settlers in Spain were perhaps hostile to Sertorius when he first reached the country. When Crassus, as a young optimate, escaped in 86/85 to Hispania Ulterior (where he had served in the time of his father's governorship) he found his friends, in a province under Marian control, cautiously unhelpful, and had soon to hide himself; but in this plight, he was succoured by a Vibius Paciaecus, a rich landowner on the southern coast—eventually emerging, on the report of Cinna's death, to start a revolt with a small local force. Crassus soon abandoned Spain for what seemed a more promising venture in

---

[1] Sulla's treatment of cities: Appian 1.96(447–9); 100 *ad fin.* (470); 104 *ad fin.* (489); with Fröhlich 'Cornelius Sulla', *P-W* iv.1555, for a summary of the other evidence. Cf. the list of Sullan colonies in Italy in Kornemann 'Coloniae', *P-W* iv.522 (β) f.

[2] Plutarch *Sertorius* 22.5.   [3] Ibid., and Appian 1.108(507).

[4] The rising in Etruria: Sallust *Hist.* 1.65–69; Licinianus p. 34 (Teubner); Florus ii.11.5–8 (iii.23).

[5] Plutarch *Sertorius* 15, with Appian 1.107 *ad fin.* (504); for other evidence, F. Münzer 'M. Perperna' (6), *P-W* xix(i).898 f.

[6] Gabba 96 *ad fin.* f. Gabba perhaps extracts too much from the material here assembled.   [7] Gabba 88 f.

the province of Africa, but Vibius Paciaecus later fought with the anti-Sertorian forces in Spain, till he was killed in 80. The story of Crassus and Paciaecus is made absorbing by Plutarch's skill; which is not to say that it is more than a slight shred of evidence for the Romans in the south and their sympathies.[1]

Nor does the control established by the senatorial forces fairly early in the Sertorian war over certain parts of the south prove strong support from the local Romans. Caecilius Metellus, the senatorial commander, was glorified by poets of Romano-Spanish Corduba, and rejoiced in praises 'pingue quiddam' (as Cicero puts it) 'sonantibus atque peregrinum';[2] but his officers are more likely to have been amused by this example of his intense love of flattery than satisfied of the loyalty of the Cordubenses.[3] Veteran settlements were established by Metellus in districts hitherto purely native, the middle valley of the Anas and the mountain region north of the middle Tagus.[4] These did

[1] The episode as a whole, Plutarch *Crassus* 4–6.2. Plutarch does not identify the troops which Crassus raised as native or Roman, or make it clear why Crassus soon abandoned Spain for Africa. But the account is full of picturesque detail, derived from Fenestella, who had it from one involved in the episode. Paciaecus sent two good-looking slave-girls to Crassus to minister to his comfort and pleasure in his place of hiding, and to communicate with himself; Fenestella had often heard one of them, in her old age, telling the story (διεξιούσης προθυμῶς, 5.6). Vibius' *cognomen*, as given in *Crassus* 4.2 and *Sertorius* 9.4, seems corrupt and Münzer (*P-W* XVIII(2)2061 f.) argues convincingly for 'Paciaecus'. That name would probably be Oscan. For this man in 80, Plutarch *Sertorius* 9.4.

[2] Cicero *pro Archia* 26. If there really was something very 'pingue . . . atque peregrinum' about the verses of the Corduban writers, the native Spanish element in the city (Strabo 141) might have something to do with it. But there is nothing Spanish or in any obvious way provincial about the Latin of the literary family of Corduba, the Annaei. Annaeus Seneca the Elder (*c.* 55 B.C.–*c.* 37 A.D.), the younger Seneca, and Lucan were all born in Corduba; but each came to Rome in early life.

[3] Gabba 93 f. treats Cicero *pro Archia* 26 as evidence of willing support for Metellus in Corduba. But it was prudence to flatter Metellus, who loved to be treated as a demi-god (Sallust *Hist.* II.70, with Plutarch *Sertorius* 22.2 f.). Nor is the local fortune of war always a safe pointer to local feeling.

[4] The settlement on the Anas appears in Ptolemaeus II.5.8 as Καικιλία Γεμέλλινον ἢ Μετέλλινα, in *Itinerarium Antonini* 416.2 as *Metellinum*, and in Pliny *N.H.* IV.117 as '(colonia) Metellinensis'. It looks as if 'Metellinum' ('praesidium Metellinum') was the original name, and colonial status was granted later, the change being reflected in the confusion of genders in Ptolemaeus; see M. I. Henderson, *J.R.S.* XXXII (1942) 7[30]. The other settlement to be attributed to Metellus is Caecilius Vicus, *Itinerarium Antonini* 434.1, where, as Schulten *Sertorius* 67[338] points out, this name is certainly to be restored for 'caelio nicco'.

not have colonial status, and it is not known what influence they gave him and his family in the region.

In any case Spain, native and Roman, soon came to look more to Pompeius, who arrived in 76, charged to press the war to a final conclusion. It was no doubt during the war that he began—in the south and where he won victories—to found his Spanish *clientelae*.[1] At the end of the war the settlement of affairs in Citerior became his task, and here he secured greater influence still. An amnesty was granted to those Roman Sertorians who made full surrender, and they were allowed, if they so chose, to return to Italy, at once or after an interval.[2] But Pompeius took a personal attitude to his defeated enemies, making it quite clear that their best hope for the future lay in becoming his *clientes*,[3] and his later influence in Citerior must have been largely based on Roman survivors of Sertorius' armies who saw their future in Italy as uncertain, and preferred to stay in the land of their long exile, under his protection;[4] some of his own soldiers may also have been encouraged by him to settle in Spain, either as colonists (since Valentia seems almost certainly a Pompeian colony of these years[5]) or in settlements of lower status.

Pompeius' *clientelae* in Ulterior—not so strong as in Citerior— were soon put to the test by Caesar, first during his quaestorship of 68, then when he went as propraetor in 61 and also during his consulship in 59.[6] The record of the benefits he conferred in the province does not mention Roman residents, though in 59 he may have offered positions in his army to men from Spain.[7] But the politician who attended, amid the preoccupations of his proconsulate, to the interests of the small

[1] Balbus of Gades received the citizenship through Pompeius, though he took his *nomen* from Cornelius Lentulus, consul in 72: see Cicero *pro Balbo* 6. Pompeius had some Spanish connections even before his arrival in Spain in 76; in 81 he granted citizenship to Hasdrubal of Gades and men of Saguntum (the Fabii) for their services in the campaign in Africa (Cicero *pro Balbo* 51).

[2] *Verrines* II.5.151 f. There was a separate amnesty for the *Lepidani* under the *Lex Plautia*, Suetonius *Divus Iulius* 5.

[3] *Verrines* II.5.153.

[4] The strength of Pompeius' influence in Citerior: Caesar *B.C.* II.18.7, with I.61.3.

[5] See 'The colonization of Valentia', at the end of this section.

[6] *B. Hisp.* 42; Plutarch *Caesar* 12; Cicero *pro Balbo* 43.

[7] Caesar *B.G.* V.27.1, Q. Iunius 'ex Hispania quidam'.

Roman *conventus* on the Dalmatian coast,[1] will not have neglected to cultivate the Romans of a far more important province; and the enthusiastic attitude towards him in 49 of the Spanish Romans (even if exaggerated in the *Bellum Civile*) indicates that he had done so in a very successful way. How deliberate he could be in such matters is seen in his dealings with a son of southern Spain; but the career of the famous Balbus shows a native and his community rising through the relationship more rapidly and impressively than any provincial Roman.

Balbus, born a citizen of Punic Gades and presumably Punic in descent, got Roman citizenship in 72, through Pompeius, for services against Sertorius.[2] It is not clear whether or not Caesar met him in his quaestorship in Spain in 68. But Balbus was Caesar's *praefectus fabrum* in 61/60 for the Spanish campaign, and Gades received important benefits through his influence with Caesar.[3] When Caesar left Spain, Balbus went with him to Italy, brought Pompeius and him together, and gradually grew closer and closer to Caesar. In 56, when Balbus' citizenship was impugned in the Roman courts, the leading Gaditani (whom Caesar continued to cultivate) showed their loyalty to both men by appearing for the defence.[4] Then in 49, while Balbus in Italy was using his ostensible neutrality to help Caesar, the Gaditani, as soon as they heard of Caesar moving south after Ilerda, revolted against Varro, made the Pompeian garrison do the same, expelled its commander, and took over for Caesar.[5] Soon, with Caesar victorious everywhere in southern Spain, they were declared Romans, and Gades became the first *municipium c. R.* outside Italy.[6]

---

[1] See below, the section on Dalmatia.

[2] Cicero *pro Balbo* 6 etc.

[3] *pro Balbo* 43: 'quis est enim nostrum cui non illa civitas sit huius studio, cura, diligentia commendatior? Omitto quantis ornamentis populum istum C. Caesar, cum esset in Hispania praetor, adfecerit, controversias sedarit, iura ipsorum permissu statuerit, inveteratam quandam barbariam ex Gaditanorum moribus disciplinaque delerit, summa in eam civitatem huius rogatu studia et beneficia contulerit.'

[4] They were sensible not only of past benefits, but of those 'quae cotidie labore huius et studio aut omnino aut certe facilius consequantur' (*pro Balbo* 43).

[5] Caesar *B.C.* II.20.1–4. The Gaditani took as signal Caesar's proclamation (19.1) calling the chief citizens of each community to meet him at Corduba on an appointed day.

[6] Livy *per.* CX; Dio XLI.24.1.

Gades was a commercial centre of the first importance. Like Utica, it had an old pro-Roman tradition, with allied status since the second Punic war. When Caesar was in southern Spain in 61/60, it was considerably, though not completely, romanized.[1] No *conventus c. R.* is mentioned; but it may be presumed that one existed (as at Utica), that its influence contributed to Romanization, and that this, as well as Balbus' services and Gades' importance, had to do with the rapid advancement of the city. But the fact remains that a city where the Romans were at the most in a minority was promoted before places (such as Italica or Corduba) where they virtually constituted the community, or were at least a dominant majority.

In the other towns of Ulterior an important part was played in the events of 49–45 by the Roman residents, though many were averse to military service and some had come to Spain to escape war.[2] In 49, even before Caesar's victory at Ilerda, anti-Pompeian demonstrations occurred in parts of the province.[3] When Caesar moved south after Ilerda, he sent ahead a proclamation to the leading men of the native and Roman communities, to meet him at Corduba on an appointed day. His report of the response need not be doubted: 'nulla fuit civitas quin ad id tempus partem senatus Cordubam mitteret, non civis Romanus paulo notior quin ad diem conveniret'.[4] While the strongest native community, Carmo, ejected its Pompeian garrison, the *conventus* at Corduba shut the town against the Pompeian governor, Varro, and put it in a state of defence.[5] Likewise one of the two legions which Varro was taking to Gades—the 'vernacula legio', made up largely of provincial Romans—mutinied so soon as it heard the news from Gades, marched to Hispalis, and camped in the forum and colonnades; the *conventus* applauded and members welcomed the men to their homes.[6] Only the other legion, brought from Italy, re-

---

[1] Cicero *pro Balbo* 43.

[2] Such as Q. Subernius of Cales. In spring 45 Cicero writes to Dolabella (*ad Fam.* IX.13.1 ff.), explaining how Subernius went to Spain to avoid war, but got caught up in it in 46, contrary to his will, on the Pompeian side. The same happened to M. Planius Heres of Cales (*ad Fam.* IX.13.2). This man may well belong to the family of the name with interests in the lead trade, for which southern Spain was the greatest source of supply (see Münzer *P-W* 'Planius').

[3] Caesar *B.C.* II.17.1–3; 18.5 f.; 21.2.   [4] Ibid., II.19.2.

[5] Ibid., II.19.3.   [6] Ibid., II.20.4 f.

mained obedient to Varro; when Italica shut its gates against him, he sent word to Caesar that he would surrender.[1]

Caesar had certainly numerous provincial clients and supporters to buttress his new regime in Spain, some connected with him directly; some, especially at Gades, through Balbus. A few are known—the Titius whom he brought into the Senate and his two sons, who became *tribuni* in his army;[2] L. Decidius Saxa, an officer in the army at Ilerda, treated by Cicero as a Celtiberian intruder into the citizenship, but certainly of an immigrant family;[3] L. Vibius Paciaecus, the settler who gave him intelligence in the emergency of 46–45.[4] But his influence in Ulterior was soon brought down from the height of 49 by the misgovernment of the man whom he left in control on his departure, Q. Cassius Longinus.

This misgovernment—of a piece with Cassius' earlier record in Spain—provoked an attempt on his life by Romans of Italica. The attempt, made at Corduba, failed, but was followed by serious disturbances among the provincials and in the army of the province, too complicated for a full account here. Since Cassius' attackers were settlers, his depredations may be assumed to have hurt, not only the natives, but this class;[5] treated, as it was, even more harshly after the failure of the plot, it played a prominent part in the upheavals of 48/47. The account of these in the *Bellum Alexandrinum* (where the author leaves Egypt to treat contemporary events in Spain) is at pains to emphasize that hatred of Cassius was not peculiar either to settlers or natives, but was provincial. Sympathy with the inhabitants of the province drew into the movement, not only the *vernacula legio*, composed of men born in Spain, but the second legion, which had 'become provincial' through long sojourn in the region.[6] These two legions had served under Varro, and the

---

[1] Ibid., II.20.6 f.   [2] *B. Afr.* 28.2.

[3] Saxa's career is fully treated by R. Syme *J.R.S.* xxvii (1937) 127 ff. He appears first as an officer of Caesar's army at Ilerda (Caesar *B.C.* 1.66.3).

[4] Cicero *ad Att.* xii.2.1 (April 46), *ad Fam.* vi.18.2 (January 45), with *B. Hisp.* 3.4.

[5] *B. Alex.* 49, especially 2–3, not specifically mentioning Romans among Cassius' victims.

[6] Ibid., 53.5: 'nemo enim aut in provincia natus, ut vernaculae legionis milites, aut diuturnitate iam factus provincialis, quo in numero erat secunda legio, non cum omni provincia consenserat in odio Cassi.'

influence on them of provincial connections may have been reinforced by residual sympathy for the Pompeian cause,[1] though the second legion did not conduct itself as boldly as the *vernacula legio* after the attack on Cassius.

As for the settlers, the *conventus* at Corduba took a leading part in the upheaval, but, though bitter against Cassius, was not anti-Caesarian, as the author of the *Bellum Alexandrinum* tells the story. For, when a certain Thorius of Italica, chosen by troops near Corduba for leader, persuaded these to write the name of Pompeius on their shields,

frequens legionibus conventus obviam prodit, neque tantum virorum sed etiam matrum familias et praetextatorum, deprecaturque ne hostili adventu Cordubam diriperent; nam se contra Cassium consentire cum omnibus; contra Caesarem ne facere cogerentur orare.[2]

In the upshot the command of the troops was transferred from Thorius to Marcellus, quaestor to Cassius, who had declared against him, but not against Caesar.[3]

Subsequent events, however, suggest that sympathy for Caesar at Corduba may have been badly damaged by the conduct of Cassius even before, in answer to this demonstration, he devastated fields and farms of the community.[4] After the arrival of Trebonius, in early 47, to take over the province, and the flight of Cassius, Ulterior was superficially peaceful for a short time; but Trebonius never overcame the discontent among troops or civilians. Whether this was his fault or not, the situation came to a head in 46, during and after the fighting in Africa between Caesar and the Pompeians.

The mainspring, initially, of the new movement was the discontented legions, whose officers got in touch with the Pompeian leaders in Africa; but it was two rich settlers, T. Scapula and Q. Aponius, who exploited the situation within the province, bringing in the provincials generally and becoming the leaders.[5] Scapula, the more important, kept a big domestic establishment

---

[1] *B. Alex.* 58.1–4, especially 2.
[2] Ibid., 58.4; cf. 59.1.
[3] Ibid., 59.1.
[4] Ibid., 59.2–60.1.
[5] Desertion of Trebonius by the two *vernaculae legiones*, *B. Hisp.* 7.4. The general attitude of the legions and the leadership of Scapula and Aponius, Dio XLIII.29.

at Corduba, now a Pompeian stronghold.[1] Cnaeus Pompeius set out early in 46 from Africa, but, when he was delayed by illness in the Balearics, Scapula and Aponius set the revolt in motion in June, and had driven out Trebonius before he arrived. In the war which followed, the differences, from place to place, of Roman sympathy do not emerge very clearly in the ancient accounts; the *Bellum Hispaniense* was a confused story (though the author clearly fought with Caesar's army) even before the mutilation of the text, whilst Dio has little detail about the provincial Romans.[2]

Immediately on his arrival, Cnaeus, following the advice given him by Cato in Africa,[3] rallied all the *clientes* of his father not already brought out in revolt by Scapula and Aponius, and thus, with their support and troops from Africa, caused most of the communities in the south to join him before Caesar arrived in November 46. The solid core of his army was the two *vernaculae legiones* taken over from Trebonius, with another raised for this war from the Roman settlements in Spain.[4] But these were torn by conflicting loyalties. At Carthago Nova, where Roman residents were certainly important, the authorities shut the gates against Cnaeus on his landing.[5] Corduba, though under the control of Pompeians and Pompeian troops, had a party anxious to work for Caesar.[6] Ursao (Urso), on the edge of the hills south of the Italica-Malaca road, an important place in the fighting, was controlled by the Pompeians, but had a Caesarian party, perhaps including local Romans.[7] Three Romans from Hasta, a small town not far inland from Gades, deserted Cnaeus' main army at the point when things started to go against him, reporting general disaffection, only suppressed

---

[1] Scapula, Cicero *ad Fam.* IX.13.1, with *B. Hisp.* 33.3. The importance to the Pompeians of Corduba appears from the general course of the war, as narrated in the *B. Hisp.* and Dio XLIII.29 ff.

[2] Dio XLIII.28–40.　　　　　　　　[3] *B. Afr.* 22, especially 4 f.

[4] For these legions, *B. Hisp.* 7.4. In the statement about the new legion raised from the settlers the reading may be either 'ex coloniis quae fuerunt in his regionibus' or 'ex colonis qui . . .'; in any case the terms are not to be taken in their technical sense.

[5] The shutting of the gates: Dio XLIII.30.1. For Roman residents at Carthago see *C.I.L.* II(1)3408, 3433 f., 3439, 3495 (shown by their orthography to be early). In 3408 the status of the three (four?) men is obscure.

[6] *B. Hisp.* 2 and 34.

[7] Ibid., 22, with the good note by A. S. Way in the Loeb edition of the Caesarian corpus p. 403 f.

by force, in his Roman cavalry;[1] but at Hispalis, where there was enthusiasm for Caesar in 49, Cnaeus' supporters resisted to the last, though the Pompeians had no regular garrison there.[2] One of those residents of Italica who tried to kill Cassius in 48 reappears in 45 as Pompeian commander at Ategua,[3] and the conspirator Scapula of 48 and the Scapula of 46 may be identical.[4]

The final Pompeian defeat at Munda was followed by a programme of rewards and punishments,[5] affecting numerous communities, *conventus c. R.* as well as native towns. Caesar appears, from a speech delivered at Hispalis to a gathering of provincial notables, to have been in no mood to distinguish, in thought or action, between native and Roman in southern Spain, assimilated, in his eyes, by their common guilt.[6] But local communities were treated as more, or less, guilty. In certain places the *conventus c. R.* comes to an end through the establishment of a *colonia c. R.* This happened at Tarraco and Carthago in Citerior, Hispalis in Ulterior,[7] but it may be that the colonization at Carthago, because it had resisted Pompeius, was carried out in a way more beneficial to the city and the resident Romans than at Hispalis.[8] Roman colonies, however, were not established wherever there happened to be private settlers in any number, and some *conventus c. R.* certainly continued in existence till Augustus promoted them to municipal or colonial status. Italica, probably because of its attitude in the upheavals, was not promoted by Caesar but received municipal status from Augustus.[9]

[1] *B. Hisp.* 26.1 f.

[2] Ibid., 35 f.

[3] L. Munatius Flaccus: *B. Alex.* 52; *B. Hisp.* 19; Dio XLIII.33.2–34.5.

[4] The Scapula of 46–45 is called by Dio, who alone gives his *nomen* (XLIII.29.3), 'Quintius'. The conspirator of 48 is called Annius Scapula in *B. Alex.* 55.2. This Annius was a man of great importance, as the Scapula of 46–45 is said to have been; there may be a manuscript error in Dio, due to the name of the other leader of 46–45, *Quintus* Aponius.

[5] Dio XLIII.39.4 f., without much detail.

[6] *B. Hisp.* 42. The manuscript breaks off in the middle of the speech. It would be rash to regard the text, even where it goes into direct speech, as the actual words used.

[7] Tarraco, Vittinghoff 79[10]; Carthago Nova, 79[4–9]; Hispalis, 74[4]. The existence of a *conventus* may be presumed at Tarraco, though nowhere attested.

[8] A plausible surmise by Vittinghoff 74 and 79.

[9] I cannot believe that Italica can have become a *municipium c. R.* in 49,

Nothing is known about the part of the *conventus* in the renewed fighting when Sextus Pompeius came out of hiding after Munda, gathered scattered survivors of the Pompeian armies, and got control of a large part of the province.[1] In mid-44 Sextus was called to Italy by the Senate to take charge of the fleet; but feelings aroused by the new war may be the background to the cruelty of the young Balbus in 43, when he was quaestor to the governor (Asinius Pollio) and magistrate of the new *municipium* of Gades. Among Romans who fell victim to Balbus were a Pompeian veteran done to death at Gades, and a *circulator auctionum* from that community lately obnoxious to Caesar, Hispalis.[2]

Just as in Italy the wealth of many *equites* brought trouble upon them in the proscriptions of Sulla and of the Triumvirate, so their property brought trouble on the rich provincial Romans in southern Spain. What they suffered at the hands of Varro in 49 was mild. They were compelled to guarantee him 120,000 *modii* of corn, 20,000 Roman pounds of silver, and the sum of 18,000,000 sesterces;[3] that is, they promised him, in terms of monetary value, something between 25,000,000 and 30,000,000 sesterces. That sum looks small compared with the 200,000,000 sesterces exacted by Caesar as a collective fine after Thapsus from the three hundred important pro-Pompeian Romans of Utica,[4] or set beside the fact that five hundred men of Gades had each the equestrian qualification, 400,000 sesterces, under Augustus.[5] But it seems that the settlers were still wealthy, when Cassius Longinus in his turn squeezed them, and it is likely that Cassius got much more from them.

There is little evidence from this period for the sources of the settlers' wealth. Strabo says that the silver mines in southern Spain, having originally belonged to the state and been leased to the companies, had become private property when he wrote;[6] Strabo is referring primarily to the silver mines near

---

without this being mentioned (like the promotion of Gades) in the sources. Obviously the town cannot have been made a *municipium* by Caesar *after* the events of 48. Italica appears on coins of the Augustan age as a *municipium* (Vives y Escudero *La Moneda Hispanica* IV.126 f.).

[1] Appian IV.83 f. (348–53).
[2] Asinius Pollio writing to Cicero, *ad Fam.* x.32.1–4.
[3] Caesar *B.C.* II.18.4.   [4] *B. Afr.* 90.2–3.
[5] Strabo 169 *ad init.*   [6] Ibid., 148.

Carthago Nova, but he is also thinking of those elsewhere. This change, which he does not date, may well have taken place in the late Republic; the Spanish gold mines remained state property.

The Cordubenses had fine fields and farms which were greatly prized.[1] Here, and elsewhere in the south, the various forms of agriculture found there under the Principate will have been practised by the settlers of the late Republic, especially viticulture and the growing of olives.[2] The river Baetis being navigable for fair-sized sea-going vessels as far as Italica and Hispalis,[3] this latter city was already a ship-building centre,[4] whilst Corduba, much further upstream, had busy river-boat traffic.[5] Hispalis had the appearance of an Italian city, possessing a forum lined with colonnades,[6] and Italica and Corduba, created in the first place by order of military commanders, are certain to have been planned and built on regular Roman lines.

Whether private settlement contributed anything like as much to social change in southern Spain as the public colonization of Caesar and Augustus, cannot be said. But the process of Romanization, which, under Augustus, Strabo notes as almost complete through a large part of Baetica,[7] was certainly well under way when Caesar established his Spanish colonies, and this was mainly due to the earlier settlers.

Note: the colonization of Valentia

In 138 B.C., according to Livy *per.* 55, 'Iunius Brutus consul in Hispania iis qui sub Viriatho militaverant agros et oppidum dedit, quod vocatum est Valentia'. This Valentia can certainly be identified with the city of this name appearing in the Sertorian War (Sallust *Hist.* II.54) and called by Pliny (*N.H.* III.20) 'colonia Valentia'—the modern Valencia, approximately three miles from the sea, as Pliny describes the *colonia*. This

[1] *B. Alex* 59 *ad fin.* to 60.1, with Strabo 141.
[2] For these under the Principate, J. J. van Nostrand *E.S.A.R.* III.177 f., olive groves in Baetica 45 B.C., *B. Hisp.* 27.1 and 3.
[3] Strabo 142 *ad init.*   [4] *B. Alex.* 56.6.
[5] Strabo 142.   [6] Caesar, *B.C.* II.20.4.
[7] 'The Turdetani and especially those around the Baetis have changed completely to the ways of the Romans, not even any longer remembering their own language. The majority of them have acquired Latin status and they have received Roman colonists, so that they are not far from all being Romans.' (Strabo 151.)

settlement of veterans of Viriathus with land in the most fertile region of the east coast compares favourably with some Roman conduct in the war; but I cannot believe with some, that the settlers were given Latin colonial status. The settlement is not in the same class as the Latin colony at Carteia in 171 B.C., since there the colonists were sons of Roman soldiers by peregrine women, not ex-enemies (see above p. 24 f.), but is comparable rather with the town of Gracchuris, founded near the upper Ebro by T. Sempronius Gracchus in 178 B.C., after he had received the surrender of the Celtiberians of the region (Livy *per.* XLI). Livy XLIII.3.1–4, by indicating the novelty of the Latin status of Carteia, rules out Latin status for the earlier foundation (something most unlikely in itself) and the Latin status of Gracchuris (Pliny *N.H.* III.24) must be of much later origin. On the assumption then, that Valentia was founded as a peregrine town in 138, it is reasonable to suppose that it still had that status at the beginning of the Sertorian War. In that war forces of Sertorius had a defeat near Valentia and the city was taken by Pompeius, only to be recovered by Sertorius and held by him till his death (Schulten *Sertorius* 112, 115 f., 138). Afranius, already closely connected with Pompeius, commanded under him in a battle on the river Sucro, south of Valentia, in 75 (Plutarch *Sertorius* 19). Some sort of connection between him and Valentia is attested in the inscription of a monument which the 'consc[r]ip(ti) et c[ol](oni) col(oniae) Vale[nt] (inae)' set up in his honour in Italy in 60 B.C., when he was consul (*I.L.S.* 1.878 = *C.I.L.* IX.5275, found between Asculum and Cupra Maritima in Picenum, where Afranius presumably had a villa). This connection might go back to the war, but it seems more likely that Valentia received colonists after the end of the war, and that Afranius had a part in the colonization (the Valentia of the inscription can hardly be the place in Narbonensis, see Goessler *P-W* 'Valentia' (5) 2153 f.). Perhaps the colonists were veterans of Pompeius' forces, but they could have been Roman or native survivors of Sertorius' armies; nor is there any indication whether their status was Latin or Roman, though Valentia had acquired Roman colonial status by the date of Pliny's Augustan source (see Pliny *N.H.* III.20, where 'colonia' unqualified must mean 'Roman colony'). But there remains some mystery about the origin and functioning of the double community attested at Valentia by various late inscriptions (*C.I.L.* II.3737, 3739, 3741 'Valentini veterani et veteres' and 3745 'uterque ordo Valentinorum'). Presumably the distinction of the two bodies began at the time when public settlers were sent to Valentia at the end of the Sertorian War to form a *colonia* alongside the original community; probably the two communities remained formally distinct, but became closely associated in practice. But what was the status of the 'veteres' in our period?

AFRICA

The province which became known as Africa was established in 146 B.C., when Carthage was taken after a siege of three years and completely destroyed. Carthage was not rebuilt till a century later, and Utica, the great pro-Roman port to its immediate north-west, became the seat of the governor. The provincial region was bounded by a line following a sinuous course from the coast near Thabraca to the sea near Thaenae, south of Leptis Minor;[1] the treaty with Leptis Magna, concluded at the beginning of the Jugurthine War, gave Rome a hold three hundred miles further east, but the line from Thabraca to Thaenae remained till in 46 the kingdom of Numidia beyond it was annexed as Africa Nova.

Despite the weakness of Carthage as a state after the second Punic War, the economy of city and territory had continued to flourish, as is clear from the early payment of the heavy war indemnity to Rome; the region taken in 146 had not only important trade from its ports, but also, in the fertile plains and undulating hill country, types of agriculture like enough those of Italy to attract farmers with the necessary capital.[2]

[1] The literary evidence for the frontier of 146 is given by Mommsen, *C.I.L.* VIII(1) p. xv. There is further epigraphic evidence, with discussion of the line of the frontier in the middle Bagradas region, in Teutsch *Das römische Städtewesen in Nordafrika* 10 f. (see especially note 32 and also map I at the end of the book). Vaga, north of the river Bagradas, was in Numidia (see Sallust *Jugurtha* 47) at the time of the Jugurthine War and remained so till the annexation of Numidia.

[2] The various regions of Roman Africa and neighbouring Numidia are clearly distinguished, with reference to their agricultural conditions and development, in ancient and modern times, by T. Frank in 'The Inscriptions of the Imperial Domains of Africa', *A.J.P.* XLVII (1926) 55 ff., especially 67 ff.

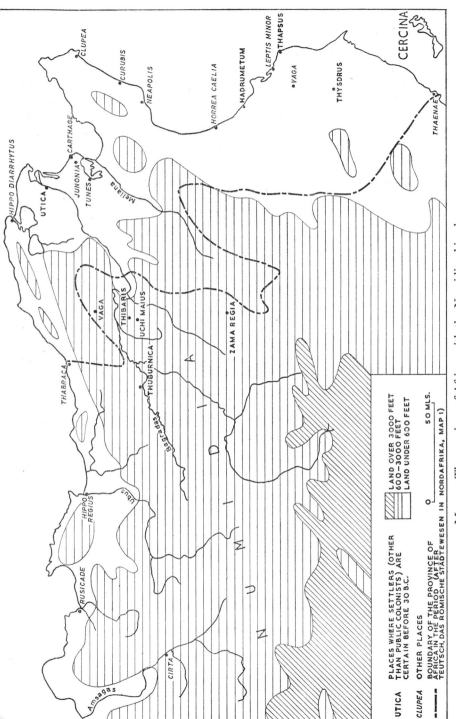

MAP III. The province of Africa, with the Numidian kingdom

UTICA   PLACES WHERE SETTLERS (OTHER
         THAN PUBLIC COLONISTS) ARE
         CERTAIN BEFORE 30 B.C.

CLUPEA   OTHER PLACES

         BOUNDARY OF THE PROVINCE OF
         AFRICA IN THE PERIOD (AFTER
         TEUTSCH, DAS RÖMISCHE STÄDTEWESEN IN NORDAFRIKA, MAP 1)

         LAND OVER 3000 FEET
         600-3000 FEET
         LAND UNDER 600 FEET

         0   50 MLS.

In the second century B.C. Italian and Roman business men were travelling beyond the imperial frontiers in various regions of the Mediterranean world.[1] They may have been numerous in Carthage before the third Punic war, though their presence there in 148 B.C. receives only passing mention.[2] In 112 B.C., at the outbreak of the war between Adherbal and Jugurtha (which became war between Jugurtha and Rome), they were active in considerable number in Cirta, Adherbal's capital, where Masinissa had turned an ordinary Numidian town into an important capital and Greeks had recently been settled by Micipsa. When Adherbal was defeated outside the walls, these *togati* took up arms, saved him from capture or death, and prevented the troops of Jugurtha from bursting into the city; but later, when they saw further resistance was hopeless, they made Adherbal open the gates—and were themselves massacred to a man.[3] The number and importance of this body is apparent from the fact that they were the backbone of the defence of Cirta and that Adherbal could not continue resistance against their wishes. Their fate certainly caused alarm and indignation among the African Romans generally, whose influence was now increasing.

The African Romans come to light as a self-assertive group in 108/7, strongly supporting Marius in his ambition to replace Metellus against Jugurtha.[4] The worst complaints against Metellus certainly came from those who had formerly visited the Numidian towns for trade,[5] convinced by Marius' propaganda that Metellus would let the war drag out, but that Marius would rapidly make their trading territory safe for them again.

Marius' chief supporters, since their voices told in Rome, must have been men of considerable wealth and standing; they were numerous in Utica,[6] traditionally founded before Carthage, long a flourishing port, and now part, or perhaps main heir to Carthaginian trade. The colonists established by C. Gracchus in 122 at Junonia on the adjacent territory of Carthage were

---

[1] Cf. their activity, *c.* 200 B.C., along the pirate-ridden eastern shores of the Adriatic (Polybius II.8.1–4, with Livy XL.42.1–5), or at Delos (below p. 100) from the close of the third century.

[2] Appian *Punica* 92.

[3] Sallust *Jugurtha* 21.2–4 and 26.1 f.

[4] Velleius II.11.2; Sallust *Jugurtha* 64.5–6; 65.4–5.

[5] Sallust *Jugurtha* 47.1–2 (Vaga); 21.2 and 26.1 (Cirta).

[6] Sallust *Jugurtha* 64.5.

probably not far below them socially,[1] and close connections, social and marital, may be presumed from the beginning between the two groups. When the Junonian settlers lost their corporate status in 121 through the cancellation of their colonial charter by the Senate,[2] they acquired a strong anti-senatorial grievance, without anyone to champion them at Rome after the death of Gracchus and the ruin of his party. So, when Marius began to fish in troubled waters, it is probable that the Junonian settlers and the residents at Utica and elsewhere were drawn closer together by the common animosity to the Senate which he encouraged.

It was the African Romans, by the support they first gave to Marius' political ambition, who enabled him to acquire glory by concluding the already half-won war against Jugurtha, so that his way was open to further military glories. From 103 Marian army families were settled in compact groups—without colonial status—on large allotments of land in the valley of the middle Bagradas, and from these groups considerable and prosperous Roman communities grew, Uchi Maius, Thibaris, and Thuburnica, and perhaps others.[3] The fact that this settlement

---

[1] For the lots of land were fairly large and C. Gracchus tended to choose for his colonists τοὺς χαριεστάτους: Plutarch C. Gracchus 9.3. Plutarch is applying the phrase to the colonists intended for Tarentum and Capua, but the people sent to Junonia were apparently of the same type. They were chosen from the whole of Italy (Appian 1.24 (104)) and received two hundred iugera each (lex agraria of 111 B.C., C. G. Bruns F.I.R.⁷, p. 83 sec. 60, with the comments of E. G. Hardy Roman Laws and Charters 43 and 72¹⁴).

[2] For which the decisive evidence is not the literary allusions to what the conservatives intended, but the phrase '. . . lege Rubria quae fuit' of the lex agraria of 111 (Bruns p. 83 sec. 59).

[3] de viris illustribus 73.1 mentions legislation by Appuleius in 103 for allocation of land to Marian veterans in Africa, on a family or individual basis, not in coloniae. It is clearly implied that the opposition was intimidated and the bill went through. The settlers, of their own or with public encouragement, came to form communities, and this appears to have been the origin, as Roman towns, of Uchi Maius, Thibaris, and Thuburnica. Late inscriptions associate Marius with these towns. I.L.S. 1.1334 and III(2)9405 (and other inscriptions) refer to Uchi Maius as 'colonia Mariana Augusta Alexandriana', I.L.S. II(1)6790 to Thibaris as 'municipium Marianum', and Ann. Ep. 1951 no. 81 (p. 29), from Thuburnica, speaks of Marius as 'conditor coloniae'. But they cannot have been founded by Marius as coloniae. This is ruled out, not only by de viris illustribus 73.1, but by Pliny N.H. v.29, describing Uchi Maius and Thuburnica as oppida c. R., and I.L.S. II(1)6790, where Thibaris is a municipium c. R. Teutsch (Da, römische Städtewesen in Nordafrika 6 ff.) does not admit de viris illustribus 73.1

met conservative resistance, which Appuleius broke, is likely to have fostered Marius' popularity, both in these new communities and among the African Romans generally.

Marius and his son naturally turned to Africa in their flight from Italy in 88; it was also natural that the force they raised there included Roman settlers as well as natives of the province;[1] they might never have got back to Italy to use this force, had they not been welcomed on the Cercina islands (just off the southernmost part of the province), where settlers were sent in Marius' consulate of 100.[2] Africa was in Marian hands from 87 to 81, but its Romans were probably divided in those troubled years. The upheavals of the period call for notice here, though the role of the provincial Romans is passed over by ancient writers, as the local prelude to the events of 49–45 B.C., when the part of the African Romans is important and better documented.

Metellus Numidicus cannot have been wholly deprived by Marius of supporters in Africa. For in 84, by which year he was probably dead, his son, Pius, tried to seize the province from the Marians, and might have succeeded, had he not fallen out with Crassus, who had brought a small force from Spain. In the event, he was soon driven out by the Marian governor, Fabius Hadrianus.[3] But the Romans in Utica, who might have supported the Marians most strongly, were soon alienated; they were squeezed of money and oppressed by Fabius, and an angry

---

as evidence, points out that the settlement was in the kingdom of Numidia, not within the province, and argues that this was unofficial colonization, without any legislation. I see no reason to reject the text; the settlements were certainly in Numidia, but this has no bearing on their origin. Full *coloniae* were established during the Republic as enclaves in the territory of allies, and by Augustus within the Mauretanian kingdom of allied Juba II (see Pliny *N.H.* v.2, Zilil as a colony of Augustus, 'regum dicioni exempta et iura in Baeticam petere iussa', with v.5); and in our case the Numidian king must have been asked to give an enclave for viritane settlement, the settlers, once established, being expected by Rome to look to the authority of the African provincial governor. For the later development of these communities see Frank *A.J.P.* xlvii (1926) 55 ff.

[1] Plutarch *Marius* 41.3, where, however, the phrase might mean other exiles.

[2] See Frank *A.J.P.* lviii (1937) 90–3, discussing the inscription published as *Inscriptiones Italiae* xiii(3)7. There seems no alternative to the reading 'Cerceinam' for 'Cerce [. . .]', but no supporting evidence exists.

[3] Plutarch *Crassus* 6.1 f.; Livy *per.* lxxxiv.

crowd burned him in his house in 83.[1] There was no punishment of the leaders, for the Marians were soon in full defeat in
Italy and Sicily, and when Cn. Domitius escaped to Africa, he
was wholly occupied in assembling and organizing the remnants
of their armies and the troops he managed to raise in the
province. Seven thousand of Domitius' twenty-seven thousand
men deserted to Pompeius when he arrived in pursuit, and
Domitius was defeated in the ensuing battle. It cannot be said
how far the defeat was due to the desperate circumstances of the
Marians, Domitius' mistake in the battle, or local Roman disaffection with Marian rule.[2]

However this may be, many provincial Roman families, at
Utica and elsewhere, now entered the *clientela* of Pompeius,
along with a number of natives.[3] This relationship was to bear
fruit later; but the African Romans, in the following decades,
were certainly divided (though not as obviously or sharply as
the Romans in Spain) by rival influences and pressures upon
them.

In 66, resident Romans, together with natives of the province,
invited Metellus Pius (who had not been concerned with Africa
since 84) from retirement, to represent them against the ex-
governor, Catiline, at his trial *de rebus repetundis*.[4] But Pompeius'
rival now for the interest of the African Romans and natives
was not Metellus, but, as everywhere, Caesar.

Caesar had not visited Africa before landing with his army
in 46. But in 46, when his position was at first difficult, various
communities, widely separated and very different in character,
were well disposed towards him from the beginning. Whilst
some Gaetulian chieftains aided the Pompeians, others, remembering benefits conferred by Marius, were ready to help
the man they heard was related to him.[5] On the Cercina islands,
in the Lesser Syrtis, where there was good farming land, Roman
settlers had been established in 100 by Caesar's father, in co-
operation presumably with Marius;[6] the Cercinates had received
Marius in 87 on his voyage back to Italy,[7] and now readily

[1] *Verrines* II.1.70; Livy *per.* LXXXVI etc.
[2] Plutarch *Pompeius* 11 ff. for the episode as a whole.
[3] Cicero *pro Balbo* 51.   [4] Asconius ed. Clark 77 *ad fin.* = p. 87 line 3.
[5] *B. Afr.* 32.3–4; 35; 55.
[6] See Frank *A.J.P.* LVIII (1937) 90–3 and above p. 46 n. 2.
[7] Plutarch *Marius* 40.14.

surrendered their important supplies of corn when Sallust was sent by Caesar to ask for them.[1] The Roman *negotiatores* and *aratores* at Thysdra gave help, as did various places—Leptis Minor, Vaga, Thabena,[2] where there may well have been Roman settlers. In some cases, this may have been from expectation of his ultimate victory rather than respect for old ties; there is evidence of a considerable body of Pompeian feeling among the African Romans, and at Utica the sympathy of the native community for Caesar was matched by equal hostility towards him among the *negotiatores*.

When Attius Varus, the Pompeian who had governed the province shortly before the civil war and knew it well, declared himself governor at the outbreak of civil war, the Romans of Utica welcomed him warmly,[3] and it was clear that Pompeius had not lost the influence he established there thirty years earlier. The native population, by contrast, had received some signal benefit from Caesar during his consulate in 59 and on this account hoped for a Caesarian victory when Curio landed to attack Varus.[4] Fear of King Juba of Numidia, the arrogantly independent ally of the Pompeians, enemy to any friend of Caesar and hopeful of Utica as a prize of victory, intensified their attitude; whilst resentment of the favour shown by Caesar to non-Romans may have made the *conventus c. R.* the more pro-Pompeian. Its help to the Pompeians, later considerable, presumably began in this year, when the Pompeians were victorious in Africa.

In consequence of that victory Africa became the base where the survivors of Pharsalus could build up a new army and

---

[1] *B. Afr.* 34.1–3.

[2] Leptis Minor (*B. Afr.* 7.1–2), Vaga (ibid., 74.1), Thabena (77.1–2). There is no mention of Romans at these places, but they are probable. In *B. Afr.* 36.2 the Italian *negotiatores* and *aratores* of Thysdra are mentioned as helping Caesar, in 97.4 the *civitas* is fined; *civitas* and *conventus* had presumably been at odds. The Leptitani who were fined (97.3) are the people of Leptis *Magna*. Thabena was somewhere on the coast, just east of the then province. Not Numidian Vaga, but Vaga near Thapsus, is meant.

[3] Cicero *pro Ligario* 3 f., describing how Attius Varus wrested Africa from the constitutionally appointed governor, Ligarius. The people described, in scornful terms, by Cicero as welcoming Varus, must have been, in the main, Roman residents.

[4] Caesar *B.C.* 11.36.1 says that in 49 the Uticenses were most friendly to Caesar, 'pro quibusdam Caesaris in se beneficiis'. *B. Afr.* 87.3 refers to a 'beneficium legis Iuliae' conferred on Utica, without further detail.

position, with Metellus Scipio as their commander and Cato as the energetic but just military governor of Utica; Caesar could move against them only at the end of 47. In the following four months of war the provincials far and wide (unless the *Bellum Africum* greatly exaggerates) were alienated from the Pompeian cause by the savage way in which Metellus Scipio compelled their support.[1] Certain Roman *conventus*, however, together with the towns where they were established, were treated by Caesar, in the hour of victory, as willing supporters of the enemy—those at Hadrumetum, Thapsus, and Zama in Numidia[2] (though at Zama the natives helped Caesar and had it recognized). Nor did terror or intimidation on the part of the Pompeians have to do with the support of the Utican *conventus* for the cause represented in their city by Cato.

The famous Utican Three Hundred were only the wealthiest and most influential members of a Roman body which may have been much larger.[3] They formed a council for raising money and supplies and helped the Pompeians considerably, so long as victory seemed possible.[4] But they were not die-hards, and soon after the news of Thapsus fear for their lives or fortunes determined them to make their own peace with Caesar (for which some may have been prepared to plot the betrayal to him of the Pompeian senators in Utica).[5] The withdrawal of their support convinced Cato that he could not stand siege in a city where the natives had been embittered by the attitude towards them of Pompeian leaders and might rise for Caesar at any moment.[6] But, while he organized the escape by sea of the Pompeian senators and fugitives from Thapsus, he had to use all his moral authority to prevent bloodshed in a city where they, the Three Hundred, and the natives hated each other more than ever.[7] Many Romans and Uticenses had their lives saved by the firmness of Cato in these last days before his suicide, and both bodies joined to honour his funeral 'propter . . . singularem integritatem et quod dissimillimus reliquorum ducum fuerat'.[8]

But the Roman residents had a testing experience when

---

[1] *B. Afr.* 26. [2] Ibid., 97.1 f.
[3] This is clear from *B. Afr.* 90.1.
[4] *B. Afr.* 90.1 mentions only money contributed by them; but see also Plutarch *Cato Minor* 59.2 f.
[5] Plutarch *Cato Minor* 59–63, especially 61–63.1. [6] Ibid., 58.1–3.
[7] Ibid., 58–65, with *B. Afr.* 87. [8] *B. Afr.* 88.5.

E

Caesar entered the city with his army a few days after these events. The officer who wrote the *Bellum Africum* appears to have been with the army on its entry, and his account suggests that he witnessed the humiliation of the Utican Romans. A mass meeting, to which both natives and Romans are summoned, hears Caesar thank the Uticenses for their loyalty and rebuke the local Romans in a caustic diatribe. This, to their ecstatic relief, ends with a lordly declaration that he will take only their wealth; at the humble suggestion of the Three Hundred a collective fine, to be paid by that body, is substituted for a penalty falling heavily on every individual.[1] Caesar was extremely angry with the Pompeian forces in Africa. But in his attitude to the Romans at Utica, as here reported, there is an admixture of contempt; he is playing with scorn on the suspense of men who, in peace, could lord it in Utica, in the war, first helped and then abandoned his enemies, and who now stand before him, hated by both sides, 'pale with fear and, for what they had deserved, despairing of their lives'.[2] They are not only made to tremble with fear, but are humbled, as Romans, in front of the citizens of Punic Utica.

The fine required of the Three Hundred was 200,000,000 sesterces.[3] That meant 670,000 sesterces from each, more than one and a half times the sum required for membership of the equestrian order under Augustus. The fine, although three years were allowed for payment, makes the sums required from Thapsus and from Hadrumetum (*conventus* and city separately in each case) look trivial.[4] Whether the wealth of the *conventus* at Utica was so much greater, or their offence so much worse, or whether both reasons entered into it, is not clear; but in any case the sum of 200,000,000 sesterces indicates great wealth.

The main source of that wealth was shipping, merchanting, and moneylending.[5] But many of the moneylenders and merchants may also have been big farmers or landowners. L. Iulius Calidus, the rich poet, friend of Cicero, Atticus, and Nepos, had landed estates in Africa, where he seems to have

---

[1] *B. Afr.* 90.   [2] Ibid., 90.2.
[3] Ibid., 90.3.
[4] Ibid., 97.2.
[5] Plutarch *Cato Minor* 59.3; 61.2.

lived from time to time.[1] Not all the landowners in Africa suggested for this period are certain;[2] but there was already a trend in some provincial regions towards large estates in Roman hands, resident or absentee,[3] and circumstances in Africa were as propitious as elsewhere for such a development. But not all those with estates in Africa will have lived in Italy, or have managed their land through *procuratores* or *vilici*; resident *aratores* are attested at Thysdra, a small town on the road running south inland from Hadrumetum.[4] There was a strong interest among the agriculturists of Carthage and her subject cities in rational farming and its methods, and a tradition of writing on these subjects. The best-known treatise, that by Mago, was rendered into Latin, by decree of the Senate, soon after Africa became a province,[5] and it seems fair to assume that in ordering this translation the Senate had partly in mind the interests of Romans taking up land in Africa; in 88 B.C. another translation was published by Cassius Dionysius, a member of the Roman *conventus* at Utica.[6] Cassius, who may have been of Greek origin, used Greek, which is not to say that he had Greek readers only in mind.

Separate notice is deserved by Publius Sittius and his private army, long active in lands adjoining Roman Africa. Entering the African war of 46 at a time critical for Caesar, they not only did him great service in their capture of Cirta—by forcing Juba

[1] Cicero *ad Fam.* XIII.6.3–4 (56 B.C.), a letter to the governor of Africa recommending Calidus, who is evidently in Africa at the time; with Nepos *Atticus* 12.4, on the proscription of Calidus by the Triumvirs in 43/42 'propter magnas . . . Africanas possessiones'.

[2] See T. R. S. Broughton *The Romanization of Africa Proconsularis* 38. The existence of the *Saltus Lamianus* in Africa under the Principate suggests strongly that the interests in Africa of Cicero's friend Aelius Lamia may have included land; *ad Fam.* XII.29 (43 B.C.) does not specifically mention estates, only his 'negotia . . ., procuratores, libertos, familiam'. 'Horrea Caelia', the name of a coastal *vicus* north of Hadrumetum (*Itinerarium Antonini* 52.5 and 58.4), must surely be derived from ownership of granaries there by the Caelii in the late Republic (cf. Cicero *pro Caelio* 73).

[3] Romans with estates in Epirus, below p. 93.

[4] *B. Afr.* 36.2.

[5] Pliny *N.H.* XVIII.22 f. Pliny does not say, in so many words, that the translation was actually made, but this emerges clearly enough. It seems to have been done by a group of men expert in Punic, under the supervision of Decimus Silanus, the Punic scholar of the time (ibid., 23).

[6] Varro *R.R.* 1.1.10. The Sextilius to whom Cassius dedicates the book must be the African governor of that name of 88; see Plutarch *Marius* 40.6, Appian *B.C.* 1.62(279), and the coins cited in *P-W* 'Sextilius' (12)2035.

back to defend Numidia—but secured for themselves a city for a settled life after the war. Although the *Sittiani* achieved recognition from Caesar as a *colonia c. R.* and the corresponding public organization, the origin of their settlement makes them, in effect, a unique kind of private emigrant.

The story starts at the time of the first Catilinarian conspiracy. Sittius, perhaps in southern Spain in 68 when Caesar was quaestor, was certainly there not much later, for his business interests in other western provinces and Mauretania, which he managed from Spain, were established before 64.[1] He was pressed about this time by creditors in Italy, found he could not recover his provincial and foreign loans in time, and had to sell Italian properties. He returned to Rome for a time, formed some connection with the Catilinarians,[2] and then went off to Mauretania before the end of 64. People said later that he was there for Catiline, to help seize the western provinces at the right moment;[3] the best defence that Cicero could offer, when he had to deal with the charge in the *pro Sulla*, was that he went before the start of the conspiracy (as if Catiline had no plans before 64!) and was owed money by the king of Mauretania.[4] He probably began at once to raise his private army, but held back in Mauretania when he heard that Catiline was doing badly.

Sittius, threatened with prosecution, then decided that it would be best not to return to Italy. But he probably kept in touch with Rome,[5] and Caesar may have been in correspondence

[1] I follow Münzer's documented account of Sittius' earlier career, *P-W* III(A) 1.409 ff.

[2] See E. Meyer *Caesars Monarchie und das Principat des Pompeius* 16–20. Unless there was damning evidence of Sittius' involvement in the Catilinarian conspiracy, Sallust would have cleared him (as later a most useful servant of Caesar), instead of implicating him, as he does (*Catiline* 21.3 f.).

[3] Sallust, *Catiline* 21.3 f., is accepted by Münzer as evidence that Sittius went to the West in 64 to help the Catilinarians. Catiline in the speech attributed to him (loc. cit.) is made to say he was in Mauretania. There is no reason to think (as Münzer does) that he went first to Spain, and to Mauretania only when he heard of his impending prosecution. Appian *B.C.* IV.54(231) gives this impression, but his account telescopes Sittius' early career.

[4] *pro Sulla* 56 ff. Cicero uses various other arguments, but they amount to little.

[5] Despite the textual corruptions, there seems no real doubt that Cicero *ad Fam.* v.17 is a letter to our Sittius. The content of the letter exactly fits the case of Sittius, and the evident reference to Publius Sulla in 2 ('cum in tui

with him during the period when he was hiring his highly effective army to African princes. That would explain the readiness of his response in 46 to the appeal from Caesar, then in serious trouble,[1] or perhaps Sittius betted on Caesar's ability to extricate himself and on the certainty of reward.

However this may be, he helped to save Caesar;[2] his seizure in the war of Juba's capital, Cirta, was recognized,[3] and the Sittiani, from homeless soldiers of fortune, became *Colonia Iulia Iuvenalis Honoris et Virtutis Cirta*,[4] with lands around that city, or were established in other settlements in the neighbourhood [5] (the Roman citizenship, with Sittius' name, being given to the non-Romans, numerous in the force, if not a majority in it[6]).

The colony was attacked, after the death of Caesar, by the dispossessed African princes and lost Sittius through an ambush,[7] then it was beleaguered in 42 in the confused civil warfare in Africa;[8] none the less it soon began to flourish. Thus a body of soldiers of fortune, under a Roman adventurer, turned the Numidian capital into a romanized city, which reached its height of prosperity in the second and third centuries A.D.[9]

The African Romans, when Caesar began his colonization, are likely to have belonged to three main classes: the men of business (most numerous perhaps in the coastal cities, but not

---

familiarissimi iudicio ac periculo tuum crimen coniungeretur'), although it does not *name* Sulla, clinches it. ('Publius tuus' at the *end* of para. 2 is presumably Sittius' son, Publius, mentioned again in 4 f.)

[1] Dio XLIII.3.2 denies that he was known to Caesar, not very plausibly.

[2] *B. Afr.* 25; 36.4; 48.1; 95.

[3] He had massacred the population on its refusal to surrender: *B. Afr.* 25.

[4] *C.I.L.* VIII(1)7041, 7071, with Appian IV.54(232 f.) (the Masinissa described as ruling Cirta was a kind of vassal of Juba). Teutsch' belief (74 f.) that the *colonia* began with Latin status is not convincing; his argument from magisterial titulature does not hold (see Kornemann *P-W* 'Coloniae' 586 f.), and the Gallic or Spanish communities given Latin status by Caesar had no such origin in military adventure as Sittius' colony had.

[5] Mommsen, *C.I.L.* VIII(1) p. 618 col. 2, points to the titles of these other settlements as evidence for their joint foundation with Cirta. Cf. in particular 6710 f. for the *colonia Sarnensis Milebitana*, named after the Campanian river Sarnus, close to Sittius' home town, Nuceria.

[6] Sittii are very common, not only in Cirta (*C.I.L.* VIII(1) 7737–95 etc.), but in some of the settlements that were associated with it (cf. Rusicade, 8153–60), Sigus (5847–56), Tiddis (6707–12), and in Africa generally (VIII(2) p. 1014 f. 'Sittii').

[7] Appian IV.54(234 f.).

[8] Appian IV.53(228), 55–6(236–42).

[9] Cf. Mommsen 'Colonia Iulia Cirta', *C.I.L.* VIII(1) pp. 618 ff.

confined to these), the well-to-do farmers who had taken up land privately, and the people of Junonia and the Marian families with farms in the Bagradas valley. There may have been other settlement by veterans; but this is speculation, apart from the fact that veteran settlers were fighting in Africa in 43–40 under Sextius, Antonius' supporter.[1]

As was seen, not all those owning land in Africa were resident; but the *procuratores* and freedmen in the province of absentee landowners, such as Caelius, may have played a part in maintaining connections between Italy and Africa. Thus M. Caelius M. l. Phileros, a magistrate in Carthage (when the city came to life again as a colony of Caesar) and in Clupea (another Caesarian colony), was probably in Africa, serving the absentee M. Caelius, years before he became attendant to Sextius in the troubles of 40. His footing both in Africa and Italy is noteworthy; an inscription recording his career was erected at Formiae, where he became Augustalis and embellished the temple of Neptune at his own expense.[2] Evidently he had made a good deal of money in Africa.

From 44 to 30 the Romans are hardly known. The province provided refuge for victims of the proscriptions—till the Triumvirs brought it under their control.[3] During the confiscations in Italy some of the dispossessed may have gone there. But what the refugee countryman in Virgil's first Eclogue says to his fortunate neighbour

> at nos hinc alii sitientes ibimus Afros

hardly adds to antecedent probability. Despite the real and harsh background to the Eclogue, this line belongs to a rhetorically contrived exchange, in which places of exile at the opposite ends of the earth are set against each other for rhetorical effect; it is followed by the improbable

> pars Scythiam et rapidum cretae veniemus Oaxen
> et penitus toto divisos orbe Britannos.

The darkness over Roman Africa in these years cannot be removed by speculative inferences.

---

[1] Appian v.26(102).
[2] *I.L.S.* 1.1945 = *C.I.L.* x(1)6104. M. Caelius Rufus, father of Cicero's friend, had African estates: *pro Caelio* 73.
[3] Appian iv.36(150) and 56(241).

SICILY

Sicily in the late Republic is known chiefly from Cicero's *Verrines*. There every aspect of the province that might heighten indignation against its mishandling—its ancient culture, its past services, and its present value to Rome—is eloquently called up by Cicero to make more telling his exposure of Verres; into that exposure are woven many details of the contemporary life of the island and its inhabitants. But the *Verrines* are not ideal material for Sicilian social history. Not all the detail fits into a pattern, and the Romans appear less than the natives.

The speeches forming the so-called second *Actio* are not less useful because Verres acknowledged defeat after the first *Actio* and Cicero did not use them. In the opening of the second of these undelivered speeches Cicero, after speaking of the services of Sicily to the Roman state, turns to the benefits derived by citizens individually from Roman possession of the provinces:

Quid? illa quae forsitan ne sentiamus quidem, iudices, quanta sunt! quod multis locupletioribus civibus utimur, quod habent propinquam fidelem fructuosamque provinciam, quo facile excurrant, ubi libenter negotium gerant; quos illa partim mercibus suppeditandis cum quaestu compendioque dimittit, partim retinet, ut arare, ut pascere, ut negotiari libeat, ut denique sedes ac domicilium conlocare; quod commodum non mediocre rei publicae est, tantum civium numerum tam prope a domo tam bonis fructuosisque rebus detineri.[1]

'Ut denique sedes ac domicilium collocare': although the settlers are mentioned after the visitors and temporary residents, Cicero certainly thought them equally important. They probably lived in many places from which no evidence survives, and—so close and attractive was Sicily—may have formed groups where now only individuals are known. A fair number of Romans appear in the *Verrines* simply as established in Sicily without indication of their place of residence.[2]

There were many Romans at Syracuse, the provincial capital, chief place of business, and a particularly attractive city, and they were probably numerous at Messana, the channel port and a place of growing importance since the first political contacts

[1] *Verrines* II.2.6.   [2] Listed by Scramuzza *E.S.A.R.* III.337 f.

between Rome and Sicily. Between Messana and Syracuse Roman immigrants lived at Tauromenium, at Aetna, the city below the mountain, and at Leontini. In western Sicily they were numerous at Agrigentum, Lilybaeum, and Panormus.[1] They do not appear, in the *Verrines* or elsewhere, in the interior.

Amid the population of the province, or even of the places where they lived, the settlers were undoubtedly a small minority; but, in a province so close to Rome, they must, by the Ciceronian age, have acquired a local importance beyond their numbers. For the community at Syracuse went back to the late third century, that at Halaesa to the early second century,[2] and other *conventus* may have had a long history. Of the Roman *negotiatores* in the island Cicero says 'inviti . . . Romam raroque decedunt';[3] obviously the head of a family rooted there could become so bound up with his home and business that he might be reluctant to travel to Rome save under real necessity. As for landowners, some estates were managed by *vilici* for absentees; but in their extortions Verres' agents or accomplices had sometimes to deal with Roman proprietors living on or near their land.[4] Many liked living in Sicily; others perhaps, like Cato Maior and Columella, distrusted the unsupervised *vilicus*.

Apart from the merchants and traders, whom Cicero indicates as temporary residents rather than settlers,[5] the Sicilian Romans fell into three main classes, the *aratores* and *pecuarii*, the *negotiatores*, and men connected with the collection of the *decumae*, the *scriptura*, or the *portoria*; some may have combined these various pursuits.

The *aratores*, large arable farmers, are specifically attested in eastern Sicily, where around Tauromenium, Aetna, and Leontini, they had 'agros . . . fere optimos ac nobilissimos'; in the case of Leontini they may well have owned much of the land in the territory of the city.[6] But some *aratores* are mentioned without their place of residence, and there is no reason to

---

[1] The Romans of Syracuse are frequently mentioned in the *Verrines*: for their number and importance see especially II.5.155 and 94; Messana: II.4.26; Leontini, Aetna: II.3.106–9; Agrigentum: II.4.93; Lilybaeum: II.5.10; Panormus: II.5.16 and 140.
[2] Syracuse, above p. 19 f.; Halaesa, above p. 20.   [3] *Verrines* II.3.96.
[4] *Verrines* II.3.60; 61–63; 66.   [5] Ibid., II.2.6.
[6] 'agros . . . fere optimos ac nobilissimos', *Verrines* II. 3.104. In II.3.109 the actual citizens of Leontini are said not to have suffered through the activities of Verres' men. The reason given is 'quod in agro Leontino praeter

think that they were restricted to eastern Sicily. The *pecuarii*—large graziers and stock-breeders—are less prominent than the *aratores* in the *Verrines*; they probably had their pastures mostly in the interior highland regions, but lived on the coast. One Roman appears as *arator* and *pecuarius*; many, no doubt, pursued mixed farming.[1]

In Messana and Syracuse, Agrigentum, Lilybaeum, and Panormus bankers and moneylenders were presumably important, if not preponderant, among the local Romans, though only at Syracuse and Panormus are their activities specifically mentioned.[2] Syracuse probably had many sojourners equally at home in Sicily or Italy or other provinces; T. Herennius—probably of south Italian extraction—was born in Syracuse, went to Roman Africa and struck roots there, but was known to more than a hundred Syracusan Romans when he visited the city.[3] Were there better prosopographic evidence, families would certainly be found rooted both in Sicily and Italy, or in Sicily and other provinces, with wide connections like to those of certain eastern families from the second century.

Under Verres a number of Roman citizens abused local tithe contracts to his and their profit.[4] These people might be supposed to be of business families settled in Sicily, or at any rate, residents; but only their misdeeds are mentioned. Cicero, by implication, treats these accomplices of Verres as apart from the Sicilian Romans generally, whilst he conveys the converse impression that the better Sicilian Romans suffered no less at Verres' hands than did the Sicilians; but it may be that more Sicilian Romans than are mentioned had corrupt part in the collection of the *decumae*. Quite distinct from these people, who secured tithe contracts as individuals, was the important Roman

---

unam Mnasistrati familiam glebam Leontinorum possidet nemo'; but a great many of those owning land in the *ager Leontinus* were Sicilians, citizens of Centuripae (3.114).

[1] When Cicero asks Carpinatius who is the so-called Verrucius in his accounts and what he does, he says 'postulo ut mihi respondeat qui sit is Verrucius, mercator an negotiator an arator an pecuarius, in Sicilia sit an iam decesserit' (*Verrines* II.2.188). Clearly 'pecuarii' were one of the main classes of Romans in Sicily. C. Matrinius of Leontini was both *arator* and *pecuarius* (II.3.60 and 5.15).

[2] Syracuse, *Verrines* II.2.73; Panormus, II.5.140, 161.

[3] *Verrines* II.1.14, and 5.155 f.; for the name, below p. 153.

[4] Fully listed with references, by Scramuzza *E.S.A.R.* III.340.

societas farming other revenues, members of whose staff figure in the *Verrines*. This company appears, in Verres' governorship, to have collected the *scriptura* throughout Sicily and, in six ports at least, the *portoria*.[1] The *pro magistro*, L. Carpinatius, managing both departments in the whole province, seems to have been permanently in Sicily; likewise L. Canuleius, the local sub-manager at Syracuse for the *portoria*;[2] other sub-managers will have been resident in particular cities. Such may have been the position in early life of P. Rupilius, later consul and sponsor of the *lex provinciae* for Sicily of 132; he was said to have worked collecting *portoria* for a Roman *societas*, then to have been employed by Sicilians who had secured the local collection of *decumae*.[3] Here is another element in the Roman population in Sicily; but there is no light on the provincial importance of these people before the governorship of Verres.

Sicily twice received an exodus of victims of political strife, in 82–81, when Marians were driven out of Italy by military defeat and proscription, and again, in and after 42, when Sextus Pompeius made it a place of refuge—and resistance—for victims of the triumviral proscriptions and confiscations; and presumably persons exiled in the normal course of late Republican politics often went to the most obvious place of residence after Rome.[4] Certainly the beauties of Sicily encouraged well-to-do Romans to visit their Greek hosts[5] or to tour the cities, inspecting their glories in architecture, sculpture, and craftsmanship. They found, when Verres had done his worst, that the local guides could often only point to the place where a statue or other noble work had stood:

. . . ii qui hospites ad ea quae visenda sunt solent ducere et unum

---

[1] *E.S.A.R.* III.340 f.

[2] L. Carpinatius, *Verrines* II. 2.169 ff.; L. Canuleius, *Verrines* II.2.171, 176 f., 182 f.

[3] Valerius Maximus VI. 9.8: '. . . P. Rupilius non publicanum in Sicilia egit, sed operas publicanis dedit. Idem ultimam inopiam suam auctorato sociis officio sustentavit. . . . Portus ipsos, si quis mutis rebus inest sensus, tantam in eodem homine varietatem status admiratos arbitror: quem enim diurnas capturas exigentem animadverterant, eundem iura dantem . . . viderunt.'

[4] But there is no certain case; some doubt exists as to P. Cornelius Lentulus, the enemy of C. Gracchus (see *P-W* 'Cornelius' (202)1375).

[5] *Verrines* II.2.23 f. and 110. Of the distinguished persons who were guests of Sthenius of Thermae (II.2.110), C. Marius and L. Cornelius Sisenna may have gone as private visitors.

quidque ostendere—quos illi 'mystagogos' vocant—conversam iam habent demonstrationem suam. Nam ut antea demonstrabant quid ubique esset, item nunc quid undique ablatum sit ostendunt.[1]

But the existence of such professionals indicates the importance of these visitors in the great cities.

Indeed many Roman residents must have been drawn to Sicily as much by the attractions of life there, or the chance of a fine house and fine things for it,[2] as by business motives. Some went to retire, 'non negotiandi . . . sed otiandi causa', as did the cultivated and ease-loving Canius mentioned by Cicero in discussion of the morals of sale of property. Canius fell in love with a country seat and its gardens overlooking the sea near Syracuse, and was ingeniously hoaxed—without breach of law —by its owner, a Greek moneylender, into paying a greatly excessive sum for the property.[3]

The Sicilian Romans, or many among them, were very wealthy. Wealth, however, could not save those whom Verres determined to despoil, insult, or destroy. C. Matrinius of Leontini, a rich farmer and grazier, went away to Rome and left his *procurator*, L. Flavius, in charge; Flavius was compelled to pay Verres sixty thousand sesterces, or allow the charge to be brought against Matrinius that he had failed to deal with dangerous unrest among his slaves and connections between them and the slave rebels in Italy.[4] Men who loved fine things had furniture, works of art, or other treasures taken from them.[5] Persons of standing were brought into court on false charges and then condemned through a carefully arranged travesty of justice.[6] Others, sitting with Verres in his judicial capacity in public proceedings, were treated with complete disregard for their social station and dignity.[7] The Roman citizens actually executed by Verres were, it appears, not settlers established in Sicily, but merchants and sea captains using the Sicilian ports, or other voyagers.[8] Some were 'homines tenues, obscuro loco nati';[9] as was P. Gavius of Samnite Compsa, crucified at Messana; but others were well-to-do and had friends and influence in Sicily; such was the African banker, T. Herennius,

---

[1] Ibid., II.4.132.
[2] Ibid., II.4.37, 43 ff., especially 44.
[3] Cicero *de Officiis* III.58 ff.
[4] *Verrines* II.5.15.
[5] Ibid., II.4.37, 43 ff., 58.
[6] Ibid., II.2.31 ff.
[7] Ibid., II.2.71 ff.
[8] Ibid., II.5.72 ff, with 154.
[9] Ibid., II.5.167.

whom Verres beheaded at Syracuse.[1] The Sicilian Romans, knowing these people and having business with many of them, should have felt their execution as a blow at themselves.

Some of the settlers ventured to resist the demands of Verres' agents, to try to help his victims, Roman or Sicilian, or to complain openly. Thus Q. Lollius, a rich landowner in the Aetna district, relying on 'equestri vetere illa auctoritate et gratia', declared that he would not pay to Verres' accomplice, Apronius, more tithe than was strictly due, and resisted strongly till overcome by brutal violence.[2] Q. Septicius of Leontini did the same, without eventual success.[3] L. Rubrius of Syracuse publicly challenged Apronius to deny the partnership between Verres and himself in extortionate tithe collection,[4] and P. Scandilius issued the same challenge, with greater persistence than Rubrius, though not to the point of endangering his life;[5] C. Servilius, a *negotiator* long established in Panormus, went about commenting bitterly on Verres' conduct, till he was beaten by Verres' lictors and died as a result.[6] But it was as individuals that the settlers protested; though Cicero mentions indignation meetings in Rome on behalf of the *aratores* in Sicily, it is clear that there was no concerted action by the Sicilian Romans during Verres' term to get the Senate to bring restraining influence to bear upon him.

Of course the *decumani* in Sicily were squared by Verres or were his active accomplices, and the *equites* generally had been excluded for a decade from the juries *de repetundis*. Even so, the contrast is striking between the apparent apathy of the Sicilian Romans as a body and the African agitation of 108, which did much to deprive Metellus of his command, or the agitation soon to begin among the Romans in Asia against Lucullus. Cicero, though he emphasizes the hatred of the Sicilian Romans generally for Verres,[7] gives the impression that, apart from a minority, they made the best of a bad business, till Verres left and he himself came on the scene.

Speaking of the relations between Rome and its citizens, and the Sicilians, Cicero says 'sic . . . nostros homines diligunt ut iis

[1] *Verrines*, II.5.155.   [2] Ibid., II.3.61 ff.
[3] Ibid., II.3.36.   [4] Ibid., II.3.132.
[5] Ibid., II.3.135–41. Scandilius was a man of note, well-known to the jury, and, if anyone, should have been able to resist Verres (cf. 135).
[6] Ibid., II.5.140–2.   [7] Ibid., II.2.15 f.

solis neque publicanus neque negotiator odio sit'.[1] The great antiquity of relations between Sicily and Italy and the peace enjoyed by the island (the slave wars apart) since annexation may have done a good deal to reconcile the Sicilians to Roman rule; the system employed for raising the *decumae* allowed Sicilians to bid for local contracts, and until Verres came, it may have worked better for them than the Gracchan system did for Asia. But, except for a passing allusion to the good relations between the Agrigentines and the local Romans,[2] Cicero gives no further indication what the relations may have been between Romans and Sicilians in times more normal than the governorship of Verres.

Campanian or south-Italian origin is suggested for the majority of the Sicilian Romans in the early first century by the nomenclature found in the *Verrines*,[3] but the total of names is not great and too much must not be inferred from an inadequate sample. It is clear that Puteoli was exceedingly important in the trade between Italy and Sicily, and Cicero emphasizes the number of Puteolan traders at Syracuse and their intense interest in the trial:

adsunt enim Puteoli toti; frequentissimi venerunt ad hoc iudicium mercatores, homines locupletes atque honesti, qui partim socios suos, partim libertos, partim conlibertos spoliatos in vincla coniectos, partim in vinclis necatos, partim securi percussos esse dicunt.[4]

It is not surprising the first witness called by Cicero (or rather to be called, had he needed to deliver the speech) is a P. Granius of the great Puteolan commercial family, active from the second century in various parts of the Empire.[5]

Yet it is unclear whether the Sicilians or Sicilian Romans were much affected, politically, by their proximity to southern Italy. Marian feeling was indeed strong in that region in the crisis of the early first century; many Sicilian Romans must have sprung from southern Italy, and south Italians were probably numerous

---

[1] Ibid., II.2.7; see also 5.8, even more emphatic language.
[2] Ibid., II.4.93.
[3] See Frank 'On the Migration of Romans to Sicily', *A.J.P.* LVI (1935) 61–5, and Scramuzza, *E.S.A.R.* III.337 f.
[4] *Verrines* II.5.154.
[5] P. Granius as witness, ibid.; for the Granii generally see my index, s.vv.

in the Sertorian forces in Spain. Possibly then, though neither the Italians in 91–89 nor the Marians in the civil war are known to have had strong support in Sicily,[1] important connections existed, at the height of the Sertorian war, between the rebel forces in Spain and sympathizers in southern Italy and Sicily. But it hardly follows that Verres, as late as 72, was faced (as has been maintained) with an underground movement of Roman Sertorians in Sicily, or that Cicero is misrepresenting when he alleges that Verres executed loyal merchants, ship-captains, and voyagers as Sertorians or as pirates.[2] Not even Verres would have used this pretext had not some Sertorians been trying to reach friends in Sicily; but these were no more than refugees of a broken movement, who had not heard or had not trusted Pompeius' offer of amnesty and protection. Here Cicero's charges should not perhaps be taken at their face value in every particular; that does not mean that the truth was the opposite of all that he says, or that, on this assumption, inferences should be drawn inconsistent with the circumstances of 72 and the entire collapse of the Sertorians in Spain.

The island was not disturbed by the war of 49–45 B.C., since Cato, who had intended to hold it, left when Pompeius left Italy. Thus the test never came which would have revealed the sympathies of the Romans there.[3] Cicero continued to regard himself as the patron of Sicily,[4] but little is known, after the prosecution of Verres, of his relations with inhabitants, and his letters on behalf of natives and *negotiatores*, extant for 46,[5] show only that he maintained his influence to the best of his ability; he continued in touch with families he had got to know as provincial *quaestor* or as prosecutor of Verres.[6]

Nothing is known of the attitude of the Sicilian Romans to the grant, or proposed grant, of Latin rights by Caesar to the Sicilian communities,[7] or to the law of Antonius, after Caesar's

---

[1] Sicily in the Social War, *Verrines* II.2.5 and II.5.8; Pompeius in Sicily, Plutarch *Pompeius* 10, with Cicero *de imperio Cn. Pompeii* 61.

[2] E. Gabba 100 f. maintains this.

[3] Pompeius had connections there, presumably established in 81 B.C.: Cicero *Verrines* II.2.23 and 110; 4.25 and 48 (Sicilians granted the citizenship through him).

[4] *Ad Att.* XIV.12.1.   [5] *Ad Fam.* XIII.30–9.

[6] Ibid., XIII.38, with 31 (where L. Flavius may well be the important witness of the same name in *Verrines* II.1.14 and 5.155 f.).

[7] Cicero *ad Att.* XIV.12.1.

death, providing for the conferment of citizenship upon them. Antonius' law, as remarks of Cicero make pretty clear, was soon treated as null and void; it cannot have affected the political progress of the Sicilian communities.[1] What did affect that progress was the war waged from Sicily from 42 to 36 B.C. by Sextus Pompeius against the Triumvirs. On the one hand, Sextus, by organizing an exodus from Italy to Sicily of combatants and refugees, introduced new Roman elements into the major cities, and promoted their social Romanization; on the other hand, the acquiescence of the Sicilians in his rule delayed their political advancement under Augustus, by impairing his regard for them.

In his organized rescue operations in 42 Sextus succeeded in shipping from Italy large numbers of men prepared to resist the Triumvirs in arms.[2] Apart from combatants, Sicily is likely to have received many refugees anxious only to escape, with their lives and portable assets, out of the range of the proscriptions and confiscations. Even if Appian exaggerates in saying that three hundred senators and two thousand knights were proscribed,[3] waves of fear must have gone through the richer classes, affecting not only those listed, but others who feared proscription for their wealth. When this method gave the Triumvirs disappointing returns in money and property, a programme of direct exactions followed;[4] but neither the proscriptions nor these had as many victims as the confiscations instituted after Philippi to get land for the soldiers due for discharge. Eighteen cities lost land; the beneficiaries were the veterans of twenty-eight legions; unauthorized, as well as official, seizures took place; and the allotments are not likely to have been small.[5] The number of the expropriated must have been very great, even if the legions benefiting were well below full strength. Crowds came to Rome 'young and old, women and children . . ., lamenting and saying that they had done no wrong, for which, though Italians, they should be driven from

---

[1] *Philippics* XII.12 and XIII.5, with the comments of How *Select Letters of Cicero* on *ad Att.* XIV.12.1 (p. 484 *ad fin.* of the *Notes*).

[2] Appian IV.36(149–54) and 85(355–7). Men escaped by every sort of device and some fought their way out of Italy with followers, gathering more en route: *op. cit.* IV.25(104–6), and 39–48(163–209) *passim*.

[3] Appian IV.5(20).   [4] Appian IV.31 f. (133–6), 34(146); Dio XLVII.14.

[5] See in particular Appian IV.3(10–12); V.5(21–3), Antonius' warning to the East after Philippi.

lands and homes like the defeated in war'.[1] No compensation in land elsewhere was given to these people. But shrewd people, in this sort of situation, find means to save the future, and many of the dispossessed certainly re-established themselves in Sicily, where Sextus was prepared to receive any victim of the Triumvirate.

Augustus' caution, as *Princeps*, in granting Roman charters to Sicilian cities, is evidently to be explained by their acquiescence in the rule of Sextus Pompeius from 42 to 36 B.C. But the political advancement of Sicily had to begin. Romans were numerous, as has been seen, and locally important there in the late Republic. They probably grew in number and in influence under Augustus. As the island, subject to the pervasive influence of the Latin language and Roman customs, became more and more romanized socially, political Romanization was finally inevitable.

NARBONENSIS

From 125 to 121 B.C. there were yearly wars with tribal peoples in and around the valley of the Rhône, particularly with the Allobroges around and east of Vienna (Vienne). The region which became provincial in 121 stretched, in the east, from the Rhône to the high Alps; on the other side of the river, it took in country to the eastern Cevennes and, in the south-west, territory bounded by the Tarn valley and the upper Garonne. The activities of the Greeks of Massilia and her colonies along the neighbouring shores had done much to hellenize and civilize the coastal districts, and it had been to protect the city that Rome first intervened in southern Gaul. Massilia remained nominally independent within the new province, and the seat of the governor was established at Narbo (Narbonne) between the sea and the hill capital of the tribal Volcae Arecomici. Narbo had an important position at the junction of the coastal route and the road inland to south-western Gaul; but, apart from Narbo itself and army veterans at Tolosa,[2] it seems likely that most settlers went, not to this western region, but to the valley of the lower Rhône and the surrounding country.

[1] Appian v.12(49).
[2] On the assumption that the men from Tolosa called to the legions by Caesar in 56 (*B.G.* III.20.2) must have included Roman veterans.

The first settlers, as in Spain, were veterans established as an organized community without the status of *colonia*: Aquae Sextiae (Aix-en-Provence) founded in 122 B.C. fifteen miles north of Massilia by Sextus Calvinus after his defeat of the local Salluvii.[1] In 118, despite fairly obstinate senatorial resistance to the law, Narbo became a *colonia c. R.*, for veterans, as the title 'Martius' given to the settlement indicates;[2] but the colony must soon have begun to attract private settlers as well, and by 80 B.C. these were numerous in the province, congregating wherever profits offered, as is clear from Cicero's private speech *pro Quinctio* in 81 and his important speech of 69 defending Fonteius' actions as governor about 75.[3] Their support in the case was important for Fonteius, the charges against whom of high-handed harshness (if not those of corruption) might be countered by reference to the emergency conditions of his term of office. For while Fonteius strove to raise supplies for the armies fighting Sertorius in Spain, control of Narbonensis was threatened by native revolts, concerted with the Sertorians and aimed at cutting communications between Italy and the forces of the Senate; though Cicero refers to a siege of Narbo,[4] it need not be supposed the life of the Roman communities in the coastal region was wholly disrupted, but parts of the interior may have been unsafe for private Romans without armed protection. As the province had comparative quiet thereafter, disturbed only by the siege of Massilia in 49 and the bloodless movements of forces in 43, little is heard of the Narbonese Romans except in Cicero's speech for Fonteius, though they can hardly have failed to be involved, in some measure, in the antagonisms of Rome and Italy.[5]

Pecuarii and *aratores*, *negotiatores* and *publicani* are the occupational classes mentioned in the *pro Quinctio* and the *pro Fonteio*.[6]

[1] Livy *per*. LXI, Strabo 180. Livy *per*. says 'C. Sextius . . . coloniam Aquas Sextias condidit'; but the town had Latin status under Augustus (Pliny *N.H.* III.36), and the language of the *periochae* must here be inaccurate.

[2] For the sources for the foundation of Narbo generally see Hirschfeld *C.I.L.* XII p. 521; for the opposition to the scheme, Cicero *Brutus* 43 and *pro Cluentio* 140; the title 'Martius' first appears in *pro Fonteio* 13, but must go back to the foundation.

[3] *pro Quinctio* 11 ff.; *pro Fonteio* 11 f.

[4] Siege of Narbo, *pro Fonteio* 46; the disturbances generally, ibid.

[5] This involvement is traceable only in the case of Massilia and of Celtic notables: see R. Syme 74 f.   [6] *pro Quinctio* 11 ff.; *pro Fonteio* 12.

The *negotiatores*, as was seen earlier, cannot have been as ubiquitous as a literal interpretation of Cicero in the *pro Fonteio* would suggest, but about 100 they may have reached even small places, such as Glanum (St. Rémy),[1] not far from Arelate on the road for the Alpes Cottiae; and there is no doubt of their economic importance. Bankers and moneylenders must have had their offices in the cities of the coastal belt, but will have done business, not only with these, but with the chiefs in the interior and their communities. Cicero is probably referring to financiers established in the province when he says that Murena, as governor, in 64 helped 'our men' to collect bad debts;[2] the load of debt which nearly drove the Allobroges to join Catiline in 63[3] was probably contracted with moneylenders settled in Narbonensis. Some of the traders supplying Gaul with wine may well have established homes in the cities on or near the coast, between their Italian source of supply and their customers, and certain of the Romans whom Caesar found doing business in the heart of Gallia Comata are likely to have lived in coastal Narbonensis.[4]

Massilia is most famous in this age as a place of residence for exiles.[5] But there is no reason to suppose that its loss to Narbo of its commercial ascendancy was sudden, and it probably had a *conventus c. R.* in the late Republic; three languages were then spoken in the city, Greek, Celtic, and Latin.[6] In the Augustan age Massiliote commerce was decayed, but it was already the foremost centre of learning in the western Empire, attracting Roman φιλομαθεῖς, as Strabo noted, in great and growing number.[7] Its vogue among these may go back to the last decades of the Republic. Strabo connects the interest of the Massiliotes in things academic with the collapse of Massilia as an important maritime city. That maritime importance probably began to decline with the rise of Narbo from the late second century, though collapse came only when Massilia chose the Pompeian

[1] H. Rolland *Glanum*, plates XL and XLI, with his *Introduction* p. 9.
[2] *pro Murena* 42.   [3] Sallust *Catiline* 40.
[4] The wine traders, see Cicero *pro Fonteio* 19 f., with Diodorus Siculus v.26.3 (thought to be based on Poseidonius). Roman men of business in Comata, Caesar *B.G.* VII.3.1 and 42.1–3.
[5] Dio XL.54.3 (Milo), with Sallust *Catiline* 34.2, Cicero *in Catilinam* II.14 and *pro Sestio* 7.
[6] Varro, quoted by Isidorus *Etymologiae* XV.1.63.
[7] Strabo 180 *ad fin.* to 181 *ad init.*

side in 49 and suffered serious loss through the stimulus given by Caesar to the rival trade of Arelate.[1]

Speaking of the peoples along the lower Rhône and in the coastal country to each side of its mouth, Strabo sums them up as οὐδὲ βαρβάρους ἔτι ὄντας ἀλλὰ μετακειμένους τὸ πλέον εἰς τὸν τῶν Ῥωμαίων τύπον καὶ τῇ γλώττῃ καὶ τοῖς βίοις, τίνας δὲ καὶ τῇ πολιτείᾳ.[2] Social Romanization, as he saw it, preceded political Romanization. For all the commercial predominance of Narbo, and despite the more obvious effects of the colonizing work of Caesar and Augustus, it may well be that this social Romanization of the lower Rhône and coastal region was due as much to commerce and private settlement as to the establishment of the famous public colonies.

Note: an alleged prohibition on new olive groves and vineyards

I have not thought it necessary to discuss above the prohibition, mentioned in Cicero *de Re Publica* III.16, on the planting of olive groves and vineyards by the 'Transalpinae gentes', in order to keep up the value of olive groves and vineyards in Italy. It is pointless to discuss at length the possible success or duration of a measure about which there is no other evidence. But the following points may be made: (1) It is most unlikely that Cicero invented the prohibition (despite the anachronism of including it in a dialogue with the dramatic date 129 B.C.). (2) If the export of oil and wine to Transalpine Gaul made a real difference to the value of olive groves and vineyards in Italy, it must have been on a fairly considerable scale; the evidence of Diodorus v.26.2 about the wine trade is confirmed by this scrap of evidence, for what it is worth. (3) The Senate, not quick to intervene in economic matters, will not have taken this step because of a hypothetical threat from Gallic production to Italian exports of olive oil or wine, but only because olive oil and wine were being produced on a rapidly increasing scale by the Transalpine Gallic communities. (4) If the native communities were cultivating the olive and the vine on a fair scale, then *a*

---

[1] Strabo 180 *ad fin.*, saying simply that by joining Pompeius the Massiliotes 'lost most of their prosperity'. The reason was that Caesar made Arelate a Roman colony, at the territorial expense of Massilia, and established thereby a rival, in addition to Narbo, to her trade and prosperity. The commercial importance of Narbo: Strabo 186 *ad fin.*

[2] 186 *ad fin.*

fortiori the Roman immigrants will have been doing so, much of the coastal region being more suitable for such purposes than for cereal crops (the Massiliotes always cultivated olives and vines rather than corn on their lands, largely unsuitable for the latter —Strabo 179). (5) Narbo, Aquae Sextiae, and Massilia will not have been affected by the prohibition. (6) Cicero does not say that the *Transalpinae gentes* were ordered to root up existing olive groves and vineyards; Varro, who mentions agricultural conditions in various provinces in the *Res Rustica* (published 37 B.C.), makes no mention of the prohibition; Strabo, writing under Augustus, describes Narbonensis as a land where the olive and the vine were widely cultivated (Strabo 178).

DALMATIA

The strip of fertile plain along the eastern Adriatic, from the modern Albanian frontier to Fiume, is extremely narrow, save in one district, and immediately overlooked by a high and steep mountain wall, cut by few valleys or passes into the wild interior. Control of the coast was difficult to achieve without control of the interior, and conquest of the interior a hard task, despite the disunity of the native peoples. Under Augustus, Strabo notes the number of good harbours and the suitability of the coast for the vine and olive, but goes on to say that the seaboard 'was poorly thought of in earlier times, perhaps because people did not know its fertility, but more because of the fierceness of the inhabitants'.[1] This obviously means that settlement began late in Dalmatia, but no more precise indication is given by Strabo's Dalmatian section, in which, clearly basing himself on an out-of-date source, he takes no explicit note of the important Roman towns flourishing on the coast at the time when he wrote.

Some of these went back beyond the Dictatorship of Caesar, but, in the light of conditions in the previous two centuries, probably not to any very early date. Illyrian barbarism in the third and second centuries is perhaps exaggerated in the traditional accounts; none the less the Greek colonial cities north of the modern Albanian frontier may always have had a bad time with the peoples of the interior and the piratical communities

[1] Strabo 317.

of the coast, and by the second century most Greek cities seem in decline or practically barbarized.[1] From Epirus Roman sovereignty was extended north in 167 to the river Narenta (the Neretva), but the region remained exposed to raids by the peoples beyond the river. This caused a number of inconclusive wars,[2] till the northern coast was conquered in 78-76.[3] It was now open to settlement, but not wholly secure against the mountain peoples of the hinterland[4] or the traditional Adriatic piracy; that, though suppressed by Pompeius in 67, revived during the civil wars and flourished till it was finally put down by Octavian in 35-33 B.C.[5]

The Greek colony on the island of Issa (roughly equidistant from Brundisium and Aquileia) flourished, unlike the others, throughout the Hellenistic period.[6] About the middle of the second century Issa claimed as subject to her Tragurion and Epetion, on the coast almost due north,[7] and presumably the land between, Salona and its neighbourhood. This district, always fought for by the powerful Delmatae of the nearby mountains, fell again into their hands, but was taken by the Romans in 76.[8] Caesar probably restored it in 56 to Issa;[9] but a

[1] There does not seem to be any adequate general discussion of this subject. Brunšmid in 'Die Inschriften und Münzen der griechischen Städte Dalmatiens', *Abhandlungen des arch.—ep. Seminars Wien* (1898) 95 ff., brings together the epigraphic and numismatic material. The nomenclature of the inscriptions seems to show that most of the Greek communities became illyrianized (cf. H. Krahe *Altillyrische Personennamen, passim*), and their coinage grows coarser and poorer. Many of them became subject to the powerful south-Illyrian kingdom in the latter part of the third century. They are litttle heard of in the second and first century B.C. In the first century A.D. Pliny speaks of their existence as a fading memory (*N.H.* III.144). For the decline, even before the fourth century, of Greek settlements on the Dalmatian coast further north, see pseudo-Scymnus 411 ff.

[2] For these wars see Patsch *P-W* 'Delmatae' 2448 f. and Vulić *P-W* 'Iapodes' 725. Victories over the Delmatae around and behind Salona had little permanent effect, as appears from the repeated renewal of war, and Salona seems to have been in their hands in 78 (see the following note).

[3] Eutropius VI.4; Orosius V.23.23.

[4] Patsch *P-W* 'Delmatae' 2449 ff.; Vulić *P-W* 'Iapodes' 725 f.

[5] Appian *Illyrica* 16.

[6] M. Fluss 'Issa', *P-W* Suppl. V.347 ff.

[7] Polybius XXXII.9.1 f.

[8] See above note 3.

[9] See Kubitschek *Jahrbuch für Altertumsk.* 1.78 ff., for a fragmentary inscription of 56 B.C., found on the mainland, recording some decision by Caesar affecting Issa; presumably the decision was about the claims of Issa on the district.

conventus c. R. may already have existed there, for Romans appear in control of the place in 49, in the first fighting in the Adriatic of the civil war.[1] Salona, in Roman times, is often 'Salonae', and will so be termed here.

A Roman citizen represented Issa before Caesar in 56, when he was considering her claims.[2] In 48 B.C. Issa was 'nobilissimum earum regionum oppidum',[3] but little is known of her population. Two inscriptions suggest the city may have been bilingual at this time,[4] though her official language was Greek; whether or not there was a Roman element in Issa, enthusiasm for Caesar, striking in these years in the *conventus* of the mainland, is conspicuous by its absence at Issa.[5]

The attachment of the Dalmatian Romans was deliberately cultivated by Caesar in his proconsulate. In the south he brought together the Romans scattered about the district of Lake Scutari, settled them in the town of Lissus (Leš), and fortified it for them.[6] The *conventus* of Lissus, as Caesar terms this community, helped him in early 48, when he was shipping troops to Epirus.[7] Before this, in late 49, the Romans of Salonae had resisted siege and storm by a strong Pompeian force,[8] which had brought over the neighbouring Illyrians and the Greeks of Issa; it was the energy and courage of the Salonitan *conventus* that saved Caesar from loss of the Dalmatian coast to its south. Fighting continued in the Adriatic, after Pharsalus, between Pompeian and Caesarian naval forces. In this the latter were helped, not for the first time, by the Romans at Iader (Zadar), with such ships as they had; Salonae did fresh service in the winter of 48–47.[9]

The Romans at Iader were among Illyrians, on what may

---

[1] *B.C.* III.9.   [2] See above p. 69.

[3] *B. Alex.* 47.3.

[4] *C.I.L.* III.3076 (bi-lingual), 3075 (Latin words, Greek turn of expression). The official inscription found on the mainland is in Greek.

[5] *B. Alex.* 47.3.

[6] Caesar *B.C.* III.29.1. Perhaps this was in 54 B.C., when Caesar visited this southern part of his Illyrian province, 'quod a Pirustis finitimam partem provinciae incursionibus vastari audiebat' (*B.G.* v.1.5–9).

[7] *B.C.* III.29.1.

[8] Op. cit. III.9. The town had walls, but these were inadequate and had to be improved in the emergency with wooden towers. Scanty remains have been found of an early gate, which Gerber (*Forschungen in Salona* I.2) assigns to the late Republican period.

[9] Iader, *B. Alex.* 42.3; Salonae, ibid., 43, especially 2.

have been an old Illyrian site;[1] the *conventus* at Salonae on ground long disputed by Greek Issa and the Illyrian Delmatae; at Lissus Romans took over a town whose population had probably long lost its former Greek character and become more or less Illyrian.[2] The other late Republican settlement now known was on a site where a Greek trading post existed in the fourth century, Narona, near the modern Metković, not far from the mouth of the river Neretva.[3]

The existence of Roman Narona in the late Republic is attested by a few inscriptions, which cannot be precisely dated. One shows that it had two *magistri*, and also two *quaestores*— who were responsible for its walls.[4] This indicates that the community was organized for effective action, but does not indicate its precise status.

In the summer of 45 and the succeeding winter Vatinius, who was conducting a difficult and inconclusive war against the Delmatae, wrote letters to Cicero from his headquarters at Narona.[5] These suggest that, with the Delmatae hostile, control even of the coastlands was insecure; the Romans of the coastal *conventus* were suffering badly at the hands of a Pompeian still at large with some sort of troops at his disposal.[6] When the

---

[1] On a promontory of what is now the Ravni Kotari ('Level Corner'), where the Dalmatian coast widens into a fairly broad tract of comparatively level country. The name 'Iader' is Illyrian, and it is likely that the district was purely Illyrian (Liburnian) when settlement began. Pseudo-Scymnus (410 ff.), writing about 90 B.C. and using much earlier sources, refers to Greek settlements there which had become barbarized.

[2] See Fluss *P-W* 'Lissos' 733 f. Lissus was very close to Scodra, capital of the powerful south-Illyrian kingdom, which grew up in the third century and lasted till the defeat of Genthius by Rome in 168 B.C.

[3] The *Periplus* of pseudo-Scylax (fourth century) 24 says that the station lay nine miles from the sea and could be reached by triremes and merchant vessels. The site of Narona (the village of Vid, two miles north of the port Metković) is about eleven miles from the present river mouth; but it is certain that the land has grown considerably through accumulation of river silt.

[4] *C.I.L.* III.1820 = *I.L.S.* II(1)7166; *C.I.L.* III.1784 records the building of a temple to 'Leiber Pater' by the freedman *quaestor*, P. Annaeus Q. l. Epicadus, on his private account. This freedman (himself, as 'Epicadus', clearly Illyrian) may be connected with a family of Aquileia (see *C.I.L.* I² (2 fasc. 1).2198 and 2202, also 2286, a freedman Annaeus in Pannonia). Q. Safinius (I².2291) has a name common in Campania (Münzer *P-W* 'Safinius'), but found also in an early inscription of Aquileia (I²(2).2212).

[5] *ad Fam.* v.9 and 10 (*a*) and (*b*).

[6] Apart from Vatinius' letter (*ad Fam.* v.10(*a*)) nothing is known of this C. Catilius. He must be either a Pompeian or an adventurer exploiting the

Delmatae heard of the death of Caesar, they resisted even more strongly, and Vatinius, in despair of success or because of the political situation, withdrew to Epirus.[1] Darkness now falls on the region until Octavian's Illyrian wars of 35–33 B.C., the accounts of which throw no light on the fortunes of the *conventus* in those or the foregoing years.[2]

It is not by any means always clear, in the western Mediterranean, when precisely a *conventus* was superseded by a *colonia c. R.* or *municipium c. R.*; but in most provinces stages appear in the process of the general supercession of *conventus* by such foundations, and one sees the relative importance, in the process, of the Dictatorship of Caesar, the succeeding interregnum, the Principate of Augustus, and the following century. In Dalmatia obscurity surrounds the beginning of the changes. In the other provinces I have left this subject aside, as it has been treated clearly and fully by Vittinghoff; here the last years of my period will be neglected if I do not add to his rather slighter treatment of the matter.[3]

Iader received its status as *colonia c. R.* from Augustus; this could conceivably have happened before he assumed that title.[4] Salonae was 'colonia Martia Iulia',[5] and, though the inscription recording this title is late, the colonization must have taken

---

troubled conditions. When Vatinius eventually captured Catilius, Cicero wrote to him asking for leniency. Vatinius, though promising to do what he could, was indignant at the request: 'Sed huiusce modi vos clientes, huius modi causas recipitis? hominem unum omnium crudelissimum, qui tot ingenuos, matresfamilias, cives Romanos occidit, abripuit, disperdidit, regiones vastavit. Simius, non semissis homo, contra me arma tulit et eum bello cepi . . .'

[1] Appian *Illyrica* 13 *ad fin.*

[2] Appian *Illyrica* 16–28 is the main source for Octavian's Illyrian campaigns of 35–33 B.C., but by no means satisfactory. If Salonae, as Strabo appears to say (315), was among the places which Octavian burned, it must have fallen into the hands of the Delmatae; but it may be through careless construction of his sentence that he seems to include Salonae in the list. In any case he is poor evidence for events in Dalmatia in this period.

[3] Vittinghoff 85 and 124 ff.

[4] *C.I.L.* III(1)2907: 'Imp. Caesar Divi f. Aug. parens coloniae murum et turris dedit. T. Iulius Optatus turris vetustate consumptas inpensa sua restituit.' This is not a late inscription, as the excellence of the lettering indicates; but it was certainly put up some considerable time after the foundation, as the reference to the state of the walls shows. It does not seem reasonable to assume that, when the *colonia* was founded, the Princeps *must* already have been *Augustus*.

[5] *C.I.L.* III(1)1933.

place before the death of Augustus, since there was little, if any, foundation of Roman colonies under Tiberius. Narona was a *colonia* in the early years of Tiberius,[1] but again cannot owe the status to him. Epidaurum (where a *conventus* may have existed in the late Republic, but is not actually attested) appears as a *colonia* (without special title) in Pliny's provincial list,[2] and may have had this title from the time of Augustus, since Pliny's lists appear, in the main, to depend on a source going back to that period.[3]

If there is any likely assumption about these colonies, it is that they were founded as a group in the same year or years. This assumption made, choice of the most probable time lies between the closing period of Caesar's Dictatorship, the years 33/32 (the close of the Illyrian war and immediately after it), and the Principate of Augustus, from 30 B.C. The various considerations will be set out fully by another author,[4] and only the outline of the argument need concern us here, without regard to the necessarily doubtful arguments from the tribal affiliations of the various cities.[5]

Against the Principate of Augustus, it seems an almost conclusive argument that Augustus, when he lists, in the *Res Gestae,* the regions where he established veterans in colonies, makes no mention of Illyricum or of any region that might be understood as including Illyricum.[6] Against transformation of the *conventus* into *coloniae* in the last years of Caesar, it may be argued that the Delmatae were then giving serious trouble, and that Vatinius had his hands full dealing with them in 45–44 B.C. Admittedly the situation in those years is not known in great

---

[1] *Ann. Ep.* 1950 no. 44; see also *Ann. Ep.* 1912 no. 45 (a late inscription, establishing the title 'Iulia') and Pliny *N.H.* III.142 ('Narona colonia').

[2] Pliny *N.H.* III.144, with *C.I.L.* III.12695 (early second century).

[3] See Detlefsen *Die Anordnung der geographischen Bücher des Plinius und ihre Quellen* 26 ff.

[4] A detailed work on Roman Dalmatia is to be published by J. J. Wilkes in Jugoslavia.

[5] If we say that a certain colony must have been founded by Caesar, because its citizens belong to a certain tribe, and another colony by Augustus, because of the tribal affiliation of its citizens, we are saying that we understand completely the system of tribal affiliation in the period. But we cannot understand the system fully so long as we are in doubt about the foundation dates of many *coloniae* and *municipia c. R.* Let us avoid so obvious a risk of circular argument.

[6] *Op. cit.* col. 28 (Ehrenberg and Jones p. 24).

detail; but one, at least, of the colonies, Iader, is without question after Caesar, and to keep the group together, if possible, would seem much the best solution. If this is to be done, there remain the years 33/32 B.C.

The same objection might be raised against these years as against dating to the Principate, that the *Res Gestae* has no mention of colonization in Illyricum. But there appear to have been circumstances, of a kind now difficult to divine, causing Augustus, when it came to presentation of his public career in the form of the *Res Gestae*, to play down events in 35–32 B.C., so far as Illyricum was concerned. In one column the recovery of the standard lost by Gabinius to the Delmatae in 47 is mentioned, together with the recapture of standards lost elsewhere;[1] but Illyricum appears neither where the pacification of western provinces is mentioned,[2] nor among the western provinces that swore the oath of allegiance to Octavian in 32.[3] If the objection is ruled out, arguments appear for 33/32. Iader may perfectly well have been colonized by Octavian in the closing stages of his Illyrian war or immediately after it. If Salonae, Narona, and Epidaurum were colonized at this time together with Iader, the function of such a line of colonies can be seen better than at any other time—to help the control of territory recently pacified along the eastern Adriatic, and to guard against any revival, by Antonius, of the strategy used there in 49–47 by the Pompeians. This would fit in with what may have been done at the head of the Adriatic; Tergeste (Trieste), Pola, on the eastern coast of Istria, and Emona, fifty miles inland, in what became Pannonia, may all have received colonists about 33 B.C.[4] But it is only at Tergeste that the evidence is really strong, and the case for this period for the transformation of the Dalmatian *conventus* into *coloniae* remains circumstantial.

The presence of settlers in the Triumviral period is attested in one inscription only. In 36 B.C., two brothers, Papii, set up a monument several miles up river from Narona, celebrating the

[1] Column 29 (Ehrenberg and Jones p. 24).
[2] Column 26 (ibid., p. 22).
[3] Column 25 (ibid., p. 22).
[4] Tergeste, *C.I.L.* v(1)525 f., with the comments of Mommsen on p. 53; Emona, Mommsen *C.I.L.* III(1) p. 489; Pola, Pliny *N.H.* III.129, with the comments of Chilver *Cisalpine Gaul* 22 f.

recent recovery of Sicily by Octavian from Sextus Pompeius.[1]
It is reasonable to suppose that they erected their monument in
the country because they had a farm or estate there; but it need
not be supposed that the Papii were *coloni* or Narona already a
colony, since landowning settlers appear in various provinces
in the absence of colonization. The Papii, whatever brought
them to the district, seem private individuals—not serving
soldiers or connected with the governor; their sympathies, in a
province under Octavian, where the Romans had consistently
supported Caesar, are only what might be expected.

[1] *C.I.L.* iii.14625 = *I.L.S.* iii(2)8893 = Ehrenberg and Jones p. 57 no. 9.

CHAPTER VI

THE WESTERN SETTLERS AND ROMAN POLITICS

SETTLEMENT began in the major western provinces—Sicily, the Spains, Africa, Narbonensis—as soon as they were severally established. The evidence about settlers happens to be most abundant in the revolutionary age. Provincial Romans now take a prominent place in the life of the western regions and in history, and make their appearance for the first time in a new region, the Dalmatian coast. The Dalmatian *conventus* may have been still young when they played their part in the war of 49–45; but elsewhere most of the *conventus* now firmly established had probably sprung up in the second century. In these several regions it seems fair, by the revolutionary age, to speak of a fully-grown provincial Roman class.

There is no indication how far, in normal times, the legionary forces in a province kept a protective eye on Roman settlers. But it seems clear that the immigrants, where they gathered in appreciable numbers, were so dominant locally that they did not normally go in danger on their streets or in their fields, even though there might be resentment at their presence among the natives. Indeed, if a typical *conventus* is to be seen in the Romans of Dalmatian Salonae, such bodies were capable of defending themselves against attack by regular forces; the combined pressure of Pompeians by sea and hostile natives by land could not break the resistance of the Salonitan *conventus* in 49–48, and along this coast as a whole the settlers defended themselves effectively against attack during this civil war.

The tenacity of the Dalmatian Romans was in self-defence and in loyalty to Caesar. But, as has been shown, the attitude of provincial Romans in 49–45 B.C. varied sharply, according to the degree of influence which Pompeius or Caesar had secured locally, the changing fortune of war, and the treatment by either side of the territories it held or gained. Earlier it had been otherwise. In 108 the African Romans, when they agitated

76

to help Marius secure the command against Jugurtha, were moved, not only by their immediate business interests in Africa, but also by the pre-disposition of their class generally in favour of Marius, whose tactics brought to a head the resentment long felt against the handling of the Jugurthine war by the nobility.[1] But in the revolutionary age, when Pompeius had the support of provincial Romans in some regions and Caesar controlled their loyalty in others, the allegiance of communities or individuals was to the great man simply as patron or protector. Such allegiance might not be very firm, but the general attitude of mind precluded even the beginnings of solidarity among provincial Romans as such, and left them with little influence on the great march of events.

All this is thrown into relief by the fortunes in our period of certain communities and families indigenous to their particular provinces. The sharpening divisions among Romans permitted many of their subjects (in both the eastern and western Empire) to acquire increased importance and standing in the world. Though provincial communities were squeezed, time and time again, of men, money, or supplies, in order that Romans might keep going campaigns of no direct interest to them, cases were increasingly common when they found the great rivals under the necessity—in effect—of bargaining for their support. Sertorius dealt sympathetically with the Spanish chieftains and communities because his outlook so directed, but equally by necessity of his situation. Pompeius and Caesar each incurred debts, as ambitious politicians, to provincials and provincial communities for help received. With Caesar the connection of services rendered and payment made is very clear. Not only his notorious relations with the Transpadani, but his dealings with other western provinces have frequently the appearance of a bargain struck when he was one of the great rivals and fulfilled when he had supreme power.[2] Yet, in spite of the important service done him in some places by provincial Romans, they do not appear in the records among the conspicuous beneficiaries of his victory. It is conceivable that he rewarded with colonial status the Dalmatian *conventus c. R.* which staunchly supported him in the war; but, as has been seen, it is still uncertain to what

[1] Sallust *Jugurtha* 65.4 f.; 73.3 ff., 84.4 f.
[2] See above, chapter v, sections on Spain, Africa and Dalmatia.

period the foundation of the Dalmatian colonies should be assigned. No provincial Roman families do as well for themselves through friendship with Caesar as some leading native families in Spain and Gaul.

In Spain the settlers connected with Caesar—the officers Decidius Saxa and Vibius Paciaecus, the senator Titius—are nonentities compared with Cornelius Balbus and his nephew. Punic Gades, Balbus' city, gets Roman municipal status in 49; Italica, a Roman *vicus* since 206, has to wait to be promoted under Augustus (partly, to be sure, but not wholly because of the attempt by Italicenses on the life of Cassius in 48). As for the Gauls, though Roman settlers in Narbonensis certainly joined Caesar's armies for the Gallic wars, it is natives that appear by name in his entourage, to give colour in 44 to the verses alleging adulteration of the Senate with outlandish figures from Comata.[1] In Africa, the Uticenses, having received some distinction by a Julian law of 59, favour Caesar's cause in 49 and in 46, receive his public thanks after Thapsus, and in 36, perhaps in fulfilment of a plan prevented by his death, attain Roman municipal status;[2] nothing is heard of honours for Romans in the province who gave him help.

These assertions are based on somewhat scrappy material, since the provincial Romans come to light only intermittently, even in the comparatively well-documented events of 49–45 B.C. With better information, it might be found that extensive use was made by Caesar of the granting of colonial or municipal rights to reward faithful service by provincial Romans.[3] These did not, however, as individuals make great stir in the world, and the contrast seems confirmed by the wide difference observable in the eastern provinces between the fortunes of the settlers and of important native families.[4]

The dispersion of Romans to the West under various forms of duress was certainly on the great scale in the last century of

[1] Suetonius *Divus Iulius* 80.2: 'Gallos Caesar in triumphum ducit, idem in curiam,/Galli bracas deposuerunt, latum clavum sumpserunt.' Cf. Syme 74 f. and 79.

[2] Dio XLIX.16.1.

[3] See Vittinghoff 79 on Carthago Nova (but *C.I.L.* II.3408 does *not* prove that the city had a constitution on municipal lines before the colonization, since there is no reason to assume that the four Romans in the inscription are *quattuorviri* of a *municipium*).

[4] See below chapter XII, section on Anatolia, 74–30 B.C.

the Republic; and a powerful impression is left by the cumulative evidence. The proscribed, the political exiles, and self-exiles, the soldiers of civil war driven from Italy in defeat make a considerable multitude of men, but not so great as the families uprooted, at different times from 82 to 30 B.C., to provide farms for the soldiers of victorious armies. The number of veterans to whom confiscated land was given in this period was probably around half a million,[1] and the number of families evicted was certainly very great, even on the assumption that one largish farm was often divided into holdings for more than one veteran. The majority of the dispossessed are commonly assumed to have settled in Rome or other cities, to live there as best they could. But it is hard to believe that dispossession on this scale did not produce movement into the provinces of some importance. In modern times evictions, starvation, or hard circumstances have sent people from Scotland, Ireland, and European countries to lands across the oceans and conditions wholly strange to them. Since little is known about the victims of the Roman confiscations and their reaction to disaster, the comparison cannot be exact; yet there seems no doubt that some of the dispossessed, as well as the political exiles, of revolutionary age must have tried to repair their fortunes in lands no long voyage distant from Italy and similar to it in essential respect.

But the atmosphere of despair produced by repeated violence may have been equally important in its results. In the sixteenth *Epode*, written in or after 40 B.C., Horace called up the mood—which must have been common at the time—of complete and final revulsion against civil war:

> Altera iam teritur bellis civilibus aetas,
>   suis et ipsa Roma viribus ruit.
> Quam neque finitimi valuerunt perdere Marsi
>   minacis aut Etrusca Porsenae manus,
>
> . . . .
> . . . .
>
> impia perdemus devoti sanguinis aetas,
>   ferisque rursus occupabitur solum.

The feeling of a curse on Rome may already have weighed on

[1] Cf. J. Kromayer 'Die wirtschaftliche Entwicklung Italiens im II und I Jahrhundert vor Christ' in *Neue Jahrb. für das Kl. Altertum* XXXIII (1914) 159–63.

many Romans in the early first century when, with the Social
War hardly burnt out, they were plunged first into civil war and
then the atrocities of the *Sullanum regnum*. When Cicero thought
of these atrocities, of the situation of Roscius and all it implied,
he came near despair.[1] Sertorius, in the desperate period when
he was driven between Spain and Africa, is said to have longed
to find the Islands of the Blest, beyond the Roman world, and
live there 'in quiet, free from tyranny and wars that would
never end'; the tradition in Plutarch has it that he was prevented
from sailing on the voyage only by the refusal of his pirate allies
to join him.[2] This may echo, not just a temporary fit of despair
in Sertorius, but a mood, common in Italy under the horrors
of the Sullan régime, of longing for escape. Such a mood may be
most poignant in the man who is least likely to take steps to
escape, in such a one as Horace when, in the sixteenth Epode,
he calls on his fellow Romans

> 'ire pedes quocunque ferent, quocunque per undas
> Notus vocabit aut protervus Africus'.

But some, stirred more and more by such feelings, at last uproot
themselves.

A combination of causes excited and maintained the movement of emigrants to the western provinces of the Empire;
ex-soldiers of forces defeated in civil war, exiled members of
factions which in turn persecuted and were themselves persecuted, men who left Italy with hopes, not always fulfilled, of
security and tranquillity, such expatriates, and with them,
victims of expropriation, surely made a considerable element
in the Roman communities, alongside people who would have
emigrated in any event from a quiet Italy, to make or improve
their fortunes.

Although the settlements sprang in part from the dissensions
of Italy and became involved in them, the western provincial
Romans in the revolutionary age are little more than an append-
age to the state and the citizen body. But this was soon changed,
in the transformation of the West which Caesar started, Augustus
and great successors of Augustus continued. The emigrants
became increasingly integrated into the state and involved in
its operation as a result of a variety of measures, among which

[1] *pro Roscio* 150 *ad fin.*   [2] Plutarch *Sertorius* 8.2–9.2.

were the organization of town life on the model of municipal
Italy and the enlistment of numerous provincials into the
re-organized administrative and military systems of the Empire. The raising, by deliberate policy, in the districts most
amenable to Romanization, of native communities to citizen
and municipal status, did indeed rob the original provincial
Roman classes of their old superiority in standing; but along
with these new citizens and the *coloni* sent out in great numbers
by a succession of Emperors, they came to form a great homo-
geneous body of Romans equal to the Romans of Italy and at
one with them in outlook and loyalties.

PART II

THE EAST

CHAPTER VII

ITALY AND THE EAST

ECONOMIC RELATIONSHIPS WHEN SETTLEMENT BEGAN

IN the West the involvement of the settlers in the struggles of the revolutionary age is seen, but the evidence for their distribution is inadequate; in the East their part in those struggles is little detectable, and one or two only are known of the people who may have gone there to escape the troubles of Italy. But the eastern pattern of settlement appears substantially, through more inscriptions and some literary evidence; the provenance of the settlers can be examined in the light of their names; and there is better evidence than in the West for their occupations and economic activities. Since people certainly went to the East in the main for economic reasons, this chapter considers the economic relations, when settlement began, between Italy and the eastern Mediterranean world and the relative advantage, for exploitation of opportunities there, which different parts of Italy and their inhabitants may have enjoyed.

These matters are touched on to some extent in J. Hatzfeld's book, *Les Trafiquants Italiens dans l'Orient Hellénique* (1919), which deals, not only with traders, but with emigrants to the East generally. This work is excellent in some respects, in others unsatisfactory. The first part, 'Histoire de l'expansion des *negotiatores* dans le monde hellénique', treats the distribution of the settlers generally, their apparent disappearance from many cities of the Anatolian coast in the first century A.D., and their appearance now for the first time in numerous places in the interior. It relates the epigraphic and the literary evidence skilfully to each other, and the local material to imperial circumstances. But the shadowy evidence for the first beginnings of settlement is handled with unconvincing confidence; the long section on the provinces in Anatolia separates adjacent places, the life of which was certainly connected; the positive dating of inscriptions where there is no certainty at all and the slips in references mar an account which makes readable things that might have been unreadable.

The second part, 'Activité, organization, rôle des *negotiatores* en Orient', considers the general importance of the movement. The chapters deal with the settlers' occupations, their provenance and social status, the organization of their *conventus*, their relationships with the Greeks, and kindred subjects. Hatzfeld treats these matters in a way at first convincing, but rises too soon into the thin air of speculation. The chapter on the economic interests of the settlers remains on solid ground, but that on the relationships between them and the Greeks is full of surmise.

Most of Hatzfeld's topics are included here, but on a scheme different from his; some (such as the organization of the *conventus c. R.*) are omitted because no evidence exists for them within my period and it seemed mistaken to apply to them, even with reserves, material belonging to the Principate. Delos is treated in a sketchy way in *Les Trafiquants*, perhaps because the author had already dealt with it fully in his long article 'Les Italiens résidant à Delos'.[1] I shall refer here, not to the Delian section of the book, but to the article only.

'Trafiquants italiens', Hatzfeld takes it, first began to venture to the East about 240 B.C., gaining confidence from the 'prosperity and equilibrium' enjoyed by Italy between the first and second Punic War; thus the occasional Italians now found in Greek lands, although not numerous, are significant as pioneers.[2] But, in fact, these men were by no means the first in the field from Italy, nor is there any reason to suppose important change, at this time, in the economic relationships between Italy and the lands to its east. These were now ancient, and must be presupposed for the intensified economic contacts that came in the second century. As well as buying from Greece, the Siceliote and Italiote Greeks had exported thither and to Greek Asia from much earlier times.[3] Inasmuch as Magna Graecia passed the peak of its prosperity about 500 B.C., Sicilians may thereafter have had more of this trade than the Italiotes; in the

---

[1] *B.H.* xxxvi (1912) 6 ff. A number of the inscriptions used, being in Latin or bilingual, were re-edited in 1918, as *C.I.L.* I²(2 fasc. 1).2232–59.
[2] Hatzfeld 18.
[3] Rostovzeff 121 ff., with his notes, and 124.

fourth century Sicily was sending corn to Athens, perhaps in large quantities. But the important trade with Greece in salted fish was in the hands of Bruttians and Calabrians, and there is no reason to think that the Italiote Greeks were now commercially negligible beside the Siceliotes.[1] Some of the merchants will have been native Italians, or Greco-Italian *hybridae* from places where Greek communities and their neighbours had virtually merged through inter-marriage or a powerful Italic people had overrun a declining Greek colony. So the Ἰταλικοὶ ἔμποροι of Polybius,[2] victims of the Illyrian pirates in 229 B.C. and occasion of the first Illyrian war, are likely to have been a mixture of Italiote Greeks, *hybridae*, and south Italians—not pioneers, but participating in an ancient trade, which piracy could not stop and which may have gained as much from the prosperity of Asiatic Greece as it lost from the depression of old Greece. No evidence exists for a marked change in the circumstances or extent of that trade about 240 B.C. The new age in the economic relationships of Italy and the East begins later, with the new political relationships of the first half of the second century.

The change had three aspects. Firstly, trade increased greatly in volume; there are no trade returns, but the great and rapid increase in traders from Italy on Delos is by itself sufficient evidence. The classes conducting the trade likewise changed in relative importance. That is to say, the Italiotes of the Greek cities in the extreme south were soon overtaken in importance by inhabitants of the coastal region from the Surrentine peninsula to the Volturnus—Campania in the later sense—mainly Greek or Oscan by extraction, but now increasingly romanized (and with Roman and Latin colonists in their midst).[3] Natives of this region were soon joined, in the movement, by men with old Roman names, many, it is certain, based on Puteoli and the neighbouring colonies, but some certainly from the Roman

---

[1] Sicilian corn, Demosthenes LVI.9 and XXXII *passim*, with A. H. M. Jones *Athenian Democracy* 95 and H. Knorringa *Emporos* 98 f., for other evidence. Bruttian and Calabrian salt fish merchants, Athenaeus *Deipnosophistae* III.116 cf., quoting Euthydemus of Athens (second or first century B.C.?).

[2] II.8.2.

[3] For the prosopographic evidence for the relative importance among the emigrants of people from different parts of Italy see chapter VIII, section 'Provenance of the Delian Ῥωμαῖοι', and chapter X (the East generally).

territory further north and even the *urbs* itself. Finally—something which had not happened before—traders became settlers, perhaps engaged, more than in trade, in banking, moneylending, and exploitation of land. There is no evidence showing precisely how this happened; but, if anything may be presumed, it is this order of development.

The local provenance of the emigrants is discussed, from the prosopographic evidence, in chapters VIII and X; but it seems reasonable to look here at Italy in the second century to see who had initial advantages for eastern enterprise when the movement began.

The new development of overseas trade sprang, in large measure, from Roman military success in the Mediterranean. Great new wealth came to Italy from war and conquest, and much passed into private hands. This caused a new demand for foreign commodities and provided more capital for foreign trade. Since the individuals enriched in this way will have been more often Romans than Italians, Roman citizens were probably the better placed, so far as capital was concerned, for overseas trade. But a man with less capital, if he understands trade and has inherited connections with the markets, may do better than the newcomer and novice with the larger capital; thus, for consideration of the advantage, for overseas trade in the second century, of a base in this or that part of Italy, one must think of the several regions involved, their commercial traditions and 'connections', and the degree of economic prosperity now enjoyed by each.

Italy north of Rome is unlikely to have had much eastern trade in the second century. I distinguish, therefore, for consideration: (*a*) the Italic peoples south of a line (arbitrary in its precise termini) from the Surrentine peninsula to Mt. Garganus; (*b*) the Greek cities of this region; (*c*) the Oscans and Greeks of Campania; (*d*) Romans (whether of Rome, the immediate territory of Rome, or in other parts of Italy) and Latins.

(*a*) The southern Italic peoples, inasmuch as they had overrun some of the Greek commercial cities and were assimilated elsewhere to the Greeks, are likely to have had a share, in the fourth and third centuries B.C., in the maritime trade of Magna Graecia. But in the closing stages of the second Punic war they were thinned and impoverished by the actions of Hannibal and of Rome, and Roman post-war policy depressed them further.[1] One would not expect them to have been excluded altogether from the overseas movement, for individuals may have been spurred precisely by misfortune to emigrate,[2] and, where Greek cities continued to flourish in the second century, the neighbouring Italians are likely to have shared their prosperity in some degree; but the Greeks themselves, for the most part, were less prosperous than ever before.

(*b*) The Greeks of southernmost Italy had already, by the fourth century, seen their best days.[3] In the second Punic War many cities were ruined or depopulated, and others lost land soon after it to Latin or Roman colonists. These, if they made roots (not always the case), were bound to promote Romanization; Brundisium, a Latin colony from 246, may have already begun to undermine the prosperity of Greek Tarentum. If certain cities, recovering to some extent after the war, retained their Greek character into the first century A.D., the region as a whole was like the patient who recovers to some extent after a serious illness, but lives thenceforth on a reduced level of energy, with no hope of regaining vitality.[4]

(*c*) Oscan and Greek Campania (far more Oscan than Greek from about 400 B.C.) saw in the second century the opening of a period of intense prosperity.[5] But the land was losing its old character. At the end of the fourth and the beginning of the third century the establishment of Roman and Latin colonies in the Latin-Campanian border country had produced a change in the character of that district.[6] After the second Punic war the process continued in the south of the region, with the establishment of Roman colonists on the coast at Volturnum, Liternum, and what had been Greek Dicaearchia.[7] This city, now Puteoli, entered on its era of great prosperity, as port of Rome, import–

---

[1] See T. Frank *C.A.H.* VIII.334 f.

[2] But no sufficient basis appears for Frank's definite statement loc. cit.: 'many refugees had crossed the seas to Greece and the Hellenistic empires'.

[3] A good summary of their position in Rostovzeff *RE* 14.

[4] E. Ciaceri *Storia della Magna Grecia* III.164–200 (second Punic war), 201–237 (post-war period).

[5] Frank *C.A.H.* VIII.346 ff. The association of Campania with the rest of southern Italy may be criticized on the grounds suggested here.

[6] Most important: Minturnae, Livy x.21.8, Sinuessa, ibid. (*coloniae c. R.*); Cales, Livy VIII.16.13 f.; Suessa Aurunca, Livy IX.28.7 (Latin colonies).

[7] Livy XXXIV.45.1–3.

export centre, and place of manufacture. It became partly romanized, partly cosmopolitan, through the great influx of foreign traders of which Lucilius speaks (c. 150 B.C.).[1] Neapolis remained Greek, because it became commercially a backwater, a city for leisured visitors, writers, and students; but in 215 Cumae—whose inhabitants were already largely Oscan in blood and *cives sine suffragio*—had received three hundred Capuans allowed to keep Roman citizenship for loyalty in the war, and in 180 Latin, by permission of the Roman Senate, had become the official Cumaean language (and permitted to auctioneers there).[2] Inland the people of Capua—the original 'Campani'—and the neighbouring Atellani had been *cives sine suffragio* since 338, and in the late third century at least one distinguished Capuan family was allied in marriage with noble families of Rome.[3] Capua, with neighbouring towns, was punished indeed in 211 for defection to Hannibal: many leading Campani were imprisoned, the status of city was taken from the humbler people allowed to remain, and Roman citizenship, even *sine suffragio*, denied them.[4] Yet, by 189 and probably earlier, the Campani, whatever elements they now comprised, were being enrolled by the Roman censors,[5] and in the next year had their right to marry Roman women confirmed (with retrospective effect for unions contracted and children already born).[6] Though need for manpower for the legions may have been a motive for the censors, it is also likely that they were so assimilated by intermarriage and Romanization with the Roman citizen body and the Latins that it was seen as absurd to deny them their old *civitas sine suffragio*. The Romanization of the region was probably further encouraged in the second century

[1] Lucilius III.123 (Marx): 'inde Dicarchitum populos Delumque minorem'. For the rapid advance of Puteoli, M. W. Frederiksen 'Puteoli' *P-W* XXIII(2) 2045 (sec. VII) ff.

[2] The loyal Capuans, Livy XXIII.31.10 f.; Cumae granted the right to use Latin, Livy XL.42.13.

[3] Livy XXIII.2.1 ff., especially 6 f.

[4] Livy XXVI.16.5–11 and 33.12–34.12. Beloch (*Campanien* 319) is wrong in taking Livy XXVI.16.6 as meaning that the entire population was enslaved. Livy says 'multitudo alia Campanorum': 'a multitude of other Capuans'.

[5] Livy XXXVIII.28.4. The Campani asked the Senate where they should be enrolled and were told at Rome. The passage suggests that this was not the first time they were called to the census.

[6] Livy XXXVIII.36.5 f.

by private movement of citizens and Latins southwards into what became the most thriving part of Italy; there may have been such among those proprietors adjacent to the local *ager publicus* who in 173 B.C. were found to have enlarged their farms by encroaching upon it without paying rent.[1] Thus it was as a land being steadily romanized that Campania prospered in the second century, with its trade shared between the natives and the incomers, and the natives, in many districts, more and more assimilated to the Romans. Some of the southern Campanian cities continued to be and feel themselves Oscan, as appeared in the Social War, but Campania as a whole was not a rebel stronghold. Among the eastern settlers men of Oscan extraction are readily distinguishable, as will be seen, by their names; but many of these people, by the middle of the second century, are likely to have been very similar, as far as language and way of life were concerned, to Romans of like social standing.

(*d*) It is wrong to suppose the Romans as handicapped, in the second century, for overseas trade and settlement. Not only did many acquire much new capital, but they could trade and settle abroad with even greater confidence than most other inhabitants of Italy; for Romans alone were truly 'rerum domini', and an assurance, beyond what Italians or Italiotes might attain, could be theirs. Local trade at Rome was no new thing; now demand for foreign commodities and slaves was growing enormously, and even Frank (who supposes that south Italians and Italiotes had a great lead in trade) thinks that the improvement, in the early second century, of harbour facilities at Rome, 'probably means that eastern shipping to Rome was increasing rapidly'.[2] This trade certainly was in fair part in Roman hands. Puteoli and other southern ports were now available to Roman merchants, who cannot have been based only on Rome and central Italy. Oscans are indeed among the earliest *negotiatores* on Delos, and Oscan-Campanian names are prominent there throughout the life of the trading community, and in the East generally. But it was Roman and Latin—not Italian traders—who in 187 obtained immunity from port dues under the treaty granted by the Senate to Ambracia, and in 180 the merchants taken by king Genthius of Illyria in the Adriatic

---

[1] Livy XLII.1.6 and 19.1 f.
[2] *E.S.A.R.* I.203 ff.

are described by Livy as Romans and Latins.[1] Again, long before the second century, moneylending must have provided profits to a fair number of Roman citizens, since otherwise indebtedness could not have become a burning issue, as it often had; now, with much increased capital, the bankers and money-lenders were well placed to enter new fields, and it may be that they reached not only Delos in the second century, but other regions, even before they fell under the sovereignty of Rome.[2] In this sphere, there is no reason at all to see Romans at a disadvantage beside Italians or Italiotes.

Latins, whether from Latium or the Latin colonies, socially assimilated to the Roman citizen body, are hardly to be considered, in this context, as very different from the Romans. They were almost as well placed as Romans for enterprise overseas; as the Senate acted, if spasmodically, to protect Roman traders, so it acted for Latins, and they were probably regarded by provincials in much the same light as Romans.

The nomenclature of inscriptions will be the main test for these presumptions about the provenance of the settlers; for their distribution, the material is partly literary, chiefly epigraphic. Whilst the sum of local references is rarely large, a single *collective* reference, literary or epigraphic, can suffice for a particular place; and where there were special local attractions, the appearance of even a few individuals or families suggests with probability a more considerable body. Conversely, since local material is nowhere abundant, even in the best documented period (the late Republic and the Augustan age), the conclusion from lack of evidence—that there can have been no settlers in a place before a certain date, or that they must have died out, departed, or become assimilated after a certain date—has to be regarded with suspicion, so far as particular cities are concerned. The fact that no epigraphic evidence is forthcoming before or after a certain date, may be due to those circumstances which sometimes destroy or bury beyond recovery the inscriptions of an entire period. Where, as is the case in Cilicia, the Republican settlers are known only through the letters of Cicero, their non-appearance later is of doubtful

---

[1] Livy xxxviii.44.3 f. and xl.42.4 f. respectively.
[2] See below pp. 95–9 and 125.

significance, since no later texts give similar detailed information about the province. What is most unfortunate, the matter of the apparent change in the pattern of settlement in Anatolia generally under the Principate is complicated by the suspicion attaching to negative evidence.

The next chapter treats the distribution of the settlers before the first Mithridatic war (including a section on Delos necessarily longer than the rest); chapter IX their reappearance, after the war, in Roman Asia and Greece and their appearance in new regions as these came under Rome. More general matters are discussed in the remaining chapters: the provenance in Italy of the settlers, their occupations and economic interests, their relations with the natives, their standing in the Roman world, and their character as seen by other Romans. The various classes of people who visited the eastern provinces 'otiandi causa' appear alongside those who settled 'negotiandi causa'. Such leisured people kept settlers in touch with Italy, as also did the wealthy men maintaining interests and establishments both in Italy and overseas.[1] The stable provincial Roman class which grew up in the eastern provinces had in many places a more fluid, but interesting fringe.[2]

[1] Atticus bought his estate near Buthrotum in Epirus before his return from Athens to Italy in 65, and visited it regularly both before and after 65 (see Cicero *ad Att.* 1.5.7, with Feger 'T. Pomponius Atticus', *P-W* Suppl. VIII.506). In Varro's book on farming, published about 37 B.C., Romans with large estates in Epirus ('Epirotae' II.1.28 and 'Synepirotae' II.5.1) are very knowledgeable about that country, and clearly belong to a class who paid regular visits to property overseas.

[2] In early 50, when Cicero was travelling towards Laodicea on Lycus to perform there his duties as governor, a certain P. Vedius, a friend of Pompeius, who was staying in the city as guest of Pompeius Vindullus, made a journey of some length to meet and escort him; his bizarre train amazed Cicero, including, as it did, wild asses and a dog-headed baboon sitting on one of the two chariots. Cicero was much tickled, when it came out, by chance, that luggage left by Vedius in Vindullus' house included miniatures of five Roman matrons of the nobility (*ad Att.* VI.1.25).

CHAPTER VIII

SETTLEMENT BEFORE THE FIRST
MITHRIDATIC WAR

THE groups of settlers, before the legislation extending citizenship in 89/88 B.C., are likely to have consisted of mixed Romans, Latins, Italians, and Italiote Greeks, with the relative importance of each element varying from place to place. Reference to 'Romans and Italians'—or to 'Italians and Romans'—would be clumsy and would beg the usually uncertain question of their relative importance, without including the Italiote Greeks. Now settlers or visitors in the East from any part of Italy were commonly Ῥωμαῖοι to the Greeks among whom they came, without distinction of status or local origin, and indeed they often applied the term to themselves. I use Ῥωμαῖοι, therefore (till 89/88), where I am not able or do not need to distinguish the various elements. It may be presumed that it was found possible in or soon after 89/88 to confer the citizenship on Latins, Italians, and Italiotes living outside Italy. I pass over, therefore, to 'Romans' after this date.

GREECE

Parts of Greece, city and countryside, became more and more depopulated and desolate between the first Roman intervention and the Augustan age. But certain cities were fairly prosperous commercially, Chalcis, Athens (though less so after the Mithridatic war), and Corinth, until its destruction in 146 B.C. Thessaly, Boeotia, Messenia, and Elis, or their best districts, produced considerable agricultural wealth throughout the period.[1] It may be assumed that an Italian or Roman attracted

[1] Polybius XXXVI.17.5, writing of his own time, speaks of 'a low birthrate and a general decrease of population, which has made cities deserted and land unproductive'. But Rostovzeff finds great differences between region and region, at this time and later (see 603–32, 739–64, 951–3, 1145–8). For a brief but discriminating account, J. A. O. Larsen *E.S.A.R.* IV.418ff. Servius Sulpicius' picture of the ruin of the Isthmian cities in 45 B.C.

to one of the commercial cities could find profitable opportunities, not only in trade and banking, but also in land, and
likewise that he would not be confined to landowning or agriculture, if he went to a city in one of the great agricultural
districts.

Far more ʿΡωμαῖοι had settled, by the middle of the second
century B.C., on Delos than in any mainland city, Corinth
possibly excepted. But I take Greece first, since there was commerce between southern Italy and the Greek lands generally
long before Italian merchants began to take an interest in
Delos.

The north-west and north-east

The Ἰταλικοὶ ἔμποροι seized in the Adriatic in 229 B.C.
by Teuta of Illyria, the Roman citizens and Latins of concern
to the Senate, when it required immunity from port dues for
their kind in the treaty of 187 with Ambracia, and the Romans
and Latins imprisoned by Genthius of Illyria in 180,[1] were
clearly merchants and sailors voyaging to the ports of southern
Illyria, Epirus, and north-west Greece, or touching at these on
longer voyages. Some such may eventually have established
themselves in one or other of the Epirote or north-western
Greek ports, but this is surmise. It is conceivable that the settlement on Zacynthus, known through its repulse of Archelaus in
the first Mithridatic war,[2] may have grown up long before; but
our only certain evidence for early *settlement* in the north-west
is Livy's account of the capture of Leucas in 197 by Flamininus,
when exiles 'of the Italic race' betrayed the desperate resistance
of the Leucadians by opening the gates to the Romans.[3]

Nor—to cross to north-east Greece—can much be made of
the slight evidence for the first beginnings of settlement in
Thessaly and the Thraceward regions. Two Roman or Italian
families were important in the early or middle second century
in Abdera,[4] but are isolated. Thessalian Larissa may conceivably

---

(Cicero *ad Fam.* IV.5.4) is shown by J. Day, *Economic History of Athens*
120 ff., to be partly misleading.

[1] For these three classes, Polybius II.8.2; Livy XXXVIII.44.4; and Livy
XL.42.4 respectively.

[2] Appian *Mithridatica* 45.   [3] Livy XXXIII.17.11.

[4] See below p. 169.

have had ʿΡωμαῖοι about 170 B.C.;[1] but this is dubious, and in Thessaly as a whole they do not appear in appreciable numbers till about 100 B.C.[2]

Corinth

The old trade between Sicily and southern Italy and Greece certainly included the Isthmus and the neighbouring regions— thus Sicilian corn went to Athens. It is not surprising, in view of the destruction of Corinth in 146 B.C., that no trace has survived of Romans or Italians trading there in the second century. But the presumption is strong, especially as there were ʿΡωμαῖοι at both Pergamum and Carthage before Asia and Africa became provinces of Rome. Strabo, furthermore, talking about Delos in the second century, says that on the destruction of Corinth ἐκεῖσε . . . μετεχώρησαν οἱ ἔμποροι, making it an even greater trading settlement than it had been before. He does not say in so many words that ʿΡωμαῖοι were important at Corinth and in this migration, but a later remark implies that they had frequented both Delos and Corinth and concentrated on Delos after the destruction of Corinth.[3]

Athens

Athens was not prosperous in the late third century B.C. But the city may have begun to recover after Cynoscephalae and Magnesia, and certainly moved towards new prosperity after the defeat of Perseus, when, in 167/6 B.C., by accepting Delos under the Roman post-war settlement, she accepted Roman protection.[4] About the year 174 B.C. a Roman citizen—a Cossutius—completed the Athenian Olympieion (which Peisistratus had not taken beyond the foundations), under contract to Antiochus IV Epiphanes, and was later honoured by the people. This man, forerunner of many ʿΡωμαῖοι, must belong to the family of Cossutii active throughout Italy and the eastern

---

[1] See Hatzfeld 23 ad fin. f. The inscription he discusses is mutilated, obscure, and of uncertain date; and it is not certain that the τηβεννοφόροι here are civilian.

[2] Ibid., 65 f., discussed below p. 150.

[3] See Strabo 486 quoted in full on p. 102.

[4] In the view of Rostovzeff, 629 ff. and 741 ff., the recovery of Athens began after Cynoscephalae and Magnesia and made further strides after the defeat of Perseus.

Mediterranean in the second and first centuries B.C. in architecture, building, and connected activities.[1] Athens had long been a cosmopolitan city, with its professions open to foreigners, but it seems noteworthy, thus early, that a Roman or Italian could secure such a contract. There were probably other ῾Ρωμαῖοι active in Athens before 124/3 B.C., when the next datable inscription is found, recording some such as ephebes.[2]

When the names prominent in Athens in this period are collated with contemporary nomenclature on Delos, it appears that many Athenian ῾Ρωμαῖοι had some sort of connection with Delos.[3] Those attested are mainly ephebes (the ephebia had long admitted foreigners) or men and women who died in Athens, recorded in funerary inscriptions.[4] No cult associations have come to light, such as are prominent in the epigraphy of Delos and certainly helped the *negotiator* there to make useful contacts during the practice of religious piety and social good fellowship. It will account for the frequency of ephebes with names connected with Delos, if it is assumed (something itself highly probable) that many ῾Ρωμαῖοι were sent by their fathers from Delos for education at Athens; as for the men and women attested in the funerary inscriptions, some of these may have retired from Delos to Athens in old age. But it would be wrong to conclude that the ῾Ρωμαῖοι at Athens in this period were all very young or old people. It may be partly accident that there are not other types of inscription, and it is difficult to suppose that there was not some sort of business community at Athens: an important Delian *negotiator* would wish to have a subsidiary

---

[1] Δέκμος Κοσσούτιος Δέκμου, *I.G.* III(1)561, Vitruvius VIII.160 (Teubner p. 148 lines 15 ff.) and 161 (p. 149 lines 12 ff.). The Cossutii were an important family (a Cossutia should have married the young Caesar, Suetonius *Divus Iulius* 1.1). They were still in the sculpture trade in Rome in the early Principate: see *I.G.* XIV.1249 f., with *P-W* 'Cossutius' (3)1674 and 'Menelaos' (18) p. 835. Cossutii are found *c.* 100 B.C. on Delos (*B.H.* XXXVI.30), Paros (*I.G.* XII(5)422 and 1049) and at Erythrae (Le Bas III.48, with Hatzfeld 107[4]). What is the date of the other Cossutius at Athens, Μάρκος Κοσσούτιος Γαΐου (*I.G.* III(2)2873, 'in Ceramico')? These places all suggest interest in marble, building, and the sculpture trade. For the export of products of art to Italy, see Rostovzeff 744 f. with 1505[13].

[2] *I.G.* II(1)471 lines 107 and 122 mentions ῾Ρωμαῖοι as ephebes; but the restoration of *C.I.L.* X(2)7350 (135 B.C.) to include 'c(ives) R(omani)', though by Mommsen, is dubious. (Inscription found in Sicily.)

[3] Hatzfeld 41 *ad fin.* ff.

[4] Hatzfeld 42. But not all the inscriptions can be securely assigned to this period.

H

establishment or a representative in the city which not only appointed the superintendent of the Delian administration, but was the obvious centre for travel on the mainland and a place much frequented from every part of Greece and Greek Asia. However this may be, it seems clear that many of the ʿΡωμαῖοι in Athens must have reached the city in one way or another via Delos (the ramifications of whose Italian-Roman community into other parts of the Greek world remain for later study).

Boeotia and Euboea

The Romans were active, diplomatically and militarily, in Boeotia on the eve of the war with Perseus, making use of the route from Creusa to Aulis and Chalcis—whence troops were shipped for the north. Chalcis was an important port of Hellenistic commerce, and the road from Creusa a commercial route.[1] It may well be that service in Boeotia before and during the war of 171–168 suggested to some Romans and Italians that they might live and make money in Boeotia or Euboea. On the mainland the earliest centres of settlement were perhaps Lebadea and Anthedon, where the Arellii are probably connected with a family of that name established on Delos in the late second century.[2] On Euboea Chalcis was probably the first centre of settlement. Among the victors in games held there about 100 B.C. are various ʿΡωμαῖοι; a number have names connected with Delos, and some were probably resident.[3] Eretria had a body of ʿΡωμαῖοι παρεπιδημοῦντες, established by the early first century.[4]

The presence of these groups is not surprising. An extensive trade was conducted by Eretria in the second century and later, and alongside the ʿΡωμαῖοι a number of other groups of ξενοί[5]

---

[1] For economic conditions in Boeotia and Euboea in the Hellenistic period see Rostovzeff 210 *ad fin.* f.

[2] Hatzfeld 40[4–7] for Lebadea and Anthedon.

[3] *I.G.* xii(9)952, also edited by A. Wilhelm *Jahr. des öst. arch. Inst.* I. Beiblatt 48 f. The inscription records results of games, apparently in the second or early first century. The names occurring are Castricius, Horarius, Herennius, Cornelius, Quinctius. All of these (except Herennius) are found on Delos, and the Castricii were important *negotiatores*.

[4] *I.G.* xii(9)234 line 28 ff.; *A.J.A.* xi(1896)173 ff., with 186 f. on the date.

[5] See J. Day 'The Value of Dio Chrysostom's Euboean Discourse for the Economic Historian' (in *Studies in Roman Economic and Social History in Honour of Allan Chester Johnson*, ed. P. R. Coleman-Norton) p. 225 f. This essay is largely concerned with our period.

are found there. The trade of Chalcis also continued to flourish in the second century, and the Euboean cities generally appear to have been comparatively prosperous in the late Republican period.[1] The trade connections of these naturally included Delos,[2] and links between ʽΡωμαῖοι on Euboea and on Delos are equally natural at the time when the ʽΡωμαῖοι were dominant on Delos.

DELOS AND THE NEIGHBOURING ISLANDS

The Mithridatic sack of Delos in 88 B.C. and the massacre of the *negotiatores* was a dividing line in the history of the island; the commercial community never flourished again quite as before the war, though temporary recovery may have been greater than is sometimes supposed. But certain features continued to belong to Delian Roman life as before 88; so, in attempting to give an account of that life, I have not rejected all post-war material or material of uncertain date.

In the following chronological table certain definite causes are assumed for the rapid expansion and rapid collapse of the commercial community; I argue the probability of these later.

166 B.C.	Delos assigned by Rome to Athens and made a free port.
165 B.C.	Complaint of the Rhodians to Rome about reduction of their revenues, due to Delian ἀτέλεια.
From c. 165 B.C.	Increasing weakness of Rhodes produces increase in piracy in the eastern Mediterranean, and hence in number of slaves offered on the Delian slave market.
From c. 165 B.C.	Sharp increase in ʽΡωμαῖοι coming to Delos for the slave trade.
146 B.C.	Destruction of Corinth and migration to Delos of ʽΡωμαῖοι formerly active there.
c. 130 B.C.	Slave revolt on the island.
88 B.C.	First Mithridatic war. Athens joins Mithridates, Delos sides with Rome and revolts from Athens. Attempt by Apellicon to recover Delos for Athens, repulsed by the Delian Roman Orbius and his force.
	Delos later seized and sacked by Mithridates' general, Archelaus; 20,000 ʽΡωμαῖοι and others killed on Delos and the neighbouring islands.

---

[1] Chalcis, J. Day op. cit. 222 f.; Carystus and Histiaea, 229–34.
[2] Day op. cit. 221, 229, 230, 232.

86 B.C.	Recovery of Delos by Rome, following on recovery of Athens.
From 86/85 B.C.	Fresh movement of *negotiatores* to Delos; restoration of the port and town begun.
69 B.C.	Sack of Delos by a pirate fleet under Athenodorus, acting for Mithridates. Restoration and fortification of the town by C. Triarius, legate of Lucullus.
67 B.C.	Destruction of the pirate fleets by Pompeius and consequent drying up of supply of captives to Delos.
By 55 B.C.	Collapse of foreign community and of Delian commerce virtually complete.

The causes of the Delian boom and the importance in it of the ʿΡωμαῖοι.

Delos' position, her virtual neutrality, and the attraction of the Apolline festivals operated, before the Roman era, to create one of the important entrepôts of the Hellenistic world, with a fairly important banking business.[1] Foreign men of business were established there by the middle of the third century, but few, if any, of these were from Italy. About the end of this century and the beginning of the next, when Delos was being drawn politically into the Roman orbit, resident Italians and Italiote Greeks, though not numerous, included men of wealth and standing.[2] Incomers from Italy, Roman as well as Italian, began to abound after 166 B.C., when Rome handed over the hitherto independent island to Athens and the Athenians, obedient to Roman desires, conferred on the port its well-known ἀτέλεια.[3] During the course of the second century they rose to numerical predominance, though other foreigners, attracted by the port régime, probably increased too. This numerical predominance, clear from the inscriptions, is more striking since their monuments must have been the particular mark of the Pontic forces in the massacre and sack of 88 B.C. It is apparent

[1] Larsen *E.S.A.R.* iv.350 *ad fin.* f. (the grain trade); Rostovzeff 231 (banking), 233, 1372[62] (trade and banking).

[2] A dedication *c.* 220 B.C. (*B.H.* XXXII.78 no. 19 line 5) records a certain Μινάτος who may well be kin to Μινάτος Μινάτου Στήϊος ʿΡωμαῖος ἐκ Κύμης, dedicant of a golden crown in the Apolline treasury in 181 B.C. Descendants are found in the later second century (*B.H.* XXXVI. 80, 'Staii'). Another early figure is ʿΗρακλείδης of Tarentum, who had descendants on Delos (*B.H.* XXXVI.42). At the end of the third century Marcus Sestius of Fregellae received a decree of *proxenia* from the Delians (*B.H.* VIII.89). A number of other early names are given by Hatzfeld *B.H.* XXXVI.102.

[3] Polybius XXX.31.10; Strabo 486, both passages quoted on p. 102 f.

from all the evidence that they were no less predominant
economically and socially on an island where the will of Rome
was the thing that counted in important matters. This predominance is clearly expressed in the metrical dedication in
which a Roman Poplius praises the merits of one of the super-
intendents of the administration appointed from Athens.[1]

Καὶ προγόνων ἀρετῆς σε καὶ εὔκλεος εἵνεκα δόξας
ἔστασεν, Γλαύκου Πειραιέως "Αροπε,
'Ελλήνων πλᾶθύς τε καὶ ἄστεα μύρια 'Ρώμας
καὶ κλυτὸς ἀρχαίου δᾶμος 'Εριχθονίου.
Τῶν μὲν γὰρ βιοτὰν αἰδοῦς μέτα, τῶν δ' ἐφύλαξας
δόγματα, τῶν δ' ἐσάους πάτριον εὐνομίαν.

The position of the 'Ρωμαῖοι, as it was before 88, is illumin-
ated by the events of that year. Roman control of Asia and most
of Greece collapsed and Athens joined Mithridates; then Delos
revolted from Athens. Apellicon, the Athenian demagogue and
commander-in-chief, brought a force of some thousand men to
take control, but was utterly defeated in a surprise attack in the
position he took up on the island.[2] The Roman organizer of this
attack has been identified, very probably, with one of the most
prominent *negotiatores* of the time, L. Orbius;[3] in which case his
force is likely to have consisted of Delian 'Ρωμαῖοι. If this is
correct (and no regularly appointed commander was in a
position to defend Delos in 88), here is clear sign of the importance of the 'Ρωμαῖοι. Later in 88 Mithridates' general,
Archelaus, a far more formidable commander than Apellicon,
came with a much larger force. He recovered Delos and, as
Appian puts it, 'other places' by force of arms, and had them
transferred to Athens, after killing a host of people living in
them. The number massacred is given by Appian as twenty
thousand, mainly residents from Italy.[4] The 'other places' of
Appian must be islands close to Delos, where 'Ρωμαῖοι settled
in comparatively small numbers. It would therefore appear that

---

[1] *B.H.* xvi.150 no. 1.
[2] Poseidonius in Athenaeus v.214d–215b = *F.G.H.* ii(A) p. 248, lines
13–29.
[3] See F. Münzer *P-W* 'Orbius' (2) 879, quoting (at end) the Delian
inscriptions for L. Orbius. In Athenaeus the leader's name is 'Ορόβιος,
but the identity of 'Ορόβιος and Orbius seems likely in the light of the
amphora mark, 'Ορόβίων, found on Delos.
[4] Appian *Mithridatica* 28.

there were approaching twenty thousand foreigners on Delos alone and that the majority were ʿΡωμαῖοι.

This rise of the ʿΡωμαῖοι to numerical predominance is not explained by the proclamation of ἀτέλεια in 167 B.C. Dues must be supposed to have been abolished equally for merchants of every nationality, and nothing suggests that anything was done for the ʿΡωμαῖοι that was not done for other traders. Traders generally, using Delos or established there, had less to pay out than elsewhere,[1] and so more and more came from various quarters; but the ʿΡωμαῖοι had no privilege, and something else must explain how, within the foreign community, they rapidly achieved preponderance.

One might suppose that the proclamation of the free port encouraged movement of ʿΡωμαῖοι to Delos because they were impressed by a demonstration of Roman ability to foster trade; the Senate had, indeed, changed, at one stroke, the conditions of commerce in an important port, in territory not yet formally under Roman sovereignty, by simple indication of its will to the nominally sovereign power. But this, if it encouraged ʿΡωμαῖοι to go to Delos, would not give them an ascendancy there; and there is nothing about this sort of thing in the sources. These do, however, suggest more tangible causes. The relevant texts, which follow, are two passages from Strabo and a passage of Polybius.

The first Strabo passage deals with the commercial expansion and collapse of Delos and with the source of supply and scale of operations of the great slave market:

Τὴν μὲν οὖν Δῆλον ἔνδοξον γενομένην οὕτως (through Apollo and his festivals) ἔτι μᾶλλον ηὔξησε κατασκαφεῖσα ὑπὸ ʿΡωμαίων Κόρινθος· ἐκεῖσε γὰρ μετεχώρησαν οἱ ἔμποροι, καὶ τῆς ἀτελείας τοῦ ἱεροῦ προυκαλουμένης αὐτοὺς καὶ τῆς εὐκαιρίας τοῦ λιμένος· ἐν καλῷ γὰρ κεῖται τοῖς ἐκ τῆς Ἰταλίας καὶ τῆς Ἑλλάδος εἰς τὴν Ἀσίαν πλέουσιν· ἥ τε πανήγυρις ἐμπορικόν τι πρᾶγμα ἐστι, καὶ συνήθεις ἦσαν αὐτῇ καὶ ʿΡωμαῖοι τῶν ἄλλων μάλιστα, καὶ ὅτε συνειστήκει ἡ Κόρινθος· Ἀθηναῖοι τε λαβόντες τὴν νῆσον καὶ τῶν ἱερῶν ἅμα καὶ τῶν ἐμπόρων ἐπεμελοῦντο ἱκανῶς (Strabo 486).

Strabo relates in the context how Diodotus Tryphon first made the Cilicians into anti-Seleucid rebels and highly organized pirates,

---

[1] Roussel 13–16 discusses the precise significance of ἀτέλεια.

exploiting Seleucid weakness, Egyptian and Cypriot hostility, and Roman and Rhodian indifference:

ἡ δὲ τῶν ἀνδραπόδων ἐξαγωγὴ προυκαλεῖτο μάλιστα εἰς τὰς κακουργίας (organized piratical attacks on shipping and coastal towns) ἐπικερδεστάτη γενομένη· καὶ γὰρ ἡλίσκοντο ῥᾳδίως, καὶ τὸ ἐμπόριον οὐ παντελῶς ἄπωθεν ἦν μέγα καὶ πολυχρήματον, ἡ Δῆλος, δυναμένη μυριάδας ἀνδραπόδων αὐθημερὸν καὶ δέξασθαι καὶ ἀποπέμψαι, ὥστε καὶ παροιμίαν γενέσθαι διὰ τοῦτο 'ἔμπορε, κατάπλευσον, ἐξελοῦ, πάντα πέπραται.' αἴτιον δ᾽ ὅτι πλούσιοι γενόμενοι Ῥωμαῖοι μετὰ τὴν Καρχηδόνος καὶ Κορίνθου κατασκαφὴν οἰκείαις ἐχρῶντο πολλαῖς· ὁρῶντες δὲ τὴν εὐπέτειαν οἱ λῃσταὶ ταύτην ἐξήνθησαν ἀθρόως, αὐτοὶ καὶ λῃζόμενοι καὶ σωματεμποροῦντες (Strabo 668 ad fin.).

Polybius gives part of the speech before the Senate of the Rhodian Astymedes in 164 B.C.:

Τὸ δὲ μέγιστον σύμπτωμα τῆς πόλεως· καταλέλυται γὰρ ἡ τοῦ λιμένος πρόσοδος ὑμῶν Δῆλον μὲν ἀτελῆ πεποιηκότων, ἀφῃρημένων δὲ τὴν τοῦ δήμου παρρησίαν, δι᾽ ἧς καὶ τὰ κατὰ τὸν λιμένα καὶ τἆλλα πάντα τῆς πόλεως ἐτύγχανε τῆς ἁρμοσούζης προστασίας· ὅτι δὲ τοῦτ᾽ ἔστιν ἀληθὲς οὐ δυσχερὲς καταμαθεῖν· τοῦ γὰρ ἐλλιμενίου κατὰ τοὺς ἀνώτερον χρόνους εὑρίσκοντος ἑκατὸν μυριάδας δραχμῶν, νῦν εὑρίσκει πεντεκαίδεκα μυριάδας, ὥστε καὶ λίαν, ὦ ἄνδρες Ῥωμαῖοι, τὴν ὑμετέραν ὀργὴν ἧφθαι τῶν κυρίων τόπων τῆς πόλεως (Polybius xxx.31.9–13).

Strabo, in 486, first attributes the second-century boom to the destruction of Corinth—after which the merchants active there moved to Delos, drawn partly by its ἀτέλεια, partly by its excellent situation for East-West trade. He then adds (having said that the festivals became ἐμπορικόν τι πρᾶγμα) that the Ῥωμαῖοι were predominant on Delos even before the destruction of Corinth. This remark is not made worthless by the confused development of the passage, but it is unfortunate that the only indication when they began to grow important is in the following remark about Athenian concern, after they took over, for the ἔμποροι. This remark is apparently to be read as closely connected with καὶ συνήθεις ἦσαν . . ., so that the ἔμποροι are primarily Ῥωμαῖοι and the implication is that the Athenians encouraged them (as indeed they were bound to do). So Strabo appears to think that the movement of Ῥωμαῖοι to Delos began to acquire importance from 166; further the passage does not take us.

In 668, Strabo implies that the trade in slaves on Delos first developed into something big in the years after 146, when, as he says, the Romans, enriched after the sack of Corinth and of Carthage, wanted far more slaves, and the Cilicians, now organized for grand-scale piracy by Diodotus Tryphon, were ready to supply them and found in Delos the obvious market. But, as has been seen, the enrichment of the Roman upper classes had begun with the opening of the second century and had gone far by its third decade, and Strabo is equally mistaken in not allowing for piracy and slave-trading before Diodotus Tryphon;[1] he either never thought about these things or was too pleased with the neat synchronism (new supply coinciding with new demand) to bother about them. But at least this is evidence about a trade of peculiar interest to Rome, and likely to attract ʿΡωμαῖοι; the substance of the passage is not called into doubt by the facility of the synchronism.

The speech in Polybius of the Rhodian Astymedes is now useful. The reported reduction, through the grant of ἀτέλεια to Delos and consequent diminution of international exchanges through Rhodes, of Rhodian revenues from 1,000,000 drachmae over a year to 150,000, may be exaggerated, but the figures need not be dismissed as corrupt. It is not to be doubted that the Rhodian economy soon became seriously and permanently weakened.[2] This weakening led, by a chain of cause and effect, to the development of the slave trade as the leading feature of the Delian economy.

Before 167 Rhodes had policed the eastern Mediterranean and kept piracy within some bounds. To do this she had maintained a great fleet. The money for this had been drawn from sources including harbour dues and charges and the revenues of subject territories. Now the former were curtailed and the latter lost, as a result of the Roman measures, and the financial basis of Rhodian naval power was undermined. Though Rome became somewhat less hostile after the Rhodian embassy of

[1] See W. Kroll P-W 'Seeraub' 1038. Though the evidence is presented rather confusedly here, Etruscan and Cretan pirates were clearly a plague to the eastern Mediterranean in the third century: cf. in particular S.I.G.² 255, Strabo 477 (the Cretans), A.M. xx.222 ff. (inscription illustrating role of Rhodes).

[2] Polybius xxx.31.9–13, xxxiii.17, with the comments in C.A.H. viii.287 ff., 291 f. (the Rhodian-Cretan war c. 155 B.C.).

165/4, Rhodes was not allowed to recover her former naval greatness. Thus the piratical Cretan communities, which the Rhodians had kept in check, became far more dangerous and, worse, there was nothing to prevent the Cilicians from making sea robbery a highly organized business. There can be little doubt that the supply of captives greatly increased in the two decades after the defeat of Perseus and the declaration of Delos as a free port; equally little doubt that the Roman upper classes (and some Italians) were already able to buy slaves on a greatly increased scale. The beginning, then, of the boom in the Delian slave-market may be assigned to this period, and its causes connected with the weakening of the Rhodian sea power.

The demand in Rome and Italy for slaves for unskilled labour could be met from western sources. But to meet the increasing call for slaves with training, education, accomplishments, or looks, traders turned to the East. If they were to buy at the lowest price the captives best suited to the Italian market, it is obvious that they had to go in person to inspect what was offered and to bargain; the keen slave-trader could not sit in an Italian port, missing the best bargains and paying more for slaves less attractive to the customer. Thus the Delian slave-market was bound to create a body of resident slave-traders, Roman, Latin, Italian, or Italiote, and it is reasonable to connect, not only the mid-century Delian boom, but the prominence of ʿΡωμαῖοι in it, with the simultaneous increase in the demand for slaves and the supply.

Strabo continues the first passage (486) by saying that Delos never recovered after the sack and the massacre of the ʿΡωμαῖοι in the first Mithridatic war. But there was some temporary recovery after the war, and it remains for later discussion how far the collapse of the commercial economy, an accomplished fact by the middle of the century, may be explained by the loss of captives for the slave market after the pirates were put down in 67 by Pompeius.

Provenance of the Delian ʿΡωμαῖοι

Hatzfeld (followed by most scholars) asserted that most of the Delian ʿΡωμαῖοι, on the showing of nomenclature, were from southern Italy, a small minority only from Rome, Latium, and central Italy. This—as he thought—bore out antecedent probability, southern Italy being commercially important in the second century, Rome and central Italy unimportant commercially. That sharp distinction ignores (as I have maintained) actual conditions in Italy. One part of the south, Campania, was highly prosperous and well placed for overseas trade, but already in the second century Campania was steadily becoming romanized and many of those who traded from its ports are likely to have been Roman incomers. The extreme south, by contrast, was not generally prosperous, for both the Italiote Greeks and the south Italic communities were thinned, weakened, and impoverished. Not only in Campania, but in whatever part of the country opportunity offered, men of Roman descent may be supposed steadily more important in commerce, banking, and moneylending, conscious of new openings abroad and well placed to exploit them. These conditions seem to be reflected on Delos, however cautiously the evidence—epigraphic only—be used.

It must indeed so be used. For the great majority of the persons attested nomenclature is the only test of provenance, since (for whatever reason) it is only in inscriptions relating to Italiote Greeks that the individual's place of origin is often mentioned. Furthermore, of two hundred and twenty-one persons of identifiable status in the inscriptions collected by Hatzfeld in 'Les Italiens résidant à Délos'[1] no less than ninety-five, on his later computation, are freedmen and forty-eight slaves.[2] It is likely that many of these first reached Delos, not from Italy, but from some part of the eastern Mediterranean, brought by pirates and sold on the slave market, so that they never saw Italy, but learned the speech and customs of their masters on the island. The probable importance of this element among the *liberti* is the first limitation to the usefulness of the evidence collected by Hatzfeld. Further, an *ingenuus* of unknown ancestry can be of servile origin, since already in the third generation change of *cognomen* may conceal the slave status of the grandfather. So among the *ingenui*—eighty-eight names out of two hundred and twenty-one—an element of servile descent must be allowed for: an unfortunately unknowable quantity.

[1] *B.H.* xxxvi (1912) 5 ff. (index 10 ff.), hereafter called *Délos*.
[2] *Les Trafiquants* 247.

Yet the majority of the *ingenui* need not be supposed of servile descent. Families are clearly traceable, with their freedmen and slaves, from generation to generation on Delos. It is most unlikely that the pioneer, or pioneering group, to whom each family must go back, was not free. In the second century the Roman bourgeoisie and the important families in the Italian towns will have kept fairly clear of the freedmen class,[1] and have been keen and energetic enough, in most cases, to supervise their affairs personally (as many of their descendants did in Cicero's day).[2] It seems unlikely that the Granii of Puteoli, when they first became interested in Delos, sent out a freedman to act for them, or that a shrewd *negotiator*, in that age, deputed to a *libertus* responsibility for carrying his interests into a new field. Thus, although the prominent Delian families made considerable use of freedmen, it is likely that the pioneers on Delos were *ingenui*.

The total number of *gentilicia*, Roman and Italian, found in Hatzfeld's list is one hundred and fifty-five. It seems fair to consider these (including those borne by *liberti* only) on my assumption that the pioneer who brought the name to Delos will usually have been an *ingenuus*.

It may be that, in some cases, individuals appearing to be eastern *negotiatores*, or connected with *negotiatores*, are in fact freedmen (or even kinsmen) of provincial governors, or received the citizenship from them. But, since Hatzfeld took account of this possibility in making his Delian index, and the number of these is not likely, in any case, to have been large on Delos, this does not seriously affect the use of his lists.

The use of nomenclature here is affected by other considerations. Few names were altogether restricted, by the second century B.C., to any one region of Italy, and it would be reasonable in but few cases to say, merely on the strength of a name, that this or that family *must* have reached its home overseas direct from one particular district of Italy. Many names that till the fifth century belonged narrowly to the highlands of Samnium were then carried into the neighbouring plain lands—more

---

[1] In the century following some of Cicero's friends in the *ordo* were proud of their ancient *equestris nobilitas*, as also were Ovid, Velleius, and others.

[2] Atticus is typical of the class; he had *procuratores*, but was far from leaving things to them (cf. R. Feger, *P-W* Suppl. VIII.516 ff.).

particularly Campania—by invading or infiltrating Samnites. Subsequently, from the late fourth to the second century, Romans and Latins were introduced, first into northern Campania, afterwards further south, by colonization and private movement; more massive colonization came later, when cities in Campania, as elsewhere, had land confiscated and given to veterans by Sulla. Conversely, native Oscans formed Roman connections or were attracted to Rome, or became romanized where they lived. Such movement and change, which, *mutatis mutandis*, affected other parts of Italy, suggest the difficulty, on Delos or elsewhere, of linking 'Ρωμαῖοι with particular parts of Italy.

Yet particular gentile names are strikingly prominent, even much later than our period, in Campania or in individual cities of Campania; if one such name is very common overseas, there is a reasonable inference about the native district of those who carried it to the provinces; the inference is even more probable when a number of such names appear overseas and make a cumulative impression.

The names in Hatzfeld's Delian index cannot be exhaustively classified, but (Italiote Greeks apart) there may be distinguished: (1) those Oscan in character and prominent in Campanian epigraphy, or belonging, before the Romanization of the region, to leading families there; (2) names attested for Campania, but also common further east or south; (3) Roman/Latin names carried into Campania by colonization or private movement; (4) Roman/Latin names with no known association with Campania. References to Hatzfeld's index need not be given, since it is alphabetical.

(1) Oscan Staii established themselves from Cumae on Delos in the early second century, and flourished there, holding to their native *praenomina*, Minatus and Ovius.[1] Trebius Loisius, an important merchant, flourishing on the island about 160, was almost certainly from Capua.[2] The Pettii seem certainly connected with Capua, Nola, Abella,[3] and neighbouring places, and the Pactumeii with Capua;[4] Campania certainly contri-

---

[1] See Münzer *P-W* 'Staius' 2136.
[2] See Münzer *P-W* 'Loesius' 965.
[3] Münzer *P-W* 'Pettius' 1381, with *C.I.L.* x.1208, 1216 (Abella), 3544 (Misenum), 4787 (Teanum), 6267 (Fundi).
[4] *C.I.L.* x.3778, 4171, 4254, 4270, 4294.

buted far more Delian *negotiatores* than this list suggests, but I reserve for (2) names common to Campania and the regions to its east and south.

(2) Such (to mention only the certain cases) include Tutorius (originally Messapic; but found as far north as Puteoli), Seius or Sehius, Cerrinius (Pompeii, but also Beneventum, Aeclanum, Bovianum, Larinum, Ausculum, and Saepinum), Heius (Nola, but also Venusia and Saepinum), Stlaccius, Ofellius (Capua and Beneventum), Vibius, and Gerillanus (the only name chiefly confined to the extreme south-east).[1]

(3) The names are not known of any of the colonists sent to Puteoli early in the second century; but the Granii, who became the leading family in the town and soon reached Delos, had close connections with Rome *c.* 100, and do not appear Oscan.[2] The Cossinii, apparently native to Tibur, had interests at Puteoli and overseas in Greece and the East;[3] likewise the Cluvii, important at Puteoli and in Campania in Cicero's day and possessing large interests in Asia, may have been established on Delos about 100.[4]

(4) Names characteristically Roman/Latin form the largest single class, not surprisingly, since, as has been seen, both Romans and Latins were already active in eastern trade in the early second century.[5] The respective importance of Romans and Latins cannot be established;[6] but from the total of one hundred and fifty-five names indexed by Hatzfeld, one may

---

[1] Tutorius, Brundisium (*C.I.L.* ix.24), Canusium (ibid., 402), Puteoli (x.1928), with Münzer *P-W* 'Tutorius' 1626; Seius (Münzer *P-W* 'Seius' 1120); Cerrinius, Pompeii and district (*C.I.L.* x.994 f., 1160 etc.), Beneventum (ix.1643, 1910, 1925), Aeclanum (ibid., 6274, 6276), Bovianum (ibid., 2573), Larinum (ibid., 740), Ausculum (ibid., 678), Saepinum (2521); Heius, Nola (x.1305), Venusia (ix.523), Saepinum (ix.2467); Stlaccius (Münzer *P-W* 'Stlaccius'); Ofellius (Münzer *P-W* 'Ofellius' (8) and (10)); Vibius (Gundel *P-W* 'Vibius' 1948); Gerillanus (see below p. 153).

[2] Münzer, *P-W* 'Granius', details the members of the family. He expresses no view on the origin of the name.

[3] See Münzer *P-W* 'Cossinius' (1), (3) and (4) with *C.I.L.* iii.574 and x.2183, 2255, 2344 ff., 2929.

[4] For the Cluvii at Puteoli and in Asia, below p. 133.

[5] See above p. 91.

[6] In the second century many names were certainly common to the Roman citizen body and the Latin communities. There were also some names now common both to the Romans/Latins and to non-Latin peoples. Such was 'Egnatius': see Skutsch *P-W* 'Egnatius' 1993 ff.

distinguish fifty-four Roman/Latin *gentilicia*, many of which were common, or prominent, in the Roman citizen body in the second century B.C.; individually they tend to occur less frequently than some of the names connected with Campania. Aemilii, Caecilii, Claudii and Clodii, Plotii, Rutilii, Sextilii, and Stertinii are relatively frequent; other Roman names found (each in fewer instances) are Antonius, Calpurnius, Cornelius, Fabius, Fabricius, Flaminius, Fulvius, Furius, Laelius, Lucretius, Mamilius, Marcius, Octavius, Porcius, Servilius, Sestius, Sulpicius, and Valerius.[1]

The Anicii on Delos, the Magulnii, Samiarii, Saufeii, and Satricanii, stand as a group on their own. These names seem to be identified with Praeneste. This city, with an ancient tradition of industry and long attached to its own Latin dialect, was still, in the second century, a proud and highly individual allied community, despite its proximity to Rome. It is not unlikely that it had its own commercial life in this period, with families such as these playing a prominent part.[2]

The Italiote Greeks can readily be distinguished, since the home-town of the individual or the family commonly appears in inscriptions. There are twenty-two in all in Hatzfeld's list.[3] As these appear to be freemen, they may be compared, for number, with the eighty-eight Roman or Italian *ingenui*. One in four can hardly be reckoned a proportion answering to the claim made for Magna Graecia; and since four are from Campania (Neapolis), a region distinct from the rest of Magna Graecia, the correct figure would be rather one in five. In southernmost Italy, Velia, Petelia, Heraclea, Locri Epizephyrii, Tarentum, Azetium are represented; from eastern Italy, Ancona. That city was far removed from Magna Graecia, on the Picene coast, but it received, in the early fourth century, a body of Greeks dis-

---

[1] To those mentioned add: Annius, Calvius, Carvilius, Cincius, Gessius, Helvius, Hostilius, Labienus, Licinius, Lollius, Memmius, Maevius, Mindius, Naevius, Numitorius, Orbius, Otacilius, Petronius, Plaetorius, Plautius, Pompilius, Pomponius, Popilius (Poplilius), Quinctius, Raecius, Titinius, Tuccius, Veturius.

[2] The Anicii, Klebs *P-W* 'Anicius' 2196; the Magulnii, Samiarii, Saufeii, and Satricanii, Münzer *P-W* s.vv.

[3] I omit (*a*) the Sicilian Greeks included by Hatzfeld (*B.H.* xxxvi.130[4]), (*b*) *hellenized* Apulians and an Oscan, included by him (ibid., notes 2, 8, 9, 10). The individuals stand out by their names and need not be listed.

contented with the rule of Dionysios I of Syracuse, and there-after, though isolated from the other Italiotes, long retained Greek elements in its life.[1]

A floating or a stable population?

One is prompted by the circumstances of Delos to ask whether the ʿΡωμαῖοι were a real settlement, with all that word implies in continuity, stability, and domestic life, or came and departed frequently, without establishing roots. Certainly they did not form a community rooted in the island in the way in which agricultural communities may be rooted in a place—with hardly any new families coming or old families leaving; on the other hand there is no reason to think that the whole composition of the body changed constantly in the course of a few years.

The port town and its surroundings were not such as to attract a wealthy man to spend all his time there.[2] For this reason, and for reasons of business, many traders probably had a footing elsewhere, in Greece or in Asia; many too may have chosen to retire elsewhere in old age.[3] On the other hand a Delian trader or banker—it is reasonable to suppose—could prosper only if he gave most of his time to Delos; and he would try to pass on his business there to a son or heir. One would thus expect to find families connected with Delos from generation to generation, but not at home there and only there in the way that a family dependent on land might be in an Italian country town.

In the last quarter of the second century the Athenians resident on Delos, the ʿΡωμαῖοι, and the other foreigners combined on a number of occasions to honour benefactors; the terms of the 'decrees' suggest, as will shortly appear, that some at least of the ʿΡωμαῖοι were regarded as permanent residents. But, by 125 B.C., it would have been strange if there had not been some permanent residents among the ʿΡωμαῖοι; what is needed is an indication how far these generally were rooted and at home on

---

[1] Strabo 241. For other evidence see P-W 'Ancona', and C.I.L. IX p. 572 (introduction to the inscriptions of Ancona).

[2] Laidlaw 239 f., 243.

[3] For the recurrence elsewhere of names common on Delos see p. 97 (Athens), 132 (Ephesus), 134 (Miletus), 136 (Cos). But some at least of the names in Asia will be due to the dispersal of the Delian Romans after the collapse of Delian commerce.

Delos. Apart from these 'decrees', inscriptions attesting the ῾Ρωμαῖοι are almost exclusively dedicatory or honorific texts, which they set up occasionally as individuals, but more often as presidents or members of the three famous *collegia*. These *collegia*, deriving their respective names from Hermes, Apollo, and Poseidon, certainly functioned as much for social and business as for religious purposes; as their members were men, men are preponderant in Delian epigraphy. Funerary inscriptions, which would have helped the tracing of family relationships, are rare on Delos. This is to be attributed to the continued operation, even in the second and first centuries B.C., of the taboo on burial there, causing the removal of the dead to Rhenaia.[1] But this special local difficulty does not mean that there is no useful evidence. The enormous growth of the town, revealed by the excavations, which changed or submerged the old pattern, must belong, in the main, to the period 166–88 B.C.[2] There were not only harbour improvements and new public buildings and quarters, but new residential streets.[3] Nothing suggests a distinct quarter belonging to the ῾Ρωμαῖοι and a few houses only can be assigned to them,[4] but it is evident that they must have had an important part in the growth of the residential quarter of Delos. The houses here are (as might be expected) very much *sui generis* in their plan and details, but still family dwellings, often with most careful attention to comfort and amenity, as though to make up for the narrowness of the streets and cramped character of the town.[5]

In the case of the Italiote Greeks, whose inscriptions, for some reason, record relationships in a way the others do not, a tree of some families may be made for three or four generations;[6] and some of the prominent Roman and Italian families can be

---

[1] The taboo dated from 426 B.C., Thucydides III.104. Its persistence in the second and first centuries B.C., Roussel 207. It was also forbidden for women to give birth on Delos. Remains have been found on Rhenaia of what appear to be special birth and death rooms, Roussel 207[4].

[2] Roussel 307 ff., especially 309 f.

[3] Laidlaw 232 ff.

[4] No distinct national quarters: Roussel 312 f. Houses identified to particular owners (Q. Tullius, Sp. Stertinius, Philostratos of Ascalon and Neapolis): Roussel 312 f.

[5] Laidlaw 239–45.

[6] See Hatzfeld's index: Ἀγαθοκλῆς Ἑρμώνος from Elea; Ἡρακλείδης Ἀριστῶνος from Tarentum; Τίτος Σατυριώνος from Heraclea.

traced for half a century or longer, though a definite tree cannot be made for them.[1] Many names occur only within a brief period, around 100 B.C., but even in these cases the recurrence of father and son or of brothers suggests that business was being done by families, not individuals.[2] As will be seen, many Delian Ῥωμαῖοι seem to have had a second footing or connections of some kind in old or Asiatic Greece; but connections of this kind would not make their community less stable, in the sense the term is used here.

The public status of the Delian Ῥωμαῖοι

When Delos was given to Athens in 167/6 B.C., the Delians were mostly expelled and Athenian settlers sent to replace them. These were allowed an Ecclesia and Boule, but from the beginning the Ecclesia seems to have passed honorific decrees only, and government to have been exercised by the Ἐπιμελήτης and the magistrates whom Athens appointed and supervised.[3] Since the honorific decrees cease about 145, it seems likely that the Ecclesia and Boule fell into desuetude about this time. About twenty years later there begins a new series of honorific decrees, made on the combined initiative of the Athenians on Delos, the Ῥωμαῖοι, and the other foreigners. In these five main formulae are found:[4]

1. Ἀθηναίων οἱ κατοικοῦντες ἐν Δήλωι καὶ οἱ ἔμποροι καὶ οἱ ναύκληροι καὶ Ῥωμαίων καὶ τῶν ἄλλων ξένων οἱ παρεπιδημοῦντες.

2. Ἀθηναίων καὶ Ῥωμαίων καὶ τῶν ἄλλων ξένων οἱ κατοικοῦντες καὶ παρεπιδημοῦντες ἐν Δήλωι.

3. Ἀθηναίων οἱ κατοικοῦντες ἐν Δήλωι καὶ Ῥωμαίων οἱ παρεπιδημοῦντες καὶ οἱ ἔμποροι καὶ οἱ ναύκληροι.

4. Ἀθηναίων καὶ Ῥωμαίων καὶ τῶν ἄλλων Ἑλλήνων οἱ κατοικοῦντες καὶ παρεπιδημοῦντες ἐν Δήλωι.

[1] The Staii from Cumae; the Aemilii; the Audii (from 150/125 B.C., no. 6, p. 18 in Hatzfeld's index, to the middle of the first century, no. 3); the Aufidii (see Hatzfeld Les Trafiquants 37 and 84); the Plotii (cf. C.I.L. III.7218, early second century, with Hatzfeld no. 4, after the Mithridatic war); perhaps the Sehii (C.I.L. III.7218); the Vibii (from c. 180 to c. 100, Hatzfeld's index); the Sextilii (Münzer P-W 'Sextilius' (22)).

[2] See Hatzfeld's index, for the Cottii and the Gerillani; the article 203, no. 12, for a dedication by Tutorii for the whole family; ibid., no. 14, for a similar dedication by A. Pactumeius; and ibid., 204, no. 16, by a Gessius for his family.

[3] Roussel 97 ff., especially 120 ff.   [4] Distinguished by Roussel 51.

I

5. Ἀθηναίων καὶ Ῥωμαίων καὶ τῶν ἄλλων Ἑλλήνων οἱ κατοικοῦντες ἐν Δήλωι καὶ οἱ ἔμποροι καὶ ναύκληροι οἱ καταπλέοντες εἰς
τὸ ἐμπόριον.

Some sort of committee may have taken the decision to
honour benefactors in the name of the various groups, and it
need not be assumed that all the groups came together in one
body at some time. If they did, it cannot have been anything
like an Ecclesia, but must have been a much more informal and
ad hoc gathering, since the formulae vary considerably, in an
apparently arbitrary way, from year to year and temporary
residents and visitors are included alongside permanent residents.
Since the formulae do not define a legally recognized body, the
terms applied to the various groups can hardly indicate their
particular status. Thus the fact that the term κατοικοῦντες is
applied to Ῥωμαῖοι, as well as to Athenians, in three of the five
types of formula (2, 4, 5) need mean only that many of these, as
many Athenians, were permanent residents on Delos, not temporary visitors (termed οἱ παρεπιδημοῦντες or οἱ ἔμποροι καὶ
ναύκληροι or οἱ καταπλέοντες εἰς τὸ ἐμπόριον, etc). The term
κάτοικος and the term κατοικεῖν connote a status in certain
legal and political contexts, but are not always so used,[1]
and the conjunction here with the obviously non-technical
παρεπιδημοῦντες and καταπλέοντες makes it the more unlikely
that they are used in a technical sense in these inscriptions.

Hatzfeld gives all the inscriptions in chronological order.[2] Re-
marking on the distinction common to all the formulae between
κατοικοῦντες and visitors (παρεπιδημοῦντες or καταπλέοντες), he
adds that the Ῥωμαῖοι are regularly included in the former class
only from 115 B.C.: thus the Athenians on Delos are always
κατοικοῦντες, but the Ῥωμαῖοι are first so called long after
many of them had become permanent residents.[3] The term,
therefore, he argues, must connote status, as well as residence—
status which the Athenians on Delos held from 167, but the
Ῥωμαῖοι acquired only about 115. But, as already noted, the
terms κάτοικος and κατοικεῖν are not necessarily technical; and as
early as 125 B.C. the formula is found Ἀθηναίων καὶ Ῥωμαίων
καὶ τῶν ἄλλων ξένων οἱ κατοικοῦντες καὶ παρεπιδημοῦντες ἐν Δήλωι,

---

[1] See Liddell and Scott, ed. Jones s.v.   [2] *Délos* 104 ff.
[3] Ibid., 107 f.

which seems to suggest that, ten years before the suggested change in 115, some of the ʿΡωμαῖοι were regarded as κατοικοῦντες.[1]

The ʿΡωμαῖοι and the Delian environment

The ʿΡωμαῖοι on Delos, as has been seen, were heterogeneous: Italians, mainly from Campania, but also from other parts of the south; Romans, but not from the *urbs* only; Italiote Greeks; freedmen, some coming from Italy, some originally bought as slaves on the Delian market. These classes, living all within the narrow port town and brought together constantly in its activities, cannot have been socially exclusive; the freedmen, it is clear, attained in Delian life the scope which the class came to enjoy earlier in the provinces than in Italy.[2] Nor can the ʿΡωμαῖοι, of whatever type, be supposed to have declined social contacts or marriage with the Delian Athenians or the various foreigners on the island. Evidence for marriage connections fails us, since the Delian inscriptions (for reasons mentioned) are not concerned with family matters. But intermarriage is probable in view of the influence and prestige among the ʿΡωμαῖοι of families that were international even before they came to Delos. Such was the family of the wealthy banker Philostratos (late second century): described by the brothers Egnatii, in an honorific inscription, as Νεαπολίτης, ὁ πρότερον χρηματίζων Ἀσκαλονίτης, τραπεζιτεύων ἐν Δήλωι, he was (as one chose to regard him) a Greek-speaking Syrian, an Italiote of Neapolis, or a Delian ʿΡωμαῖος.[3] Likewise the family of the rich Simalos (c. 100 B.C.) had a footing in Tarentum, in Cyprus, and in Athens, as well as connections with Egypt and its court. Families like that of Philostratos and of Simalos, whose members could go to distant lands without need of introduction, had powerful advantages in commerce. If there is exaggeration in the eulogy of Simalos as προσφιλὲς Αἰγύπτου κοιρανίαις ἔρυμα καὶ ʿΡώμας ὑπάτοισι,[4] there

---

[1] Ibid., 105, first inscription.

[2] Ibid., 155.

[3] See Durrbach *Choix* p. 212 no. 132. Philostratos was obviously important among the ʿΡωμαῖοι: cf. the dedication in honour of him and sons by the Ἰταλικοί, *B.H.* XXXVI.210 no. 25 *bis*; his own dedication to Apollo and the Ἰταλικοί, *B.H.* VIII.128; and the other inscriptions quoted by Durrbach op. cit. 214. His son was an ephebe at Athens in 93/2 or 92/1, *B.H.* XXXI.438 no. 29, with Roussel 373 for the date.

[4] Stolos, an Athenian, συγγενὴς of Ptolemy Soter II, set up a statue in

can be no doubt that the success of his family and their like impressed the 'Ρωμαῖοι, and promoted the trend towards a social tone more Greco-oriental than Roman or Italian.

Even with Italiote Greeks excluded, the great majority of the inscriptions are either Greek or bilingual—Greek and Latin. This is explicable partly by the presence in number of freedmen from the eastern Greek or Greek-speaking lands, but also by the fact that Greek was the official public language of Delos and the common language of the various groups there. 'Ρωμαῖοι of every class were bound to use Greek increasingly, even among themselves, and Greek is found no less in the inscriptions recording *ingenui* than in those relating to freedmen. Certain families flourished on Delos through several generations, and Latin, significantly, is little found in their inscriptions. Some 'Ρωμαῖοι, by contrast, appear as isolated individuals; Latin is used rather more commonly in the inscriptions relating to these, and it may be that they were short-term residents on Delos who did not acquire Greek as a habit. Although the *liberti* appear mostly in Greek inscriptions, some are found in inscriptions in Latin; these, presumably, came to Delos from Italy.

The evidence of cults likewise indicates that most 'Ρωμαῖοι were influenced deeply from the beginning by their Greco-oriental environment. The point is not that Apollo, Hermes, and Poseidon loom large. Their cults, or those of the gods identified with them, had long been important for natives of Italy; and these three deities—the patron of the island and its commercially profitable festivals, the god of commerce, and the sea-god—were bound to have honour among merchants, bankers, and sea-captains. It is rather the manifest interest of the Delian 'Ρωμαῖοι in oriental deities, coupled with their lack of interest in the traditional Roman-Italian deities whom many might have honoured at home.

Though Italians and Romans must be presumed to have

---

honour of Simalos, with verses on the base, which open (Durrbach *Choix* 205 f.)

’Αλκινόου μελάθροισι προσείκελα δώματα ναίων,
Σίμαλε . . . .

and continue with a variety of flowery compliments, including that quoted in the text. For the other evidence about Simalos, including the Tarentine connections, see Durrbach 206 f. The young men of this family also are found at Athens: Durrbach 207.

taken with them to Delos the *Lares familiares* and *Penates*, it is not clear how far these cults were observed by them in the cosmopolitan port town. Liturgical paintings found in certain Delian houses have been identified by a scholar with the Italian–Roman cult of the household deities;[1] in the opinion, however, of P. Roussel, rites of Greek character could have been performed against the background of these wall paintings, nor is the nationality of the owners of the houses known independently.[2]

The Delian *Κομπεταλιάσται* are another matter. Their cult of the *Lares compitales* came from Italy. But it was practised there by slaves, and there are no *ingenui* (of course) or even freedmen in the Delian association. Though the slaves who introduced this cult to Delos must have come from Italy, the association used Greek.[3] This is not evidence for any important or enduring Roman–Italian strain in the religious life of the *Ῥωμαῖοι*.

The eastern cults satisfied the craving, already felt in Italy, for the new and exotic in religion, and some of their Delian votaries may have felt that practice of them could ease their dealings with the foreigner or in his land. The foreign deities honoured among the *Ῥωμαῖοι* are Egyptian or Syrian. Syrian Atargatis or *Ἁγνὴ Ἀφροδίτη* is prominent and some of her worshippers are wealthy men, of standing on Delos.[4] Among the benefactors of Sarapis and his temple are the Oscan Minatus Staius from Cumae (*c.* 180 B.C.), founder of a Delian family, and another Campanian who traded from one end of the Mediterranean to the other, Trebius Loisius (157 B.C.).[5] The Aemilii, active on Delos *c.* 150–100 B.C., include dedicants to Syrian and Egyptian deities.[6] Examples need not be multiplied; the vogue of these deities only foreshadows later developments in Rome and Italy.

It remains clear, however, that the *Ῥωμαῖοι* were a body with a sense of separate identity. They alone among the foreigners

---

[1] M. Bulard *La religion domestique dans la colonie italique de Délos, passim.*

[2] Roussel 277 f., 313[1].

[3] *Délos* 157 f. with notes.

[4] The Syrian deities, Roussel 253–63; the interest in them of the *Ῥωμαῖοι* 255[3], 260, 411 (inscr. no. 5), 412 (inscr. no. 8), 414 (no. 16), 422 (nos. 29 f.).

[5] For the Egyptian deities on Delos, Roussel 249–252, with 251 for the interest of the *Ῥωμαῖοι*; Minatus Staius, *Délos* 80 (no. 3); Trebius Loisius, ibid. 46 f. and *B.H.* IV.183 (full text).

[6] *Délos* 10 f.

are distinguished by name in the honorific decrees of 125–88 B.C. Correspondingly, the frequent conjunction, in dedications, of 'Italiceis'/'Ἰταλίκοις with the name of a deity is an indication of a feeling of corporate existence.[1] The three important cult associations,—the Apolloniastae, the Hermaistae, and the Posei-doniastae—undoubtedly helped the *negotiator* to maintain profit-able contacts while practising religion and 'good fellowship'.[2] But they also helped to maintain some sort of corporate sense among the Ῥωμαῖοι. It was not so much that they existed specifically for these (though no other members are found), but that the three associations could combine on occasion to act in concert for all the Ῥωμαῖοι.[3] One object thus achieved was considerable, and helpful to the whole body. This was the con-struction, about the end of the second century, of a great colonnaded square, probably known as the Ἰταλικὴ παστάς.[4] Such work presumes a fair degree of corporate spirit. It seems exaggerated to call the square 'a sort of Italian enclave on Greek soil';[5] but it was evidently the great social and business resort of the Ῥωμαῖοι. The work, though a corporate effort, also called forth the interest of individuals acting singly or in small groups. Such contributed to the adornment and improvement of the square, and, after its destruction in 88, helped, on the Roman return, to restore it.[6] This square appears to have been much like its counterpart in an Italian port; there were public baths, niches were adorned with statues, and honorific dedi-cations abounded. It is not surprising that the dedications alluding collectively to the Ἰταλικοὶ were found in the main here.[7]

The occupations of the Delian Ῥωμαῖοι

As the evidence of Strabo suggests, many, perhaps the majority, of the Delian *negotiatores*, in the boom period, must

---

[1] *Délos* 132, with 118[4].
[2] Ibid., 154 ff.
[3] Ibid., 156 *ad fin.* f., Laidlaw 202 ff. especially 207 f.
[4] *Délos* 110 ff., 117 ff., with Laidlaw 208 f.
[5] As does Hatzfeld, *Délos* 118.
[6] Restoration, *Délos* 114 f., Roussel 329 f.
[7] General character of the square, *Délos* 118; baths, *B.H.* XXXI.439 no. 30, with XXXIV.403 no. 54; games, ibid. Provenance of inscriptions relating to the 'Italici', Hatzfeld *B.H.* XXXVI.118[4].

have been slave-traders—which is not to say that they did not pursue other trades as well. But for these other occupations of the ῾Ρωμαῖοι the evidence is scanty.

Public and private banking were important in the pre-Roman period, and it is reasonable to suppose that bankers increased in number and importance with the second-century increase in Delian trade. A Sicilian banking family moved from Tenos to Delos in the early second century—probably a sign of expanding activity there.[1] Various ῾Ρωμαῖοι soon became prominent in the field: the Aufidii (benefactors of Tenos in her difficulties in the early first century),[2] the Apulian Gerillani,[3] the Oscan, Marcus Minatius (benefactor of the association on Delos of the Poseidoniastae of Berytus[4]), and the cosmopolitan man of business, Philostratus, belonging equally to Ascalon, Neapolis, and Delos.[5] These are known from Delian inscriptions; from R. Herzog's full investigations into *tesserae nummulariae* it would appear possible that the Delian Pomponii, Novii, Paconii, Fulvii, and Magulnii had part in the banking business.[6] But it would be wrong to assume that banking at Delos in the second century fell altogether into the hands of the ῾Ρωμαῖοι; Greeks and others had part in it.[7]

An association of *olearii* (ἐλαιοπῶλαι) is attested in several inscriptions, its membership of ῾Ρωμαῖοι including southern Italians and Italiote Greeks;[8] it is conceivable that there was export of oil, and also of wine, from Italy to the East via Delos, in the second and earlier first centuries, but the trade could have been the other way, and in any case the evidence—*amphorae* found on Delos and their marks—does not really indicate its scale.[9]

---

[1] *Τίμων Νυμφοδώρου* and his son: *I.G.* xii(5)816 f., with Hatzfeld *Les Trafiquants* 28 f.

[2] *Délos* 19 'Aufidii', with *I.G.* xii(5)860.

[3] *Délos* 37 'Gerillani', especially no. 3.

[4] Text and discussion of the inscription by M. N. Tod *J.H.S.* liv.140 ff.

[5] Durrbach *Choix* p. 212 no. 132 and above p. 115.

[6] For these *tesserae* generally, R. Herzog *P-W* 'nummularius'; for Delos, his table on 1422 ff., nos. 1, 4, 6, 7 f., 41; with the comments on 1434 ff. and 1439 ff.

[7] As Rostovzeff 798 suggests; for the contrary evidence, *E.S.A.R.* iv.359.

[8] *Délos* 143[1].

[9] *Pace* Laidlaw 204.

The neighbouring islands

The Cyclades cluster in a semi-circle, Andros, Tenos, Delos, Naxos, and Amorgos forming the diameter—in a straight line north-west to south-east—Ceos, Melos, and other islands making the arc on the south-west; none is more than sixty miles from Delos. There was some settlement on certain of these islands near to Delos.

Tenos had some commercial importance about 200 B.C., its sacred bank of Poseidon corresponding to the bank of Apollo on Delos. A Sicilian was conducting a private bank there at this time, perhaps on some scale, since he lent money to the League of Νησιῶται, the federation of island cities revived in the early second century under Rhodian protection. But his son appears to have moved the bank to Delos, no doubt because Delos was now enjoying a boom and greatly overshadowing Tenos.[1] During the years of the Delian boom little evidence appears of ῾Ρωμαῖοι on Tenos, but this may be accident, in view of the presence of Romans and Italians on some of the other Cyclades.[2] Tenos in any case was flourishing in the period of the Delian decline and collapse. A number of ῾Ρωμαῖοι are now found, some holding magistracies, and it may be that one Delian-Roman banking family, the Aufidii, finally moved their business to Tenos, with which they had had dealings for some time.[3]

Amorgos, an island with three ports and a spinning industry, had a body of ῾Ρωμαῖοι from the early first century to the early Principate, including members of a family once prominent on Delos, the Babullii.[4] On Naxos seven of thirty-two names in an ephebic list of the late first century B.C. are Roman, and a few other ῾Ρωμαῖοι are found, including a Babullius.[5] Babullii appear again on Paros, Melos had some Romans, and Roman names appear on Andros, Thera, and Syros.[6]

Names found on Delos in the boom period appear on these islands: apart from the Babullii, Arellius, Aufidius, Ofellius, Poppilius (Poplilius), Sulpicius, Sextilius. Though not all the inscriptions can be dated, their appearance may be due in part

[1] Hatzfeld 28 f.

[2] Ibid., 37, 'L'île de Ténos subit le contre-coup de la prospérité de Délos', may depend too much on negative evidence.

[3] Ibid., 84 ff., with notes.   [4] Ibid., 89 f.

[5] Ibid., 86 f.

[6] Hatzfeld 87 f.

to scattering of ʿΡωμαῖοι after the Delian collapse, since 'Delian' names appear also, in the later first century and under the Principate, in cities of the Anatolian mainland.

ROMAN ASIA

This province, as established in 129 B.C. after Roman acceptance of the territory of Attalus III under his will and suppression of the revolt of Aristonicus, consisted of Mysia and Lydia, Ionia, and Caria (to which Phrygia was added in 116). It included the great off-shore islands, Lesbos, Chios, Samos, and Cos.

The coastal belt of this region and its island fringe were richer than Greece in places where a settler could engage lucratively in commerce, finance, or the exploitation of land. The cities had long been enriched by their fertile soil and other natural resources, and in the Hellenistic age profited greatly by their strategic commercial position, which made the region a clearing-house for different parts of the eastern Mediterranean and near-Eastern worlds, and indeed for lands further apart.[1] The towns were attractive, and the great cities had an exuberance of display and luxury such as was not distasteful, by the later second century, to many Romans, certainly not to Campanians and Italiote Greeks. The climate of Ionia was proverbially excellent, and there everything tempted the visitor to settle. Along the north-western coast, from the Hellespont to the Bosporus, the cities were also attractive, set, as they were, in a fertile region connected equally with Asia and with Europe, in which great land and sea routes converged and crossed.[2]

The southern coast had received settlers in multitudes when the Greeks first crossed to Anatolia, and the Black Sea shores were settled in the Greek colonial age; yet they were comparatively unattractive now to the ʿΡωμαῖοι. Unlike the migrating

[1] For an admirably succinct account of the structure of Anatolia and the economic consequences see Sir C. Wilson *Notes on the Physical and Geographical History of Asia Minor*; fuller, D. Magie 34 ff., 42 f. (on the road system of western Anatolia). Economic developments in the Hellenistic period, Rostovzeff 81, 129 ff., and especially 158 ff., 532 ff. (adverse effects of the Ptolemaic occupation of western Anatolia and counter-balancing factors), 562 ff., 654 f., and 804 f. (Pergamene kingdom).

[2] The Hellespontine and Propontic cities in the Hellenistic age: Rostovzeff 585 ff. The communications of the region, Magie 41 f.

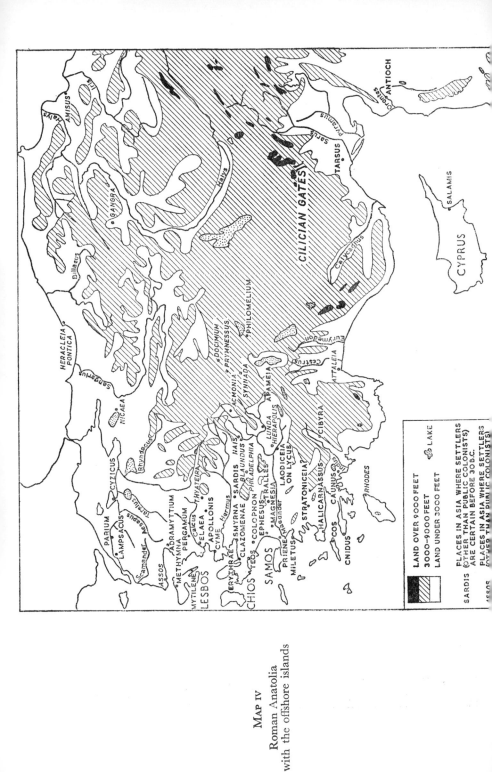

Map IV
Roman Anatolia
with the offshore islands

Greeks, who came under pressure, in such hosts that some had to make do with poor land or positions, the Ῥωμαῖοι came as individuals in comparatively minute numbers and mostly in conditions of peace, could choose the best place each for his purpose, and think of amenities. Everything told in favour of the western coast and islands and the north-west.

The Black Sea shore had indeed good land and other natural wealth, the south its fertile coastal plains in Pamphylia and Cilicia. But in the south, till the eastern corner and the Cilician Gates are reached, lofty ranges, through which passes are few and difficult, obstruct access from the sea to the central tableland. Though the northern mountain ranges are mostly lower and further from the coast, the river channels are usable only here and there for roads, so that the main routes traverse chiefly highland country. Only a few of the northern and none of the southern coastal cities (except in the south-eastern corner) were well-placed for trade with the great Anatolian hinterland or through it with more distant regions.

Thus Cilicia Tracheia, Lycia, and Pamphylia might still have failed to attract Ῥωμαῖοι, even had many of their ports not been in the hands of the Cilician pirates for long periods before 67 B.C.[1] In the north Romans eventually arrived here and there along the Black Sea, but even in the first century A.D. Roman groups are rather few further east than Bithynia, in Paphlagonia and Pontus.

By contrast, the west and the north-west, in addition to their other advantages, had much easier access to the interior, from a coast better supplied with good harbours. This was decisive, because the interior, though poor country, provided fine highways linking the various parts of Anatolia with each other and the lands beyond. Thus the major western and north-western ports became stations for a trade with the West handling, not only Anatolian products, but the luxuries from further east of ever greater interest to wealthy Romans and Italians.[2]

The great advantage of the west coast lay in its good connections with the interior. For the main trade artery ran from

[1] Cilicia was probably little more than a theatre of war till 67 B.C.: see below p. 137.
[2] For the history of the trade of Ephesus and Miletus etc. with regions further east, Rostovzeff 804 ff., with 654 ff.

Ephesus over a slight upland to the Maeander, up that valley, and then by the valley of its tributary, the Lycus, to Apamea (Celaenae). This road was easily accessible from the coast further north—that is, from Smyrna and the neighbouring towns—and from the country to its south, and gave by far the best access to the interior tableland, by Apamea and passes over the mountains beyond Apamea. From Apamea one highway led north-east to Ancyra and Paphlagonia-Pontus; another east to Caesarea-Mazaca and Melitene-by-Euphrates; another south-east through Pisidia and Lycaonia to the Cilician Gates, Tarsus, and Syria. By these routes men travelled to the remoter East and returned with its products.[1] At the same time the Phrygian region, of which Apamea was the centre, had great natural wealth. Thus Apamea became, by the Augustan age and probably earlier, both the clearing house of Phrygian commerce and an important link in trade between West and East.[2]

Asia, as Cicero could say in 67 to the popular assembly, sent revenues greater than any other province:

nam ceterarum provinciarum vectigalia, Quirites, tanta sunt, ut eis ad ipsas provincias tuendas vix contenti esse possimus, Asia vero tam opima est ac fertilis, ut et ubertate agrorum et varietate fructuum et magnitudine pastionis et multitudine earum rerum quae exportentur facile omnibus terris antecellat.

Business men found here a superb field for investment, some residing in the province to manage their interests, others supervising them through agents:

partim ipsi in Asia negotiantur, quibus vos absentibus consulere debetis, partim eorum in ea provincia pecunias magnas conlocatas habent.[3]

So Cicero summed up the natural wealth of Asia and its attractions for the *negotiatores* at a time when the province had

---

[1] See the journeys of Moschion of Priene, *I. von P.* 108, lines 155 ff. and especially 167 ff., with the comments of Rostovzeff 805 and 1520[71]. His embassies were probably to secure help for Priene in its difficulties, but they suggest that he had far-flung connections, formed in commerce.

[2] Many Jews lived at Apamea in the middle of the first century B.C.: Cicero *pro Flacco* 66–9. Probably the city already had the prosperity and bustle characteristic of it under the Principate (see Jones 69 f.). Strabo 577 calls it ἐμπόριον μέγα τῆς ἰδίως λεγομένης Ἀσίας, δευτερεῦον μετὰ τὴν Ἔφεσον. αὕτη γὰρ καὶ τῶν ἀπὸ τῆς Ἰταλίας καὶ τῆς Ἑλλάδος ὑποδοχεῖον κοινόν ἐστι. αὕτη can only mean Ephesus.   [3] Cicero *de imperio Cn. Pompeii* 14 and 18.

endured for twenty years, and was still enduring, the economic consequences of war and piracy.

Distribution and number of the settlers by 88 B.C.

The Asian Ῥωμαῖοι are known in this age as *publicani* and moneylenders only. There is no reason to doubt that there were already Roman and Italian landowners, merchants, and traders, but, since little is known of these, this is not the place to discuss the resources which they exploited. The material damage done by the revolt of Aristonicus to the land and other resources of Asia was soon repaired;[1] the Roman state, from the beginning, allowed the *publicani* and moneylenders to exploit the Gracchan tax-farming system to the full, at the expense of the provincials; and the bitterest resentment against the Ῥωμαῖοι resulted. But for the present my subject is only their number and distribution.

Though they are found first in 133—in Pergamum[2]—they had presumably been visiting that city and the other western cities for some time, many from or *via* Delos. In 88 there were Ῥωμαῖοι not only at Pergamum, but at near-by Adramyttium, at Ephesus and Tralles, at Caunus on the Carian coast, on Cos and on Chios, perhaps already established in these places for some decades. Appian, who mentions these Ῥωμαῖοι in relating the massacre of 88,[3] is telling only particularly horrifying or dramatic episodes; the full list of settlements would be longer.

The number of Ῥωμαῖοι killed in 88 is put at 80,000 by Valerius Maximus, and by Memnon of Heraclea Pontica, who is more reliable than Valerius, but wrote his local history after Caesar, perhaps much later. 150,000 were killed according to Plutarch, probably an inflated figure.[4] It need not be doubted

---

[1] Cf. the remarks of Rostovzeff on the war (808–11) with those he makes on economic conditions forty years later (823–6).

[2] A number of Ῥωμαῖοι appear among the πάροικοι granted the citizenship by Pergamum in or about 133, when the city used the πάροικοι against Aristonicus: *I. von Perg.* 1.249 lines 14 ff., together with Prott and Kolbe *A.M.* xxvii.107 ff. and inscrs. nos. 116, 118, 127, 131, 135 ('. . υἱός must indicate a Ῥωμαῖος, even where the name is missing). In 127 B.C. the local Ῥωμαῖοι were included in the benefactions of the gymnasiarch Diodorus (ibid., xxix.152 no. 1, lines 11 and 19, dated in xxxii.248 f.).

[3] *Mithridatica* 23 (the Romans on Chios, ibid., 46).

[4] Valerius Maximus ix.2.3 ext.; Memnon 31.9 (= *F.G.H.* iii B, p. 352, lines 16–21); Plutarch *Sulla* 24.7.

that the great majority of the ʿΡωμαῖοι perished; the doubt, since numbers were commonly exaggerated, is whether there can have been as many as 80,000 ʿΡωμαῖοι to be massacred, even if one includes (as one should) Romans, Italians, and Italiote Greeks, *ingenui* and *liberti*, men, women and children. Memnon wrote at least fifty years after the event and the exact source of his tradition is unknowable. His figure may perhaps have come into circulation two or three decades after the massacre. For, in 66, Cicero, driving home the reasons for stopping Mithridates, asks rhetorically:

maiores nostri saepe pro mercatoribus aut naviculariis nostris iniuriosius tractatis bella gesserunt; vos, tot milibus civium Romanorum uno nuntio atque uno tempore necatis, quo tandem animo esse debetis?[1]

Had a precise figure been current, Cicero would surely have used it, here or elsewhere. But these doubts cannot be controlled; only few inscriptions survive and the most interesting, which records ʿΡωμαῖοι at Priene, cannot be dated certainly to this period.[2]

---

[1] *de imperio Cn. Pompeii* 11.

[2] *I. von P.* 123, line 9, read by Hatzfeld (48 *ad fin.*) in connection with *I. von P.* 112: I can accept the identification of persons here proposed, but not the over-fine inference about the dates.

CHAPTER IX

THE REVOLUTIONARY AGE
(85–30 B.C.)

ANATOLIA

Conditions affecting settlement

Romans are now found in a considerable number of cities, both in Asia and in the new provinces soon added to the Empire. It would be mistaken to gauge the increase in their numbers by simply contrasting the number of settlements attested by Appian for 88 and the abundant and widely distributed evidence for 85–30 B.C.; despite the paucity of local references, the total number of ʿΡωμαῖοι in Asia before 88, whether or not it was 80,000, was certainly considerable. But one may believe that numbers did increase, since, for one thing, Romans are now found in regions previously not open to them, or, at any rate, not entered by them.

Despite the events of 88 in Asia and on Delos, there is little reason to think that Romans were deterred from Asia, to an appreciable extent, by the anxieties and troubles of the two decades after the war. Although the second Mithridatic war opened with a massacre of those active in central Phrygia,[1] it does not seem generally to have restricted their activities by land; as for the sea, the pirates, though in alliance with Mithridates they became more and more formidable, can hardly have paralysed shipping to the extent suggested by Cicero in the *de imperio Cn. Pompeii*[2]—or for a very short time only. Had shipping been generally paralysed for a length of time, Italy would have known not merely the threat of famine, as indicated by Cicero, but the actuality—not suggested by him or others—and the pirates would have been at a loss, having killed the goose that laid their golden eggs.

In the first decade after the peace of 85 many Roman citizens

---

[1] Appian *Mithridatica* 75.
[2] 31–3, 54 f.; and 44 *ad fin.* (threat of famine).

made huge profits out of the troubles of the time, as money-lenders exploiting the inability of the provincials to raise the sums demanded by Sulla from Asia, and in other ways easy to conceive. For Romans of any standing enjoyed, as such, a position of special advantage in the provincial system, and were not slow in Asia to exploit it, as is best seen in Plutarch's account of their activities before Lucullus' arrival in 74.[1] But the gains of the moneylenders, as will appear, were curtailed by Lucullus' measures in 71; it is unlikely that their profits were again, for any long period, as great as they had been. Soon too Pompeius' victory over the pirates and his successes against Mithridates improved conditions for productive investment and for trade, giving increased security by sea and land, extending the area where Romans could trade under the protection of Rome, and perhaps stimulating commerce along the routes from Syria and Roman Asia to the far East.[2] Abuse of the tax-farming system by the *publicani* and usurious exploitation of the financial difficulties of individuals and communities did not cease, but were now restrained from time to time by governors, and are unlikely to have been the mainstay of the provincial Romans in the same degree as earlier.[3] Many eastern communities were financially drained in the years 49–30 by the exactions and extortions of the belligerents in the civil wars; but the Asiatic provinces were not ruined as regions when they were taken over by Augustus, after his defeat of Antony.[4] Even then their physical resources were not widely impaired, no great tracts were depopulated, trade connections were not lost, the skill of the peoples survived, and most of Anatolia and Syria was in a better position than was Greece; there economic life was stagnating or declining, but the economic unification of the Levant generally with Italy and the West continued through the troubles of the first century B.C.

Distribution of the settlers

In the first two decades of this period detailed information is scanty, but it is clear that the Romans came again to Anatolia

[1] Plutarch *Lucullus* 20 f.

[2] E. H. Warmington *The Commerce between the Roman Empire and the East* 18 ff. and 32 (Pompeius).

[3] Rostovzeff 1018 f., and below chapter XII.   [4] Rostovzeff 1018.

very soon and in fair numbers. By 80 they seem to have returned to Chios, and in the following year Lampsacus had a
body of *negotiatores*;[1] by 74 Roman moneylenders had numerous
provincial communities long in their toils, and there were
Romans in the heart of Phrygia; in 66 the residents in Asia
were a class of importance in the eyes of Cicero.[2] Though it is
only after this that their distribution begins to be traceable, it is
reasonable to suppose that the mid-century pattern was already
forming in the period 85–66 B.C.

The western coastal region: The region most attractive to immigrant Romans was the coast and coastal belt from Pergamum to Miletus, with its great offshore islands. To this area
may be added Cos and a few coastal cities of Caria.

Aeolia and Mysia: By 60 B.C., and probably earlier, new settlers were established in Pergamum, ranking in importance
with the Romans of Smyrna and of Tralles.[3] Some of the young
Romans in membership of the flourishing ephebic organization are certainly sons to these families;[4] but the Romans of
Pergamum make first collective appearance when they dedicate
a statue to Augustus in conjunction with the Pergamenes.[5]
Connections with the Roman community at Elaea, the port for
Pergamum, must be presumed. A notable Roman benefactor of
that city (*c.* 60 B.C.) was also important at Ephesus and in the
province generally;[6] the wealthier eastern *negotiatores* were by
no means confined, in their business and other activities, to the
particular city where they lived.

Lesbos early became a favourite refuge for exiles and a resort

[1] Romans at Chios, to be inferred from *S.I.G.*[4] II.785 lines 18 f.; Lampsacus, Cicero *Verrines*, II.1.69.

[2] Moneylenders, below p. 174 ff. Romans in Phrygia p. 136 ff. Cicero on the Romans in Asia, *de imperio Cn. Pompeii* 18. [3] Cicero *pro Flacco* 71.

[4] The fragmentary ephebic lists of Pergamum were first published by W. Kolbe in *A.M.* XXXII.415 ff. and P. Jacobsthal, ibid., XXXIII.384 ff. Jacobsthal observes (385) that the lists appear to cover the period from *c.* 133 B.C. to the latter part of the first century B.C., and that the ʿΡωμαῖοι are more numerous in the later lists (no. 6, p. 388 is rightly dated by Jacobsthal about 30 B.C.). The Roman names are listed by Hatzfeld (117[8]), with references, but in irrational order. *A.M.* XXXIII.414 no. 54 ('vivo L. Culcius Opimus sibi aedificavit et libertis suis') may be early, but there is not sufficient evidence for the date of A. Ravius (ibid., 411 no. 47).

[5] *I. von Perg.* II.383.

[6] L. Agrius L. f. Publeianus, *A.M.* XXIV.205 no. 12 (Elaea), *C.I.L.* III.14195[39] (Ephesus), Cicero *pro Flacco* 31 (without *cognomen*).

for travellers or statesmen looking for rest or a more secluded
place than the busy mainland cities.[1] But Roman settlers are
not found till 45, when Caesar cancelled a special exemption
from tax or dues they had secured at Mytilene.[2] About 34 B.C.
these Romans at Mytilene dedicated a statue to the governor,
M. Titius, their *patronus*.[3] Whether the Romans at Methymna
should be assigned to this period is doubtful.[4] Few Romans
appear later on Lesbos, perhaps because of assimilation, perhaps because of loss of their inscriptions, together with most of
the island's epigraphy: if Roman money-makers no longer
came in numbers, spenders perhaps abounded, attracted by the
beauty, climate, and cultural associations of the island.

Ionia, Lydia, Caria, Rhodes: Most of the cities of western Anatolia were impressive or attractive, those of Ionia particularly
so. 'Quid tibi visa Chios, Bullati, notaque Lesbos', as Horace
asks the traveller,

> quid concinna Samos, quid, Croesi regia, Sardis,
> Zmyrna quid et Colophon, maiora minorave fama?
> cunctane prae Campo et Tiberino flumine sordent?
> an venit in votum Attalicis ex urbibus una,
> an Lebedum laudas, odio maris atque viarum?
> 'scis Lebedus quid sit; Gabiis desertior atque
> Fidenis vicus; tamen illic vivere vellem[5]

Probably Smyrna and Ephesus had most Romans. Ephesus was
founded, not where might seem natural, at the mouth of the
Maeander (whose valley is all important in the communications of Anatolia), but at the mouth of the Cayster, a few miles
away, since the harbourage was better there.[6] The great trade

[1] For the exiles, Magie II.958[74].
[2] *I.G.* XII(2)35 (col. b lines 26 ff.) = *I.G.R.* IV.33 (col. b line 27 ff.).
Those who had secured exemption can only be the resident Romans
(compare the case of Chios below p. 176).
[3] *C.I.L.* III(1)455 = 7160. A Greek inscription, *I.G.* XII(2)88, gives a
mixed list of Roman citizens (some probably of Greek origin, as the two
Iulii, lines 8 and 23, and the Pompeius, line 3) and Greeks. This may be late
first century. *I.G.* XII(2)111, containing Roman names, has not been dated.
[4] *I.G.* XII(2)517. See also *B.H.* IV.433 no. 20 and *A.M.* XI.287 no. 53.
[5] *Epistles* I.11.1 ff.
[6] The silting up of the harbour was already serious in the second and first
centuries B.C. (Livy XXXVII.14.7 and Strabo 641), but not disastrous till
much later.

route ran south-east over a few miles of upland country to the plain of the Maeander valley near Magnesia, thence up the valley, by Tralles and Laodicea, to Apamea. From Ephesus Smyrna lay less than fifty miles north by a good road, so that it too was not badly placed for travel or transport by the Maeander valley. The Sardis–Philadelphia road provided another way from Smyrna to the main trade artery, which it reached at Laodicea on the Lycus, and the Hermus basin generally was at her command. Thus both cities were admirably placed for trade, whether with the Lydian interior or with Phrygia and lands beyond, via Apamea.

Smyrna, with its excellent harbour, possessed other attractions. It had good land; it was well-planned, splendid, animated; there was an old pro-Roman tradition, which the Smyrniotes upheld to some extent in the first war against Mithridates.[1] The city became one of the three great centres of Roman activity in Asia, with Pergamum and Tralles.[2] An early inscription records a Sicilian Greek, Apollonios of Catana, and his wife—who belongs (not surprisingly) to Apamea.[3] Only one Smyrniote Roman of the first century B.C. is more than a name —the wealthy and influential banker, M. Castricius, mentioned by Cicero in the *pro Flacco*. His business embraced more than one city and perhaps other provinces.[4] Castricii were important in the second century Delian–Athenian business world and in Chalcis and Boeotia; these Castricii, the banker of Smyrna, and the banking Castricii of Italy and Sicily known to Cicero are probably connected.[5] Other names from Smyrna (Titinii, Gesii, Seii) indicate connections with Delos,[6] but it is unclear, without precise dates, whether these belong to the Delian boom or the dispersion of the Delian Romans following on the collapse of the commercial community in the middle first century B.C.

The neighbours of Smyrna—Clazomenae, Erythrae, Teos,

---

[1] Early relations of Smyrna and Rome, Livy xxxviii.39.11; in the Mithridatic war below p. 174.

[2] Cicero *pro Flacco* 71. The inscription mentioned by Hatzfeld 109[1] adds nothing.

[3] *C.I.G.* ii.3142 line 32.

[4] Loan to Tralles, *pro Flacco* 54; funeral honours at Smyrna, ibid., 75; possible interests in Sicily, *Verrines* ii.3.185.

[5] The Castricii on Delos, *B.H.* xxxvi.24; in Chalcis and Boeotia, above p. 98 n. 3; in Italy, Cicero *ad Att.* xii.28.3; 30.2 (45 B.C.).

[6] For references see Hatzfeld's index of names, *Les Trafiquants* 383 ff.

and Lebedos on the peninsula, Temnos and Cyme up the coast, Chios off shore, Magnesia and Sardis in the Hermus valley— were less important than Smyrna. But they were not mere satellites. Most of these districts had their own riches and trade.[1] Romans were living on Chios, as landowners, in the early first century, at Cyme, owning land, about 60, and at Clazomenae about the middle of the century.[2] At Erythrae some of the inscriptions mentioning Romans probably belong to the late Republic.[3] On the landward side of Smyrna, however, there is no certain trace of Romans, apart from two names at Sardis; a Bruttius (clearly a freeman) and an Arruntius. These, however, may be earlier even than 133 B.C.[4]

Ephesus, its harbour silted up, has today long been displaced by Smyrna as commercial port for the Maeander valley and the neighbouring regions. But in the second century B.C. the silting had only started; the city, replanned and rebuilt by Lysimachus and Antigonus, was full of vigour when ʿΡωμαῖοι first began going to Asia.[5] In 88 the Greco–oriental Ephesians, never friendly towards Rome, engineered or allowed the massacre of all the ʿΡωμαῖοι. None the less settlement began again after the withdrawal of Mithridates. Among the settlers, as at Smyrna, may have been families connected with Delos;[6] little is known about the Roman community in the revolutionary age, but it

---

[1] For the Erythraean peninsula, Magie 1.46; Sardis, ibid., 47; Chios, ibid., 45 f.

[2] Chios: Appian *Mithridatica* 46; Cyme: Cicero *pro Flacco* 46, and for an important Roman landowner there under Augustus, *C.I.G.* II.3524; Clazomenae: Horace *Sermones* I.7 especially 4 f.

[3] Hatzfeld 105. The most interesting is *I.G.R.* IV.1545 = *C.I.L.* III suppl. 7112. The L. Marius M. f. Aemilia from Caieta, here honoured by a number of communities acting in conjunction, was presumably resident at Erythrae. The form and details are puzzling, and Hatzfeld's discussion 105 f. is not satisfactory (good photographic reproduction needed). But L. Marius was pretty clearly a *negotiator*.

[4] Buckler and Robinson VII.105, no. 105, with 106, no. 107. See the editor's note on no. 105 for dating.

[5] Ephesus under Attalus II 'second capital of the Pergamene kingdom, a centre of its steadily growing commerce': Rostovzeff II.804.

[6] Connect P. Veturius P. f. Rodo, *magister* of an Ephesian *collegium* (*Ephesos* II.182 no. 74), with P. Veturius of Delos (*B.H.* XXXVI.90); but the inscriptions cannot be dated so precisely *c.* 100 B.C. as Hatzfeld thinks (47). The Gerillani found much later at Ephesus *may* have originally arrived from Delos (see *B.H.* XXXVI.37), but Hatzfeld (102) ignores the fact that *I.B.M.* 546 probably belongs to a much later period (see the editor's note), as do other Gerillani at Ephesos (ibid., 502, 533, 573).

probably had a continuous history from its revival after the first Mithridatic war to the early Principate.[1]

Since the Maeander–Lycus route was the main commercial artery of western Anatolia, Tralles was bound to become a centre of Roman settlement, lying, as it did, about thirty miles inland from Ephesus, where the road to the Carian and Lycian ports branched south from the highway. Ῥωμαῖοι, with their families there, died in the massacre of 88. Newcomers replaced them after the war, and about 60 the Roman community ranked with those of Pergamum and of Smyrna.[2] The rich banker, M. Castricius, may have regarded Tralles (to which he lent money) and Smyrna as equally his home.[3]

Between Ephesus and Tralles, Magnesia ad Maeandrum seems to have had a Roman community in the late Republic. The Numerius Cluvius given extravagant honours by this Magnesia is to be identified with a Cluvius important in Puteoli and other Campanian cities, and was certainly connected with M. Cluvius, one of Cicero's banker friends, who came from Puteoli.[4] Cicero's friend was creditor of five cities in western Caria, and may have resided occasionally in Magnesia, a convenient base for transactions with such cities. The Cluvii were a family of the same type as the Castricii, perhaps more powerful, the sort that would have particularly good hope of help from a governor in the extraction of debts.[5]

South of Ephesus, though the cities were less important commercially than those to the north, the coastal region had a number of Roman communities in the revolutionary age. Whereas before the Mithridatic war these are certain only at Caunus and Cos, they are now found at Priene, Miletus, and Cnidus, on Samos and Cos, and possibly at Halicarnassos and Iasos. The

---

[1] The 'Italici qui Ephesi negotiantur' honoured L. Agrius L. f. Publeianus (*C.I.L.* III.14195^{39} = *Ephesos* II.173 no. 58), probably to be identified with the L. Agrius of Cicero *pro Flacco* 31. In 29 B.C. Augustus 'ordained that temples should be created in honour of Rome and Caesar his father in Ephesus and Nicaea, and laid on the Roman residents the duty of attending to their cult' (Dio LI.20.6–7). For a Roman resident and notable benefactor of Ephesus under Augustus, *C.I.L.* III(1)424 = 14194.

[2] Cicero *pro Flacco* 71. [3] *pro Flacco* 54 and 75.

[4] *I. von Magnesia* 118 no. 139; Münzer *P-W* 'Cluvius' (6) and (7), based on *C.I.L.* X.(1)1572 f.

[5] M. Cluvius' loans to Carian cities, Cicero *ad Fam.* XIII.56. (51/50 B.C.), letter to the then governor of Asia.

evidence is epigraphic, partly uncertain in date. Interesting points, however, emerge. Names typical of Delos are common. At Miletus certain families can be traced from the late Republic to the early Principate; on Cos the Romans continued to flourish through the first century A.D. In both places they became more and more hellenized, holding important magistracies and priesthoods and inscribing their records in Greek. At Didyma (Branchidae), on the territory of Miletus, the cult of Apollo continued in the Roman period under Milesian presidency, with an annual festival and games. Here a number of Roman youths appear in lists of ephebes (covering the late Republican and the Augustan age), with a gymnasiarch who may be Roman; some are presumably *ingenui*, others freedmen.[1] Not all these youths will have belonged to Miletus, but some will, and families are found which gain local distinction. A Mussius first appears in a late Republican ephebic list;[2] in another inscription, perhaps later, the people of Miletus honour Aulus Mussius Aper for 'the unrivalled excellence of his character' and 'his talent in rhetoric, poetry, and the arts generally', which is described as 'manifold in its brilliance' and 'defying all comparison'.[3] The Samiarii may have come about this period; a later inscription in the name of Miletus honours a boy of the family for character, success in artistic (or athletic) contests, and affection towards his Greek trainers. Samiarii were important in Praeneste and are found at Delos, and it is not fanciful to trace this young man's forbears from Praeneste to Delos and from Delos to Miletus.[4] Other names found on Delos appear in ephebic lists of Miletus.[5]

Priene had a Roman community—mentioned in three long and tortuous inscriptions, in which the city pays extravagant

[1] The inscriptions were published in *I.B.M.* iv (p. 88 ff.) and by Reinach *R.E.G.* vi.153. Full references are given by Hatzfeld 104². *I.B.M.* assigned the body of inscriptions to Didyma, Reinach to Iasos; Rehm *Milet* iii.239 f. argues the case for Didyma.

[2] *R.E.G.* vi.195 no. 42 line 8, assigned by Hatzfeld, *loc. cit.*, to 53 B.C.

[3] *R.E.G.* vi.181 no. 20; the same man appears in no. 21.

[4] The honorific inscription, *R.E.G.* vi.183 no. 26; for other Samiarii at Miletus, Hatzfeld 104²; the Samiarii on Delos, *B.H.* xxxvi. 73; at Praeneste, Münzer *P-W* 'Samiarius'.

[5] i.e. Annius, Caltius, Clodius, Gessius, Laelius, Nonius, Octavius (see Hatzfeld's list *loc. cit.*).

honour to Αὖλος Αἰμίλιος Σέξτου Ζώσιμος for benefits conferred by him upon it and the ξένοι in his capacities as gymnasiarch and as magistrate.[1] Individual Romans of Priene appear elsewhere in inscriptions and *graffiti*,[2] but it cannot be said whether they led among the ξένοι; these included Athenians, Thebans, Rhodians, and natives of other Asian cities.

The peninsula at the head of which Cnidus stands is long and rocky, with no easy road to the mainland. But there was export trade from its two harbours, particularly in local wine, and this trade may have been the attraction for Romans, about 50 B.C. or earlier.[3] Caesar, touching at Cnidus in pursuit of Pompeius, declared it *civitas libera*, gratifying his Cnidian protegé, Theopompus. Theopompus, who got Roman citizenship now or later, took some concern for the local Romans, and they combined an expression of their gratitude with a public dedication in honour of Apollo Carneios.[4]

There remain Samos, Cos, and Rhodes. Samos was taken by the pirates soon after the first Mithridatic war and so damaged that the city had to be restored under the governorship of Quintus Cicero.[5] The island had long lost its importance, and it is not surprising that few Roman citizens appear; these are of uncertain date.[6] On Cos, by contrast, the settlers were important. Cos had fertile land, a good climate, and a foreign trade, not only in the famous silks and local wine, but in other necessities and luxuries; of the silk and the wine much went to Italy, which was already using the latter about 160 B.C.[7] The Roman–Italian community existed before the first Mithridatic

---

[1] *I. von P.* 112–14. A certain C. Cestius Heliodorus, mentioned in 112, is probably freedman of C. Cestius, the *eques* active in Asia *c.* 60 B.C. (Cicero *pro Flacco* 31 and *ad Att.* v.13.1).

[2] *I. von P.* 106 no. 113 lines 1 and 10; 109 no. 114 line 1. These *could* be Greeks who received the citizenship. But there is no doubt about the ʿΡωμαῖοι appearing in the *graffiti* (161 ff.): see nos. 626, 697 f., 709–13, 715, 730.

[3] For the trade of Cnidus, Magie 816¹⁰³.

[4] *B.H.* xxxiv. 425 no. 1, restored in *B.H.* xxxvi.667. See also *P-W* 'Theopompos' (4) and (5).

[5] Damage, Appian *Mithridatica* 63; restoration, Cicero *ad Q.f.* 1.1.25.

[6] About 200 B.C. its situation 'far from brilliant', Rostovzeff 672 *ad fin.* Its wine, unlike that of Chios, had not a high reputation, Strabo 637. The inscriptions are hardly worth mention.

[7] See Magie 51 f. for an excellent note on Coan products and trade. Cato *de agri cultura* (*c.* 160 B.C.) 158.2 attests use of Coan wine in his time in Italy

war and was spared by the Coans in 88.[1] It appears next under Caesar, when an inscription proclaims its amicable relations with the Greeks;[2] then under Augustus, combining with Coans and μετοίκοι to honour a physician:

... Τοὶ κατοικεῦντες ἐν τῷ δάμῳ τῶν Ἀλεντίων καὶ τοὶ ἐνεκτημένοι καὶ τοὶ γεωργεῦντες ἐν Ἀλέντι καὶ Πέληι, τῶν τε πολειτᾶν καὶ Ῥωμαίων καὶ μετοίκων, ἐτείμασαν ... Ἰσίδωρον Νεικάρχου ἰατρὸν δαμοσιεύοντα[3]

This strongly suggests that the Romans, or some of them, were landowners (perhaps wine-growers). Few, if any, inscriptions are certainly assignable to our period, but names typical of the Delian Ῥωμαῖοι (as Paconius, Seius, Granius, Castricius) are common, and suggest that Cos may have received Delian-Roman families in the years of Delian decline and collapse. Some of these families retained their identity throughout the first century A.D., when they were supplying priests of the cult of Halasarnian Apollo.[4]

Rhodes, as is well known, drew many Roman students, travellers, and exiles, but produces no sure trace of *negotiatores*. It cannot even be taken as certain that the Roman citizens whom the Rhodian authorities dared to crucify in 43 A.D. were business men; Dio's reference reveals neither the reason nor the number and class of Romans involved and it is not obvious that Roman absence should be attributed (as Hatzfeld thought) to Rhodian hostility towards foreign men of business.[5] Italians and Romans were prepared from the beginning to face dangers for trade. It is more likely that they simply saw better chance of profits elsewhere; further speculation is fruitless.

Phrygia and inland Caria: Romans were resident in 74, with their wives and children, in central Phrygia. They were massacred, according to Appian—the only source for their presence and fate—by the invading troops of the Mithridatic general, Eumachus.[6] Newcomers presumably took their place (as newcomers took the place of the victims of 88) after Eumachus was ex-

[1] Tacitus *Annals* IV.14.
[2] *Ann. Ep.* (1947) p. 26 no. 55; the restoration is considerable, but there does not seem any doubt about it.
[3] *I.G.R.* IV.1087. [4] Hatzfeld 99 f., with notes.
[5] Dio LX.24.4; Hatzfeld 153 ff., especially 156 f.
[6] Appian *Mithridatica* 75.

pelled by Deiotarus. The economic centre of Phrygia was Apamea, a city of great commercial importance, from which important highways radiated to distant regions; though Romans are not certainly attested here before Augustus,[1] it is hard to doubt their presence in the late Republic, since *negotiatores* were active, about 50 B.C., in far more remote places— L. Oppius, agent of one of Cicero's banking friends, at Philomelium, and the art dealer, M. Aemilius Avianius, at Carian Cibyra.[2] But the Roman residents were probably not yet so numerous as in the Augustan age. In the late Republic Romans are not found on the Maeander route east of Tralles; yet, as will be seen, they appear, from the Augustan age on, in cities as remote as north-Phrygian Prymnessus and Docimium.

Cilicia: Cilicia was a very small province (if more than a theatre of operations) till the pirate fleets were destroyed in 67 B.C., and Cicero is not misrepresenting when he says of Pompeius then '. . . ad imperium populi Romani Ciliciam adiunxit'.[3] The Roman settlers, first attested in letters Cicero wrote as governor in 51–50,[4] presumably began to arrive in the years after the annexation by Pompeius. They were probably concentrated in Tarsus and other cities of Cilicia Pedias; some of the people Cicero has in mind may have been living in cities (such as Apamea and Cibyra) in Phrygian and Carian regions then included in the province. Cicero, in his letters, distinguishes civilians and veterans who had settled on discharge from service in the province.[5]

In view of the threat of Parthian invasion Cicero called the veterans to his army soon after his arrival. These provided a useful force, 'firmam manum',[6] but civilians appear also to have been conscripted.[7] The *publicani* of Cilicia feature prominently in Cicero's letters, but bankers and moneylenders must also be

[1] Apamea in the early Principate, Hatzfeld 167.
[2] L. Oppius, Cicero *ad Fam.* XIII.43 f., 73 f.; Aemilius Avianius below p. 197. The moneylender, A. Sextilius (Cicero *pro Flacco* 35), may have been living at Phrygian Acmonia at the time of Flaccus' governorship, but this is uncertain.
[3] *de imp. Cn. Pompeii* 35; cf. Jones 202 f., with Badian 'Sulla's Cilician Command', *Athenaeum* XXXVII (1959) 284 ff., for Cilicia before 67.
[4] Cicero *ad Att.* v.18 etc.
[5] For the regular presence of troops in Cilicia in the previous decades, Smith 22 *ad fin.* f.
[6] *ad Fam.* xv.4.3.   [7] *ad Att.* v.18.2.

presumed; the Roman citizens who made a corner in grain in 50 in Cilicia west of Taurus may have been, not corn-dealers, but simply *negotiatores* exploiting the opportunity presented by a bad harvest.[1]

Cyprus belonged to the province. Here, alongside *publicani*, there were some few *negotiatores*, but not enough for Cicero to go in person to administer justice.[2] But they were prosperous enough; Pompeius, in his flight in 48, was able to extract from them and the *societates publicanorum* a considerable sum of money and two thousand men, whom he armed.[3]

The north-western coastal region: It is not clear what was the beginning of settlement at Ilium, which had long been connected by legend with Rome when it came under the patronage of Caesar's family in 89 B.C.[4] Only isolated names are found at Parium, just inside the Propontis, and at Cyzicus.[5] But these may represent larger bodies, for a fair body of Romans had already gathered at Lampsacus by 79—the *negotiatores* who dissuaded the angry Lampsacenes from attacking Verres when he grossly abused the privileges of his *libera legatio* in that year.[6]

Beyond Lampsacus and Cyzicus Roman men of business penetrated into Bithynia before it became a province in 74;[7] in this year, so soon as the region became provincial under the will of Nicomedes III, *publicani* entered and took up collection of the revenues, only to find themselves swallowed up, almost at once, in a new Mithridatic invasion.[8] On the Roman recovery of the province the system was restored, and about 50 the *Bithynica societas* was particularly influential.[9] Various Romans with Bithynian concerns looked to Cicero for his interest, more particularly when he was governor in Cilicia and in touch with

[1] *ad Att.* v.21.8.   [2] *ad Att.* v.21.6.
[3] Caesar, *B.C.* III.103.1.
[4] The settlement, *I.G.R.* IV.190 (not closely datable); the beginnings of the legend, see particularly Livy XXXVII.37.2 f.; Lucius Caesar and Ilium in 89, *I.G.R.* IV.194 = *I.L.S.* III.8770.
[5] Parium, Cicero *ad Fam.* XIII.53; Cyzicus, *I.G.R.* IV.135 = *S.I.G.*[4] II.763. For a Cyzicene poet of the Augustan age, Erucius, perhaps son of a settler by a Greek wife, see Cichorius *Römische Studien* 304 ff.
[6] *Verrines* II.1.69.
[7] Suetonius *Divus Julius* 49.2.
[8] Especially at Heraclea. Here, according to Memnon (*F.G.H.* III(B) p. 355 sec. 38), the citizens claimed exemption from tribute; the *publicani* insisted on collecting it and were massacred at the outbreak of war.
[9] Cicero *ad Fam.* XIII.9, letter to the quaestor of Bithynia.

neighbouring governors;[1] these men probably congregated in the capital, Nicaea, which had a permanent Roman community by the early years of Augustus.[2] Bithynia became the base for penetration into Pontus, where many Romans were taken by surprise, early in the civil war, by Pharnaces' irruption into the province and reign of terror.[3] Three hundred miles east from Nicaea, Amisus, the great Pontic port (not among Caesar's colonies in the region), has a Roman community associated with it not long after Actium.[4] This can hardly have been of recent or sudden growth; it is only with the Augustan age, however, that inscriptions attesting Romans become common in Bithynia,[5] and Pontus has revealed little trace of their presence and activities at any period.

Developments in the early Principate

Under Augustus and in the early Principate, Romans penetrated to various new districts in the Phrygian-Carian interior and to parts of the north-east. Some few cities in Phrygia and Caria, despite lack of evidence, may be presumed to have had Roman residents earlier—Apamea almost certainly, and probably Laodicea on Lycus.[6] But the contrast is striking between the list of Roman bodies attested in the late Republic and that emerging from the evidence for the early Principate.

Roman communities are found existing throughout, or for some part of the first century A.D., in the following places where they already existed in the late Republic: Pergamum, Ephesus, Tralles, Miletus, Cos, Cyzicus (if there was a Roman body there

[1] See ad Fam. XIII.62, with ad Att. v.1.2 and 19.1; ad Fam. XIII.29.4; XIII.63 (with XIV.4.2); XIII. 64.1.

[2] Dio LI.20.6.

[3] Bell. Alex. 41 and 70.

[4] I.G.R. IV.314 where |the people of Amisus and οἱ συμπολιτευόμενοι Ῥωμαῖοι honour Augustus as τὸν ἑατῶν σωτῆρα καὶ κτίστην. The background to the inscription is the recent vicissitudes of the city, especially the tyranny of Straton under Antony (see Strabo 427, with F. Cumont Studia Pontica III.1 f.). Romans acquired citizenship at Athens in our period, and, no doubt, became citizens of other cities where they happened to reside; but this expression is not found under the Republic. In the Principate συμπολιτευόμενοι Ῥωμαῖοι appear at Attaleia in Pamphylia (S.E.G. VI.646, Ann. Ep. 1941, no. 147, with R. Syme Klio XXVII.141 f. for the date, A.D. 6–7) and Isaura (I.G.R. III.292 and 294).

[5] Hatzfeld 172 f.

[6] See Cicero ad. Att. VI.1.25 for a Roman established at Laodicea.

in the late Republic).[1] But no trace is found of communities, or even of individuals, at Smyrna, or in the towns of the Erythraean peninsula, at Cnidus or Halicarnassos, on Chios or on Lesbos (after the early years of Tiberius), or in Cilicia.

Inland the new centres of settlement were: Thyateira in Lydia; Hierapolis, just north of Laodicea on Lycus; Lunda between Laodicea and Apamea; Philadelphia, on the road from Smyrna to Apamea via Sardis; Blaundus, Nais, and Acmonia, on the road from Philadelphia through Phrygia to Bithynia; Prymnessus, on the way from Apamea to Nicaea; Docimium, just to the north of Prymnessus; cities in Paphlagonia; Stratoniceia, on the road from Tralles to the Ceramic Gulf:[2] Apamea, as already suggested, must have had some Romans before Augustus, but their number was probably small, since inscriptions attesting Romans first appear in his time.[3] Roman citizens, that is to say, now appear in new parts of Anatolia, in the same way as they appear for the first time in certain places in the Peloponnese where there is no trace of them earlier. The local πραγματευόμενοι Ῥωμαῖοι probably now included, in many places, Greeks who had received citizenship;[4] but the majority must still be Romans from Italy, with an admixture now perhaps of new citizens from the western Mediterranean.

In one city only of the west coast a new Roman community appears in the first century A.D.: Assos, on the southern shore of the Troad.[5] This isolated development is perhaps to be explained as an offshoot of the colony of Augustus at Alexandria Troas, which prospered greatly. The Roman community at Assos appears to have been prosperous (and emphatic in its public devotion to the imperial house), but nothing is known about it after the middle of the first century A.D.

---

[1] Pergamum, Hatzfeld 164; Ephesus 160; Tralles 170; Miletus 160; Cos 151; Cyzicus 163.

[2] References in Hatzfeld (not all are accurate and the dates of some inscriptions are simply assumed). Hierapolis 166 *ad fin.* (referring to an inscription since published as *I.G.R.* iv.818); Thyateira 165 f.; Lunda 169 *ad fin.*; Philadelphia 166; Blaundus 169; Nais 168; Acmonia 168; Prymnessus 169; Docimium 170; Stratoniceia 172. The Romans in Paphlagonia were important by 4/3 B.C.: see Cumont *Studia Pontica* III.75, inscr. no. 66, with p. 178, inscr. no. 172.

[3] Hatzfeld 167.

[4] Fairly numerous, as is well known, in Anatolia.

[5] For the inscriptions, see Hatzfeld 161 ff.

As has been seen, Romans no longer come to light, under the early Principate, in a number of western Anatolian cities where they are attested earlier, but are found now in cities elsewhere, especially in Phrygia, where they are not attested in the Republic. What reasons may there be?

In no single city are Romans attested, in the Republic, by a multitude of inscriptions. There has been considerable investigation by archaeologists on the sites of some of the Roman cities of Anatolia, at others little or none; thus, in some cases, it may be accident that inscriptions are extant revealing Roman settlers in the late Republic, but none attesting them for the early Principate (especially where a modern town, by wholly covering the ancient site, minimizes the chance of epigraphic finds). Again, in certain places, Roman settlers are attested only by references in Cicero; if Romans do not appear later, little can be inferred from this negative fact, since no source provides for the early Principate the relevant kind of material found in the correspondence and speeches of Cicero. Of course, in some cities the Roman community may have faded out in the early Principate. In such cases the explanation cannot be the disappearance of Roman *names* through complete hellenization and adoption of Greek names. To be sure, some Roman families may have disappeared through failure of the male line and marriage of the daughters with non-citizens; but, where the male line persisted, immigrant families, however socially hellenized, were tenacious of their Roman name, which they had strong reasons of advantage and prestige to wish to retain. This has been seen on Cos, where hellenized Roman families are a feature of the first century A.D. But some of the families which made large and quick profits in tax-collection, moneylending, and banking in the late Republic may have returned to Italy, when conditions, from Augustus on, no longer allowed so much money to be made rapidly. Some families may have moved from the coastal cities to the new centres of settlement in the interior, but there seem no economic or social reasons to suppose that this happened on a significant scale. It hardly seems possible to discuss this question further; on the evidence not even the magnitude of the problem can be assessed.

Hybridae, as has been noticed, soon became numerous in the West. Evidence about them is lacking in the East, but the anecdote of Horace about an eastern *hybrida* suggests how, already in the later revolutionary period, the sharp distinction between Roman and Greek may have begun to get blurred.[1] In 42 B.C. a rich *negotiator* of Clazomenae—named Persius—had an embittered lawsuit in Asia with a proscribed exile, the Praenestine, Rupilius Rex, and, during the hearing before Brutus, outsmarted Rupilius' 'pus atque venenum'. Persius, obviously a Roman citizen, is introduced by Horace as 'hybrida . . . . Persius', but in his moment of triumph before Brutus he is 'Graecus'.[2] He is called 'Graecus', because this is the triumph of Greek wit over cruder Italian invective; but he could hardly have been so called had the word not already received an extended usage in the context of the Greek East. If a 'hybrida' such as Persius could be termed 'Graecus', it was a slight step for hellenized Romans in the East to be classed, in the social context, with *Graeci*, and this, one may presume, happened.

DELOS

Strabo says that Mithridates' general Archelaus made havoc of Delos in 87; there was no one on the island when the Romans recovered it, and since those days it had been in a poor way.[3] But, as epigraphic evidence indicates, Romans and others returned to Delos, and commercial, social, and religious activities revived at least in some degree.[4] One of the pirate fleets that joined Mithridates in his third war with Rome did indeed sack Delos again in 69.[5] Yet even after this there was some renewed activity, after C. Triarius, legate to Lucullus, had restored and fortified the port.[6] Since new communities have, in favourable circumstances, risen upon the ashes and ruins of the old, it may be that Strabo is exaggerating the situation after 87, and that some alternative or further explanation should be sought for the extinction by 50 B.C. of Delos as a centre of Mediterranean commerce. May it not be that, as an expansion in the slave trade, due to coincidence of demand and supply, produced the

---

[1] *Sermones* I.7. [2] Ibid., I.7.32.
[3] Strabo 486. [4] See immediately below.
[5] Phlegon of Tralles 12, *F.G.H.* II(B) p. 1164.
[6] Ibid., with *B.H.* XXXII.418 no. 10 (inscription by the Athenians in honour of Triarius), and Durrbach *Choix* p. 248 f. nos. 159 f.

boom after 167, so a failure in the sea-borne supply of slaves, after Pompeius destroyed the pirate fleets in 67, ruined the slave-market, and, by ruining the staple trade, ruined the Delian economy as a whole? Such an explanation would be preferable to the suggestion that the competition of Puteoli ruined Delos (eastern merchants taking their commodities direct to a western centre of exchange and so cutting out the eastern entrepôt); and more satisfying than vague reference to the changing direction of trade currents. For, though Puteoli appears already to have entered on its great age before 120 B.C., Delos was flourishing, and perhaps flourishing more than ever, in the years 120–88 B.C.; as for reference to changing currents of trade, this begs the question. But the inadequacy of our evidence for the economic trends on Delos in the years 86–60 B.C. precludes certainty.[1] It would be necessary to show that a *vigorous* recovery was nipped by the failure of the slave supply. This is uncertain. The evidence does not rule out the possibility that the Romans who re-established the commercial community after 86 were not doing very well when the sack of 69 dealt a fresh blow (on Delos and elsewhere) to confidence in the future of the port. A precise answer would demand a graph of the Delian economy. But it seems safe to believe that failure of the sea-borne supply of slaves, after 67, if it did not ruin a flourishing port, materially contributed to final collapse.

It may be noted that an exceedingly mutilated inscription, recording some Roman decision in 58 B.C. for the rehabilitation of Delos, mentions exemption from *vectigalia*;[2] but it is far from clear from the defective text that ἀτέλεια had been withdrawn from Delos at some date and was now restored, and there is no evidence here for loss of ἀτέλεια as a factor in the decline of the island in the foregoing decades.

---

[1] Discussion of the material by Hatzfeld *B.H.* xxxvi.124 ff., especially 128. The new families coming after 86 B.C. seem, as Hatzfeld says, less important than those wiped out in the war, and there is some impression of declining prosperity. But there is evidence of a foreign community as late as 53 (ibid., 129[2] = *C.I.G.* ii.2287) and the Roman *Hermaistae* were active in 57–55 (*B.H.* xxxiii.504 no. 19, with 522–5).

[2] *B.H.* xlvi.198 ff. = *C.I.L.* i[2](2 fasc. 2–3).2500 = Durrbach p. 252 no. 163.

SYRIA, ARABIA, EGYPT, CYRENE, CRETE

Syria was one of the regions with which the Delian ʽΡωμαῖοι dealt,[1] and it is not surprising to find a body of *negotiatores* at Antioch in 48.[2] The tax-farming companies in the province certainly operated on a large scale, had considerable staffs, and much ready money there.[3] But there is no further information about either *negotiatores* or *publicani* (apart from the difficulties of these latter, in 57–54 B.C., with the governor), and it seems profitless to speculate on reasons for this.[4] Certainly there may have been traders with far-flung interests and experience of exotic lands among the Romans doing business in Syria and neighbouring lands. Petra, the city of the Nabataean kingdom, a place very much on its own, approached only through narrow, rocky gorges, was a centre of trade not only with Arabia, but also, via the Red Sea or the Persian Gulf, with more distant lands. Romans, with other foreigners, were active here under Augustus,[5] in a city of merchant Arabs where life was hellenized in a splendid, but superficial, fashion. But they make no appearance after the Augustan age; lands much further east were visited in the Principate by merchants from various parts of the Empire, but these were not, so far as appears, natives of Italy.

Romans visited Alexandria for purposes of business during the last century of the Republic, especially from Delos, and others toured the land to see its wonders. But no stable community of Romans can be traced at Alexandria or elsewhere;[6] the visitors perhaps stayed only a short time among people whom the Roman upper classes disliked. This was not the case with all Romans. Soldiers of the army led by Gabinius into Egypt in 55 B.C. to restore Ptolemy Auletes were left behind when he withdrew. Caesar says of them in 48 B.C. ʽ. . . iam in consuetudinem Alexandrinae vitae ac licentiae venerant et

---

[1] Laidlaw 211 f.   [2] Caesar *B.C.* III.102.6.

[3] Cicero *de provinciis consularibus* 10, with Caesar *B.C.* III.31.2. I have assumed that there was more than one *societas* operating in Syria.

[4] Syria had, of course, many foreign traders, and trade between Syria and Italy became most important. F. M. Heichelheim *E.S.A.R.* IV.205 treats the subject of foreign traders in Syria under the Principate, but no private civilian settlers from Italy appear; Tacitus *Annals* II.82 refers unspecifically to *negotiatores* reaching Rome from Syria, and *C.I.L.* X(1) 1797 attests only traders, not residents.

[5] Strabo 779 *ad fin.*   [6] See Hatzfeld 50 f. and 143 ff.

nomen disciplinamque populi Romani dedidicerant uxoresque duxerant, ex quibus plerique liberos habebant'.[1] It took less than a decade, that is, for the rank-and-file of Gabinius' force (who were joined by fugitives from justice, exiles, and escaped slaves) to begin to be absorbed into their environment. They were not repelled, as were Romans of the upper classes, by the Egyptians, and had no special desire to remain Roman.

There may have been Roman residents in Cyrenaica before the territory became a province in 74 B.C. For, when Ptolemy Apion bequeathed his kingdom to Rome in 96 B.C., the Senate took over the crown lands (though it left the cities for the time being to their own devices) and sent a *quaestor* to collect the revenue falling to Rome.[2] The *quaestor* presumably used the services of *publicani*, and these may have been important, along with dealers in corn, in the Roman group which comes to light in an honorific inscription of 67 B.C.[3]

Nothing further is heard of Roman residents till the famous Edicts of Augustus. At that time, they were neither numerous nor wealthy, and there were only two hundred and fifteen of all ages with assets above 10,000 sesterces. Their hostility to the Cyrenean Greeks and the readiness of some of them to rig prosecutions against the Greeks (a practice which the Edicts were intended to stop) are well known.[4] Since the Cyrenean Romans tended to be poor, the guilty individuals may have been something like 'poor whites', unsuccessful and jealous men, hoping to blackmail rich Greeks by false accusations, or profit in some way by their conviction. The causes known elsewhere for hostility between Romans and natives are different; but these may well have varied from province to province.

A fair number of inscriptions of the early Principate record Roman citizens.[5] Among them there appear Stlaccii, worth noting because this is the gentile name of the two brothers

---

[1] Caesar *B.C.* III.110.2.   [2] Sallust *Hist.* II,43 p. 75.

[3] Published by Joyce Reynolds, *J.R.S.* LII (1962) 98 no. 4, with comment on 101.

[4] *The Cyrene Edicts*, sec.1 *passim*. Some of the inscriptions attesting Romans have been thought earlier than the Cyrene Edicts; but, in the case of many, it is not clear whether they are dated by years of the Actian era or regnal years of *Principes*.

[5] See the name index to *Supplementum Epigraphicum Graecum* IX; other relevant inscriptions will appear in the collection of the epigraphy of Cyrenaica to be published by Joyce Reynolds and R. G. Goodchild.

recorded in the Cyrene Edicts as appearing before Augustus in a foolish and embarrassing situation,[1] and because Stlaccii appear among settlers elsewhere in the eastern provinces.[2]

Although the merchants of Italy were adventurous, the organized piracy of the Cretans and their internal wars may account for the absence of any evidence for trade and settlement till the defeat of the pirates and the pacification of the island in 68/67 B.C.[3] Military veterans—from the forces used in 68/67 or left to help control Crete afterwards—soon began to settle.[4] Civilian settlers come to light first under the Principate, at Gortyn. Crete probably gained in commercial importance from the Augustan age, with the growth of trade between Italy and the ports of Egypt and Syria. In this natives of Campania, especially Puteolans (though merchants at Puteoli tended more and more to originate from the East), must have retained a part. So the Granii active in Crete in the first century A.D.[5] are presumably connected, if remotely, with the great Puteolan Granii of the previous century, who already traded from one end of the Mediterranean to the other.[6]

GREECE

Athens

When Greece became provincial in 146 B.C., the status of Athens was not formally changed; but the supremacy of Rome became increasingly irksome to the Athenians. In 88, after nearly sixty years of what came to seem oppressive subjection, Athens joined Mithridates. The capture and sack of the city by Sulla in 86 was a calamity, but a new period opened after the disaster, with some degree of recovery.

The ʽΡωμαῖοι resident in Athens in 88, if not killed or driven out after the city joined Mithridates, are likely to have had a bad time then and during the siege by Sulla; and the Athenians suffered greatly. Yet conditions in the following years and feelings on either side did not prevent Romans from settling again very soon. Some stayed briefly in Athens, as visitors or students,

---

[1] *The Cyrene Edicts* II.
[2] See J. C. G. Anderson *J.R.S.* XVII (1927) 39.
[3] For these conditions, Rostovzeff 785 f.   [4] Caesar *B.C.* III.4.1.
[5] Hatzfeld 157⁶⁻⁷, 158¹⁻².   [6] Cf. *P-W* 'Puteoli' 2046.

so that the city became, in Cicero's phrase, 'domicilium studi-
orum'.[1] Others established themselves permanently. Already in
79, Cicero, studying in Athens, found Romans, who had taken
Athenian citizenship, sitting as jurors or as Areopagites.[2] Con-
firming Cicero, Romans appear in inscriptions as demesmen or
tribesmen, *prytaneis* or *thesmothetae*.[3] New Roman names are
found after 86. Some inscriptions indicate links with Delos,
where, after the massacre, there was now a new community.
But many of these new *gentilicia* are missing on Delos, and there
were now probably more Romans in Athens who had not come
via Delos and had no special links with it.[4]

Among the Romans who came immediately after the war
was Pomponius Atticus. Atticus abandoned Italy to find abroad
the security and dignity he could not find at home. He chose
Athens because Athens would allow him to maintain and increase his patrimony and at the same time consorted best with
his tastes in life. He stayed till 65 B.C., and might have remained
permanently had not Cicero persuaded him to return to help
him in his candidature for the consulate. Though Atticus stood
far above other *equites* in importance and influence, he was
typical in many ways of the *equester ordo*, at home and abroad,
and his relations with the Athenians call for later mention.

As, in the second century, the Roman citizen, Decimus
Cossutius, was entrusted by Antiochus Epiphanes with the
completion of the Olympieion of Peisistratus, so about 60 B.C.
the brothers C. and M. Stallius were put in charge, by Ario-
barzanes of Cappadocia, of the rebuilding of the Odeon of
Pericles;[5] the Stallii (who had a Greek, Melanippos, associated
with them) might be from southern Italy.[6]

Boeotia and Euboea

The epigraphic material for Boeotia and Euboea is not easy
to use. Most of the inscriptions relate to individual ῾Ρωμαῖοι, a
few to local groups. Hatzfeld assigns inscriptions with confidence
to dates between the late second century and Augustus. In many

[1] *de Oratore* III.43.
[2] *pro Balbo* 30.
[3] Hatzfeld 74[7], 75[1, 4, 5, 10, 12].
[4] Ibid., 74 f.
[5] *I.G.* III(1)541.
[6] See *P-W* 'Stallius'.

cases this precise dating is quite conjectural; but there is some material clearly belonging to the late Republic.

By the middle of the first century Chalcis had numerous Romans, among them families probably connected with Delos.[1] Eretria perhaps had a number of ʿΡωμαῖοι παρεπιδημοῦντες already in the early first century, and others came to Oreos and to Carystos.[2]

On the Boeotian mainland Thespiae, perhaps because of its position near the route from the Corinthian gulf to Chalcis, had the most important group of families. An interesting inscription was found here, in which the children of the local Romans join with those of the citizens and the resident foreigners to honour the magistrate supervising education.[3] Thespiae was the home of a *negotiator* whom Cicero particularly liked for his personal qualities and literary interests.[4] The port for the city was Creusa, seven or eight miles south on the Gulf, and there is evidence of Romans here, but not before the Principate;[5] again on the Gulf, just inside the Megaris, Pagae had a Roman community about 60 B.C., apparently the only Roman body in this region after the destruction of Corinth.[6] Apart from Thespiae, some Boeotian cities were visited by Romans for their games and festivals—Orchomenos, Oropos, Acraiphia, and Coronea.[7] At Acraiphia, a Roman—Publius Cornelius P. f.—was ἀγωνοθέτης

[1] See *I.G.* XII(9)916. The league of Euboean cities appears from this to have established a cult and gymnasium in honour of M. Iunius Silanus, quaestor of Antonius in Greece in 34 (cf. *I.G.* III(1)568 and Münzer *P-W.* 'Iunius' no. 172 p. 1096). The *hegemon*, *tamias*, and priest of Silanus were Greeks, the *grammateus* a Roman (Τίτος Σεπτομίος ὁ Τίτου) and likewise the gymnasiarch (ʾΑῦλος Σαλάριος Μανίου υἱός), also a number of the honorary gymnasiarchs (lines 10, 11, 13 f., 25–8, 31 etc.). These are likely to have belonged to families established in Chalcis. Names reminiscent of Delos are found—Tutorius, Plotius, Vibius etc. See also *B.H.* XVI.94 and 108 no. 14.

[2] Oreos and Carystos *C.I.L.* III.12290 and 12287 respectively.

[3] *I.G.* VII.1862; cf. line 14 for the date.

[4] *ad Fam.* XIII.22.1.

[5] Δέκμος Στερτίνιος ʾΕισίων (*I.G.* VII.1826, Hatzfeld 68[6]) occurs in another inscription, dating him to the Principate.

[6] A. Wilhelm *Jahr. des öst. arch. Inst.* X.17 ff. gives a more complete text than was available to Dittenberger (*I.G.* VII.190), and establishes the date as between 67 and 59 B.C.

[7] Orchomenos, *I.G.* VII.3195 line 22; Oropus, ibid. 416 line 34, line 50, line 14 etc.; Acraiphia, ibid. 2727 lines 1–5; Coronea, ibid. 2871 line 14, 2873. These inscriptions are probably to be assigned to about 80 B.C. (see Dittenberger's note on no. 416).

of the three-yearly Σωτήρια at their first celebration after a
break in the series due to war—probably the first Mithridatic
war.[1]

The Peloponnese

Patrae, the important port on the western Achaean coast,
was for a number of years the home of M'. Curius, the friend of
Cicero and Atticus, a *negotiator* of importance and a less shadowy
figure than most provincial Romans.[2] Other *negotiatores* are not
attested at Patrae, which was not a particularly attractive place,
but presumably there were some, for Aigion, the lesser port
further east, had a body of Roman men of business by 74 B.C.[3]
This city was important in the great days of the Achaean
League and, having a good harbour, was well populated under
Augustus,[4] though not a rival of Patrae.

At Argos, two inscriptions in the name of the resident *Italici*
honour, respectively, two nobles, Q. Caecilius Q. f. Metellus and
Q. Marcius Q. f. Rex; since both these men were concerned, in
69–67 B.C., with war on the pirates, the honours accorded may
be in recognition of services to commerce.[5] Cleitor, in Arcadia,
had Roman Paconii in the late Republic (perhaps connected
with the Delian Paconii).[6] At Elis, where there was a Roman
body at this time or later,[7] M. Mindius (a rare name) may likewise be linked with the Mindii of Delos.[8] About 80 B.C. Gytheon
in Laconia was the home of wealthy Roman bankers, whose
generous benefactions to the city, and the involved inscription

---

[1] *I.G.* vii.2727; for date see Dittenberger's note.

[2] For M'. Curius see below p. 195 f.

[3] *B.H.* lxxviii.82 ff., where J. Bingen establishes the date by reference to
the career of P. Rutilius Nudus, whom the *negotiatores* of Aigion honour in
the inscription. Patrae was more important, but Cicero did not like it
(see *ad Fam.* vii.28.1).

[4] Its prosperity under Augustus, Strabo 387.

[5] *C.I.L.* iii.531 and *I.G.* iv.604 = *C.I.L.* iii.7265; with comments of
Hatzfeld 78.

[6] *C.I.L.* iii.497, 'Paconiae Q. f. uxsorei Gemin.' *C.I.L.* does not make it
clear whether the inscription is mutilated. No evidence for Geminii, as
assumed by Hatzfeld 78.

[7] *Olympia* v.335, not precisely datable.

[8] Mindius was half-brother of L. Mescinius Rufus, Cicero's *quaestor* in
Cilicia (*ad Fam.* v.20.2). When Mindius died (*c.* 46 B.C.), L. Mescinius was
involved in a dispute with his wife Oppia about the property (*ad Fam.*
xiii.26 and 28). Oppii among the *negotiatores* on Delos and in Asia,
Münzer *P-W* 'Oppius' 737 (11 f.) and 747 (35).

recording them, are noticed in a later chapter.[1] In Messenia, inscriptions attesting Romans relate to a special war-tax imposed on settlers, as on Greeks, by Roman authority, perhaps in 39 B.C.[2] It seems likely that the Roman wealth subject to this tax was in land, and Roman landowners appear in another inscription.[3] This foreshadows the appearance, in the early Principate, of Roman residents in the interior of the Peloponnese, at Megalopolis and Mantinea, where their resources can hardly have been other than land and stock. Romans are again found at Elis in the early Principate, and at Argos under Claudius or later.[4] Thus Roman bodies survived in some places in the Peloponnese at a time when they seem either to have left other parts of Greece, to have died out, or been assimilated into the local population.

The north-east

During the first century B.C. ʽΡωμαῖοι are found not only in the chief city of Thessaly, Larissa, but in Demetrias, Olooson, and, to the south, at Heraclea on the Malian Gulf.[5] As to Macedon, since the province Macedonia was now co-extensive with old Greece, the Romans of whom Cicero speaks as active in Macedonia about 57 B.C. need not have belonged in the main to Macedon proper.[6] But the veterans settling in this decade or earlier[7] may have chosen regions near the north-eastern frontier, where most of their service is likely to have been done;[8] Beroea, north of the Haliacmon, had Romans about this time, owning land.[9] Other Romans, settled about a hundred miles east, at Amphipolis and near Pangaeus, were perhaps

[1] S.I.G.[4] II.748.

[2] I.G. v(1)1433 lines 14, 26, 46, with 1432. The date 39 B.C. is maintained by I.G. v. (introduction p. 15), alluding to Dio XLVIII.39.1 and Appian B.C. v.77 (325 ff.) (on Antonius' exactions then). A. Wilhelm (Jahr. des öst. arch. Inst. XVII.1 ff.) and Rostovzeff (III. 1507[20]) think between 103 B.C. and the end of the first Mithridatic war; no trace has been found of Romans or Italians in the Peloponnese as early as this.

[3] I.G. v(1)1434, possibly later.

[4] Elis, Olympia 335; Argos, I.G. IV.606.   [5] Hatzfeld 65 f.

[6] Cicero in Pisonem 96 and 98.   [7] Caesar B.C. III.4.1.

[8] For the regular presence of troops in this region from the second century, Smith 22.

[9] Hatzfeld 55[5] (quoting the relevant inscription) thinks that the Piso honoured is probably the enemy of Cicero, governor 57–55 B.C. (read ʽB.H. XXXIII' for ʽB.H. XXXII' in his note).

connected with mining there, though the scale of the mine workings is now not clear.[1] When the civil war opened, one of Pompeius' legions in the Balkans consisted of veterans from Macedonia[2] (with others from Crete), and when in 48, after Pharsalus, Pompeius had an edict posted at Amphipolis 'uti omnes eius provinciae iuniores, Graeci civesque Romani, iurandi causa convenirent', the Romans he had in mind (unless his object was simply 'ut quam diutissime longioris fugae consilium occultaret') must have belonged to Amphipolis and the neighbouring regions.[3]

This is adequate evidence for Romans in various parts of a large, fertile, comparatively prosperous region. Yet in the next age no trace is found of resident Romans, apart from the public colonies of Augustus, at Philippi, Dium, Cassandrea, and Pella, and the Romans of Thrace, mentioned in a solitary (perhaps Augustan) inscription, giving no indication of their number or distribution.[4]

---

[1] *C.I.L.* III.14204 f.; for the mines in Roman times, O. Davies, *Roman Mines* 234 ff.

[2] Caesar *B.C.* III.4.1.

[3] Caesar *B.C.* III.102.2 f.

[4] *B.S.A.* XII.177 f. no. 2; with discussion of the date etc. in Hatzfeld 57 f.

CHAPTER X

THE PROVENANCE OF THE SETTLERS

THE ʿΡωμαῖοι on Delos are here excluded because they have already been considered and because they formed a special kind of short-lived body. The present material is the names listed in Hatzfeld's index of *gentilicia* in his book,[1] with those not appearing before the first century A.D. ruled out, so far as possible. The same sort of reservations apply to use of this material as in the case of the Delian material; yet, taken as a whole, it leaves a definite impression, even with the necessary reservations made.

On Delos the great majority of the ʿΡωμαῖοι attested are traders of the period prior to 88. In the East generally, though there was considerable settlement before that date, most of the evidence is from the age of Cicero and Caesar (if not from later periods). The most prominent type of settler in the revolutionary age was the banker, moneylender, or agent of a *societas publicanorum*, and such was the tradition of banking and money-lending at Rome and the importance of Rome in financial fields that the prominence of Roman names in the East is not surprising. Whilst the political distinction of Roman, Latin, and allied communities disappeared and the Italic peoples became more and more romanized, it is still possible to distinguish sharply in this period the Roman/Latin and the Oscan-Campanian element among the emigrants.

When all doubtful cases are excluded, the good Roman names—listed below[2]—number over fifty. Some occur once only, or infrequently, but the following appear fairly frequently

[1] I have not thought it needful to give page references to an alphabetical list. The user of this index will find numerous mistakes in detail and printer's errors (especially 'av. J.C.' for 'ap. J.C.', or *vice versa*).

[2] Acutius, Aemilius, Annius, Antonius, Aquillius, Arruntius; Caedicius, Caecilius, Caelius (Coelius), Caninius, Canuleius, Cestius, Castricius, Clodius, Cluvius, Cornelius, Curtius; Decimius; Flaminius, Flavius, Fulvius, Fufius, Furius; Laelius, Licinius, Livius, Lutatius; Manlius, Marcilius, Marcius, Munatius, Mummius; Octavius, Oppius, Orbius; Papirius, Pinarius, Plotius, Popilius (Poplilius); Quintius, (Quinctius); Rabirius, Rupilius; Septimius, Servilius, Sestius, Sextilius, Sulpicius; Terentius, Titinius, Trebellius, Trebonius; Valerius, Varius, Veturius.

in different places in Asia or Greece: Aemilius, Caecilius, Castricius, Cornelius, Furius, Licinius, Lutatius, Sextilius. All of these (except Lutatius) occur also on Delos. Other good Roman names found in Asia and Greece (and also on Delos) are: Antonius, Flaminius, Fulvius, Laelius, Marcius, Octavius, Oppius, Orbius, Plotius, Popilius (Poplilius), Quinctius, Servilius, Sestius, Sulpicius, Titinius, Trebellius, Valerius, Varius, Veturius. The Cluvii and Granii, whose home in Italy was Puteoli, are probably of Roman, not Oscan origin,[1] and the Cossinii may have belonged, in Italy, to Puteoli and to Tibur.[2] The Laenii, a family based on Brundisium but with important interests in Asia, seem of Roman, not south-Italian origin.[3]

As on Delos, there are a number of names of Oscan character and closely connected with Campanian cities: such are Calavius (Capua), Epidius (Nuceria), Magius (Capua), Pactumeius (Capua).[4] But, again as on Delos, other names appear which were widespread in our period both in Campania and the region to its east and south: Bruttius, Cloatius, Herennius, Ofellius, Pontius, Seius, Stlaccius, Tutorius, Vibius.[5] One name is associated with the extreme south-east, Gerillanus; the Gerillani appear to have come from Brundisium, Tarentum, and the neighbourhood, to Delos,[6] and from there, when the prosperity of the island collapsed, to Ephesus and Cos.

It will be observed that names altogether peculiar to Campania do not bulk large here; this still leaves it probable that most of the provincial families bearing Oscan names came from Campania, and comparatively few from towns of the Samnite highlands or the extreme south. An attempt could have been made here to give a complete analysis of the names in Hatzfeld's index. Thus names terminating in '-enus', probably

---

[1] For the Cluvii see above p. 133; for the Granii p. 109.

[2] See above p. 109.

[3] See the remarks of Münzer *P-W* 'Laenius' *ad init.*

[4] See Münzer *P-W* 'Calavius', 'Epidius' (1), 'Magius' p. 438 and nos. (5) and (12), 'Pactumeius' 2154 f. Magii were also important in Samnium.

[5] Bruttius, Henze *P-W* 'Bruttius' 911 f.; Herennius, Münzer *P-W* 'Herennius' 661 f.; Pontius, Münzer *P-W* 'Pontius' 30 and nos. (4), (5), (7), (11), (12), (16), (21); Cloatius, Mommsen *Unteritalische Dialekte* 270. For Ofellius, Seius, Stlaccius, Tutorius and Vibius, see above p. 109.

[6] Tarentum, *C.I.L.* ix.6165; Uria near Tarentum, ibid. 224; Brundisium, ibid. 49 f., 122, Canusium, ibid. 338 col. 1 line 34. Once at Puteoli, *C.I.L.* x.2482.

connected in origin with Picenum, and names ending in '-idius', '-iedius', and '-edius', characteristic of the central highlands, could have been listed. Such names are found in the East, but they do not bulk large. Some are very obscure (as 'Aborienus', 'Acorenus', and 'Tettasidius') and it seemed unlikely that such analysis would give any definite results.

The possession from 88 B.C. of the Roman citizenship by the former *socii*, including the Italiote Greeks, may obscure the origin in Italiote cities of many of the *negotiatores* attested in the East in the first century; for, Delos apart, it is only in old Greece that a substantial proportion of our inscriptions belong to the period before 88. Yet it seems significant that, outside Delos, the number of obvious Italiote Greeks is a mere fraction of those found on Delos, who are not indeed very numerous. This answers to the obvious presumption that the Italiotes, belonging to declining cities, will have been a declining force in overseas trade. Yet one element among the ʿΡωμαῖοι in Asia in 88 is distinguished, in the only literary evidence, as Italiote Greek, or at least springing from the hellenized or semi-hellenized towns of southern Italy.

When in 88 Mithridates overran Anatolia and the anti-Roman party in Athens gained the ascendancy, the peripatetic philosopher and demagogue, Aristion, returning from the mission to Mithridates on which he was sent, reported sheer disaster to the Roman forces and urged the Athenians to join the king at once. The episode was later related by Poseidonius in his *Histories*, with a verbatim, or ostensibly verbatim, account of the speech of Aristion before the Assembly;[1] in this speech Aristion, driving home the hopeless terror of the ʿΡωμαῖοι in Asia, declares οἱ μὲν θεῶν ἀγάλμασι προσπεπτώκασιν, οἱ δὲ λοιποὶ μεταμφιεσάμενοι τετραγώνα ἱμάτια τὰς ἐξ ἀρχῆς πατρίδας πάλιν ὀνομάζουσι.[2] The meaning of οἱ δὲ λοιποὶ . . . is clear: that many of the ʿΡωμαῖοι in Asia were Italiote Greeks or from semi-hellenized Italian communities used to wearing the square cloak, or freedmen of eastern Greek origin; that these people had been wearing the square cloak, till 89/88, but so soon as the

---

[1] Preserved by Athenaeus in the *Deipnosophistae* v.211 d ff. = *F.G.H.* II(A) p. 243 ff. Poseidonius calls him Athenion, his father's name (see *C.A.H.* IX 244⁴).

[2] Athenaeus *op. cit.* v.213 b = *F.G.H.* II(A) p. 246 *ad init.*

grant of the citizenship to the Italian *socii* was reported in Asia, the emigrants assumed the *toga*, without waiting to be officially enrolled as citizens; now, with the Greeks everywhere going over to Mithridates, they hoped to elude or appease their hostility by resuming the Greek cloak and each calling himself once more citizen of the town to which he originally belonged. There is no reason to doubt that Aristion said something of this sort, and the passage, for all its flourish of rhetoric, confirms, what is clear from other evidence, the Campanian or south-Italian origin of many of the ʿΡωμαῖοι in the East. But this should not be pressed too hard; the people mentioned first are those manifestly associated, in the eyes of the local Greeks, with Rome, who could neither conceal that fact nor appease their enemies and whose only, little-availing, resource was to cast themselves and their dependents on the altars of the gods.

CHAPTER XI

THE OCCUPATIONS OF THE PROVINCIAL ROMANS

IT is probable that people from different parts of Italy tended to pursue different occupations in the provinces, but this cannot be established. What follows is a résumé of existing information about the occupations followed by the eastern provincial Romans. Some, there can be no doubt, specialized in one way of making money rather than another, in banking and moneylending, in trade, in agriculture, or in industrial production: others, having large capital, combined various forms of investment (as Atticus did), and it is not clear whether the general investor or the specialist was more common in the East.

BANKING AND MONEYLENDING

Rome, as is well known, was the financial, though not the commercial, centre of the Empire, and much lending to provincials and provincial communities was done, from Rome or Italy, by principals who did not leave the country but had agents to attend to the details overseas and exact payment. But there were Roman principals operating on the spot in provincial cities: as the Aufidii on Delos and Tenos, the Cloatii at Gytheon, Atticus at Athens, Appuleius Decianus at Pergamum, C. Castricius at Tralles, N. Cluvius at Magnesia, and—active in various parts of Asia—the 'togati creditores' who sat on the governor's *consilium* at the trial of Philodamus of Lampsacus in 79 B.C.[1] Of the many *negotiatores* commended by Cicero to provincial governors, without indication of their business or place of residence, most are likely to have been resident bankers or moneylenders. Whether these local financiers were comparable in their scale of operations with those of Rome cannot be said. The magnitude of the Asian debt in 84–71[2] does not indicate, for the money may perhaps have been advanced in part by the *publi-*

---

[1] *Verrines* II.1.73 (see below p. 175).　　　　　　[2] See p. 174.

cani or by moneylenders in Italy, through their provincial agents.

Atticus would not have gone to Athens, despite all it had to offer him culturally, had it not been a good place for the management of his money: 'ne illa peregrinatio detrimentum aliquod afferret rei familiari', as Cornelius Nepos puts it, 'eodem magnam partem fortunarum traiecit suarum'.[1] His position as patron and protector of Athens—necessarily expensive—cannot have been achieved and maintained by the use of capital, but only by shrewd and diligent moneymaking.[2] The range of his activities at this time cannot be guessed; if banking and moneylending were his mainstay, an important sideline was certainly the dispatch to Italy of 'old masters' in sculpture, with imitations by craftsmen, a trade flourishing in the first century B.C.[3]

STAFF OF THE SOCIETATES PUBLICANORUM

The staff required by a *societas* for tax-farming operations must have been considerable in heavily populated provinces with numerous large cities, such as were Asia, Bithynia, and Syria. The *magister*—the chairman—remained in Rome, but the *pro magistro*—the managing director for operations in a particular province—had to be on the spot; thus P. Terentius Hispo, *pro magistro* for the Asian *scriptura* and *portoria*, appears to have resided at Ephesus from 51 to 47, if not longer.[4] The responsible positions in the organization must have been filled in eastern provinces, as they were in Sicily, by Roman freemen or freedmen, and many of these will have spent long periods in provincial towns, as their like did in Sicily.[5] It could hardly be otherwise, since the collection of the *decumae*, from the initial *pactiones* to the final accounting, took up the major part of the year, whilst the collectors of the *portoria* obviously had to live

---

[1] *Atticus* 2.3.

[2] Ibid., 4.3. Cf. R. Feger, 'T. Pomponius Atticus' *P-W* suppl. viii.516 ff.

[3] Cicero secured sculpture through Atticus during the latter's stay in Athens and after his return; see *ad Att.* 1.3.2 (67 B.C., and above p. 97 n. 1).

[4] Cicero *ad Fam.* xiii.65, with *ad Att.* xi.10.1. Cf. *ad Fam.* xiii.9.3 for a friend of Cicero, Cn. Pupius, on the local staff of the *societas* operating in Bithynia.

[5] Organization of the *societates* in the Anatolian provinces, Broughton *E.S.A.R.* iv.538 ff.

close to their work, whether this was in the ports or at stations inland. Some *societates* in the East exploited mines, salt-works, and the like, and handled transport business;[1] these activities too must have required some Roman staff on the spot.

TRADE

Whilst 'negotiator'/'negotiari' were not always used in one sense only, the *mercator* was strictly the merchant. In our period he probably went in person to do his business, using his own ship, if he went by sea, or possibly leading several ships; it does not seem to have been usual for merchants to employ vessels belonging to companies interested only in shipping as such.[2] *Mercatores* soon made their way beyond the western frontiers into Numidia and free Gaul, and they appear to have been equally enterprising eastwards. South Italian and Italiote merchants were busy in the Adriatic about 230 B.C. (as they must have been from much earlier times), Roman and Latin merchants early in the next century.[3] On Delos the slave-traders and their employees were probably in a majority among the ʿΡωμαῖοι, but traders in olive oil are attested,[4] and there must have been other classes of trader; Cicero, speaking in 67 about the interests of Rome in the East, mentions as a motive for past wars the punishment of those who had injured *mercatores* and *navicularii* under her protection.[5] It is not clear how far, at this time, these *mercatores* had their houses and homes in eastern cities. But a distinct class of Romans, with commercial rather than financial interests, comes to light in Asia in 59, when the *societas publicanorum* tried to exact *portorium circumvectionis*—presumably demanding duty a second time, when goods, having failed to find a buyer at one port, were sent on to another; in referring to the dispute over this (the outcome of which is not known) Cicero says that he has sympathy with the case of the

---

[1] Broughton *E.S.A.R.* iv.540 ff. For realgar mining in Paphlagonia by a *societas publicanorum*, Strabo 562.

[2] A good discussion by T. Frank, *An Economic History of Rome* 243 ff., though the part of Romans in sea-trading is underrated.

[3] Polybius ii.8.2; Livy xl.42.4.

[4] See above p. 102 ff. for the Delian slave-traders and p. 119 for the traders in olive oil.

[5] *de imperio Cn. Pompeii* 11.

provincials, who seem to have thought the attempt illegal, and with the *negotiatores*, also indignant at it.[1] Here Cicero is using the word as it was used quite often in the next century; these people must be the Romans engaged in commerce in the province, merchants, traders, shopkeepers and the like, who would lose money through such a duty.

Within this commercial class, the *mercator* was seen, in literary convention at least, as the supreme type of avarice-crazed contempt for danger; certainly some Roman *mercatores*, in the late Republic and the Augustan age, made long, hard, perilous voyages to eastern lands. Such frequented Arabian Petra in the time of Strabo;[2] Horace is probably not exaggerating wildly when he apostrophizes the 'Indian Merchant'.

> impiger extremos mercator curris ad Indos,
> per mare pauperiem fugiens, per saxa, per ignes.[3]

Trade with India became important only under Augustus, and it is obscure how large a part Roman citizens had in it, but trade by Romans in regions such as Bithynia and Caria had certainly long been considerable when Horace spoke of it in a similar context.[4] Yet it is not clear whether the typical Roman merchant in eastern trade established for himself a permanent base and home in one of the Greek cities, or whether he did not, in his sort of life, lose all real desire for a settled home. As Horace sees him, he decides, in the hour of danger at sea, to retire at last to his native countryside, but having done so, at once grows restless again for gain:

> luctantem Icariis fluctibus Africum
> mercator metuens otium et oppidi
> laudat rura sui; mox reficit rates
> quassas, indocilis pauperiem pati.

LAND

One would expect to find some of the Romans owning land. There was much good land in the East close to cities providing excellent markets and harbours for exportable products; well-to-do Romans were in a position to acquire estates, stock, and

---

[1] *ad Att.* II.16.4.
[2] Strabo 779 *ad fin.*
[3] *Epistles* I.1.45 f.
[4] Ibid., I.6.32 f.

slaves on advantageous terms; some would feel that they had not arrived socially till they had the cachet conferred by landed property.

In Asia a protégé of Cicero living in Ephesus owned land in the territory of that city or of Colophon; Romans owned land in the territory of Parium in the Hellespont and near to Cyme in Ionia; a rich *negotiator*, involved in the case against Valerius Flaccus, got land near Apollinis, north of the Hermus, after being in business for many years in Pergamum. The Romans on Chios and Cos included landowners; these, and the Roman landowners on the mainland coast, may have produced wine on a large scale.[1]

In Greece, Roman landed proprietors are found in our period at Beroea (in Emathia), and perhaps in Messenia.[2] Both territories had land suitable for the investment of considerable capital. The wealthy men who went in for large-scale grazing in Epirus in the time of Cicero and Varro—Atticus, and Varro's 'Epirotae'[3]—probably visited their estates only at intervals and had bailiffs in charge. On the other hand the Romans who appear in the early Principate at Megalopolis and Mantinea (some certainly graziers and stock-raisers) were residents.[4]

There are traces of other occupations. Romans, without rivalling the Greeks in the field, supervised the copying or imitation of Greek and Hellenistic sculpture—probably more common than original work—for the avid Roman market. They have also been found in the marble trade; and two architects—one highly praised by Vitruvius—are known at Athens.[5] It may well be that the influx under the early Principate of Romans into the inland cities of Phrygia and Lydia is partly to be explained by the prosperity of the staple industry—wool and woollen products—but evidence is lacking to confirm this reasonable surmise;[6] the evidence connecting these new im-

---

[1] The importance of wine production seems certain in view of the viticultural tradition of these districts. Local evidence for landed ownership: Colophon, Cicero *ad Fam.* XIII.69; Parium, *ad Fam.* XIII.53; Cyme, *pro Flacco* 46; Apollonis, *pro Flacco* 71 ff.; Chios, Appian *Mithridatica* 46; Cos, *I.G.R.* IV.1087.

[2] Beroea, Hatzfeld 55[5]; Messenia above p. 150.

[3] Varro *R.R.* II.I.28; 'Synepirotae', II.5.I.

[4] Hatzfeld 150[7-9]. In note 8 the reference should be *I.G.* V(2)515.

[5] See above pp. 96 and 147, with Hatzfeld 228, and Rostovzeff 744 f. with 1505 f.   [6] Hatzfeld 225 ff.

migrants with local industries or crafts is too tenuous for discussion.

TRAVELLERS, VISITORS, AND STUDENTS

Visitors and students had a considerable impact on the life of a number of provincial cities, and some certainly settled in the end. They were apart from the clash of interest between the natives and the *negotiatores*, but in touch with both classes. Thus, being usually of some standing in the world, they will have helped to bring about that reconciliation of provincial Romans and natives, the course of which is difficult to trace, but which seems a fact by the first century A.D. But that theme requires a view, reaching into the Augustan age and beyond, of the emergence of the Greco-Roman world of the mature Principate; this is not the place for an excursion into so large a subject, to which a recent book makes an admirable contribution.[1]

As soon as military and political travel had shown Romans the Mediterranean world, and Greek culture had captured their imagination, the taste for travel in the East for its own sake was quick to develop. Among great Romans, the first enthusiastic traveller known is L. Aemilius Paullus, whose tour of Greece after the defeat of Perseus was thorough and extensive;[2] Scipio Aemilianus, when he made his great political progress through the eastern Mediterranean in 141 B.C., will certainly have taken pains to see everything near his route that was worth seeing.[3] Even much lesser Roman nobles had encouragement to travel in the ceremony with which they came to be received, whether within the Empire or in client kingdoms; something entertainingly exemplified in instructions sent in 112 B.C. from a senior to a junior Egyptian official, indicating in detail the welcome to be given to the senator, L. Memmius, on his forthcoming voyage up the Nile.[4] Perhaps it was about this time that Romans began

---

[1] *Augustus and the Greek World* by G. W. Bowersock; see chapter VI ('Romans and the Hellenic Life') 75 ff. for the importance in the Augustan age of the people here considered.

[2] Livy XLV.27 f., Polybius XXX.10.3 ff., Plutarch *Aemilius Paullus* 28. His purposes, of course, were primarily political.

[3] Full examination of this journey in *P-W* 'P. Cornelius Scipio Aemilianus' 1452. The party travelled up the Nile to Memphis.

[4] *Tebtunis Papyri* (1902) no. 33.

to pass from touring the Greek lands to extended visits; thus the young man rudely teased by Scaevola in Athens in 119 for hellenizing proclivities had obviously struck roots after going there in the first place as a student.[1] Though in 85 the state of Italy was the proximate cause of Atticus' withdrawal to Athens, he would, even in happier times, have made a lengthy stay there for the satisfaction of his intellectual and philosophical interests; Cicero's tour of two years from 79 for the study of rhetoric and philosophy included not only Athens and Rhodes, but cities in Roman Asia.[2] Many comparatively obscure men went to Athens to study in the first century. Some were seeking (as Atticus sought) a place which would be at the same time safe, good for business, and suitable to their intellectual or artistic tastes; such a man was L. Saufeius, rich *negotiator* and Epicurean, friend of Cicero as well as Atticus.[3] Some were not so shrewdly averse to war, or positively eager, in 44/43, to become officers under Brutus when he started building up, from Athens, the forces needed for the war he saw coming in the East.[4]

Horace, then twenty-one, is the most famous of these. There was also Cicero's son. It is not clear whether a typical Roman student in Athens is to be seen in Marcus, idle, dissipated, but full of promises when brought to book, as appears in a most interesting letter from him to Tiro.[5] One at least of Marcus' friends was quite different, and Marcus makes a great point of his devotion to this worthy companion.[6] 'Nam quid ego de Bruttio dicam?' he says to Tiro, and goes on—

quem nullo tempore a me patior discedere; cuius cum frugi severaque est vita tum etiam iucundissima est convictio; non est enim seiunctus iocus a φιλολογία et coditiana συζητήσει. Huic ego locum in proximo conduxi et, ut possum, ex meis angustiis illius sustento tenuitatem.

EXILES

Exiles sometimes went to western provinces, more often to the East. In the early first century Metellus Numidicus spent the first part of his banishment at Rhodes, before going on to

---

[1] See below p. 166 f. [2] Plutarch *Cicero* 4.5.
[3] P-W 'Saufeius' (5) 256 *ad fin.* [4] Plutarch *Brutus* 24.2.
[5] Cicero *ad Fam.* XVI.21, especially 2 and 6.
[6] Ibid., XVI.21.4.

Tralles,[1] and Rhodes and Mytilene came to be held the places that could make exile most bearable. Mytilene had various amenities, Rhodes, besides beauty, a tradition of higher education and the presence of men distinguished in rhetoric, philosophy, or learning, which brought many visitors, so that an exile was almost certain to meet educated fellow citizens or have studious friends visit him. Cicero wrote in 46 to a friend that, if Rome were still a *civitas*, he wished to stay there as a *civis*, if it was not, to live there in effect an exile, but an exile in a place 'non incommodiore . . . quam si Rhodum aut Mytilenas me contulissem';[2] he again couples Rhodes and Mytilene in another letter of 46, to M. Marcellus, in exile at Mytilene at the time.[3] In 44 D. Brutus and C. Matius speak in letters of Rhodes as the obvious place for exile, should it come to that.[4] In Horace, Rhodes and Mytilene are the jewels of the East for the traveller, and the proverbial places of exile.[5] It was natural for Tiberius to choose Rhodes when he felt compelled to withdraw from Rome in 6 B.C.; and, since Mytilene was Agrippa's base in his first eastern mission, it was easy for later writers to misrepresent his stay in the East as semi-exile.[6]

Exiles also went to old Greece. Some chose Athens, especially perhaps men of Epicurean tendencies, such as T. Albucius, the butt of Scaevola in 119, Memmius, the patron of Lucretius, and—voluntary exiles—Atticus, and his Epicurean friend, Saufeius. In 62 P. Autronius and others associated with Catiline went there, thus deterring Cicero from going there in 58.[7] But Italian exiles, in the second century, were established on the island of Leucas[8] (perhaps simply as the nearest suitable place); C. Antonius, Cicero's consular colleague, went to Cephallenia;[9] Cicero in 58 finally chose Thessalonica (about which as a city the desperate letters say nothing), whilst Maenius Gemellus, a faithful *cliens*, withdrew to Patrae;[10] earlier one of the Mummii

---

[1] Livy *per.* LXIX; Plutarch *Marius* 29.12; Valerius Maximus IV.1.13.

[2] *ad Fam.* VII.3.5.

[3] Ibid., IV.7.4.

[4] Ibid., XI.1.3 and XI.28.8.

[5] *Odes* 1.7.1, where they head the list of beautiful places in the East praised by Roman travellers; *Epistles* 1.11.17. Further references, Magie II.958[74].

[6] See Syme 342, disposing of the notion that Agrippa was in exile.

[7] Cicero *ad Att.* III.7.1.   [8] Livy XXXIII.17.11.

[9] Strabo 455 *ad fin.*   [10] *ad Fam.* XIII.19.2.

had gone, surprisingly, to Delos.[1] Indeed, all the main cities of Roman Asia and of Greece may have received Roman exiles. If some, the sort whom Lucretius pictures, were broken by their fate, others took exile more philosophically and enjoyed the intellectual life of Athens, Rhodes, or Mytilene.

One political exile shows how the feuds of Rome could be transmitted to the provinces. A certain C. Appuleius Decianus —no doubt connected by adoption with the famous tribune, but offspring of a friend of Marius—was tribune in 98. He seems to have been loyal to Appuleius after his death, prosecuting a follower who had deserted him, as he prosecuted— without success and not necessarily for like reasons—one of the Valerii Flacci. Later he had to go into exile—perhaps after a charge of *maiestas*—because he expressed regret about the death of Appuleius. He went to Asia. His son, also C. Appuleius Decianus, remained in Asia, prospered over thirty years as a *negotiator*, and eventually got an estate near Apollonis. L. Valerius Flaccus, son of the Flaccus prosecuted by the elder Decianus, governed Asia in 62. Either, because of the enmity between the fathers, Flaccus did things to anger Decianus, or Decianus wished to avenge his father's failure; for, when Laelius prosecuted Flaccus, on his return to Rome, for extortion, Cicero, Flaccus' counsel, had to deal with Decianus as *subscriptor* to Laelius.[2] In the *pro Flacco* the *negotiator* appears—in what may be partly Ciceronian vilification—as one who has cut himself off, not merely from Rome and Italy, but from the main centres of Roman life in Asia, dresses as an eastern Greek, yet oppresses, in a scandalous way, the respectable Greek community of Apollonis, where he has secured his estate by outrageous means.[3]

L. Aemilius Paullus, though brother of the Triumvir Lepidus, was driven into exile by the proscriptions of 43, going to Brutus in Asia. Here he settled in Miletus, and remained there even when he was invited later by the Triumvirs to return to Rome.[4] He may be only one of many exiles who, after establishing themselves in a new home in a pleasant city, preferred, though given the chance, not to return to Italy.

[1] Appian *B.C.* 1.38(168), confusing him with the destroyer of Corinth.
[2] All this material is drawn from E. Badian 'P. Decius P. f. Subulo', *J.R.S.* XLVI.95 f.; this man was probably the natural father of the elder Decianus.
[3] Cicero *pro Flacco* 70 ff.   [4] Dio XLVII.8.1. and Appian *B.C.* IV.37(155).

CHAPTER XII

THE RELATIONS OF THE SETTLERS
WITH THE LOCAL INHABITANTS

BETWEEN the second century B.C., when ʿΡωμαῖοι first began to
settle in Greek or Greek-speaking regions, and the early Principate, relations between them and the natives changed completely. But the manner and tempo of the change have to be
traced from evidence mainly indirect. In the background must
be seen what the Romans felt about Greece and the Greeks
generally. Respect for the great history of Greece, admiration
for her artistic and intellectual achievement, enthusiasm for
Greek thinkers and writers—past and present—appear in the
Republican period coupled with political or social contempt
for the mass of Greek or Greek-speaking peoples of the day. Yet
the same man—Cicero, for instance—could look quite differently on different sections of the Greeks;[1] advanced philhellenism, as found under the Principate, embracing things
Greek in general, has its origins in the Republican period.[2]

In old Greece and the Aegean islands there is some light on
what may be called the social philhellene, the man who, start-
ing perhaps from an interest in Greek culture, came to like the
company of Greeks, or to help their communities with generous
benefactions; but there is little evidence for the general relationships of the ʿΡωμαῖοι and the natives. In the Anatolian provinces,
by contrast, there is some light on general factors which may
have helped in the eventual improvement of relationships, but
little evidence about individual philhellenes.

[1] Compare Cicero's favourable remarks about the Sicilian Greeks
(*Verrines* II.2.7 f.), or about the Athenians, Spartans, and Massiliotes (*pro
Flacco* 62 ff.), with his ordinary sweeping references to the *levitas* etc. of
Greeks. In the *pro Flacco* he treats the Asiatic Greeks with contempt, to
discredit their hostile witnesses; there is a more kindly reference to them in
ad Q.f. 1.1.6.
[2] See, *passim*, Bowersock *Augustus and the Greek World*, a book full of useful
observations about philhellenism as a factor in the development of the
Empire from the second century B.C.

GREECE

In the early second century, with Greek influences beginning
to permeate the whole life of Rome, even people suspicious of
those influences could not turn away altogether from Greek
culture and rhetoric. A dichotomy of attitude is found even in
the elder Cato. After advising his son, in a book dedicated to
him, that Greek culture has some profit in it, if too much time
is not given to it, he goes on to say that he found the contemporary Greeks 'nequissimum et indocile genus'.[1] Yet, as
concerns Greek culture, he certainly came to it earlier than
some people alleged[2] and in politics he defended certain Greek
communities strongly.[3] The truth may be that in some of his
hardest remarks about the Greeks he wished to provoke, and
that he really disliked most a certain class of Romans inclined to
swallow Greek social tastes and fashions whole along with Greek
culture. This type of man was still disliked in certain conservative circles at the end of the century. Thus Mucius Scaevola,
the augur, whilst he despised the artifices of a certain kind of
rhetorice, might not have endorsed Cato's advice to his son with
its patronizing note about Greek culture ('illorum litteras inspicere, non perdiscere'), but could not stomach the hellenizing
type of young Roman who forgot that he was a Roman. In
119 B.C. he stopped at Athens on his way out to govern Asia. A
certain T. Albucius had gone there and had become, in Cicero's
words, 'doctus litteris Graecis . . . vel potius paene Graecus',
wishing 'se plane Graecum dici'.[4] He called on Scaevola and
paid his respects; Scaevola made mocking reply in Greek—
χαῖρε, Τίτε—and his lictors, soldiers, and *amici* took up the
words.[5] He must have found Albucius' form of philhellenism
objectionable, and have made himself offensive to Albucius by
his words and manner and by the licence given to his people to

[1] Fragment quoted by Pliny *N.H.* xxix.14: 'dicam de istis Graecis suo
loco, M. fili, quid Athenis exquisitum habeam et quod bonum sit eorum
litteras inspicere non perdiscere. Vincam nequissimum et indocile genus
illorum. . . .'
[2] Plutarch *Cato Maior* 2.5. Chapter 2 is a criticism of the idea that he was a
late learner in Greek; but see also R. Helm *P-W* 'M. Porcius Cato' 145 f.
[3] The Macedonians, evidence in *P-W* 'M. Porcius Cato' 132; the
Rhodians, speech in their defence, Aulus Gellius vi.3.7.
[4] Cicero *Brutus* 131; *de Finibus* 1.8.
[5] Lucilius ii.88 ff. (Marx) = volume 1 p. 8.

take them up. Albucius was annoyed to the point of prosecuting
Scaevola, when he returned from Asia, for misconduct as
governor; when the prosecution failed and he himself fell upon
misfortune and exile, he returned to Athens and there 'animo
aequissimo philosophabatur'.[1]

The trial of Scaevola was taken by Lucilius for the subject of
his second book. The fragment containing Scaevola's explanation of his offence to Albucius owes its preservation to Cicero;
since the affair was recent, it may be presumed to be based on
Scaevola's actual speech. The lines run:

> Graecum te, Albuci, quam Romanum atque Sabinum,
> municipem Ponti, Tritanni, centurionum,
> praeclarorum hominum ac primorum signiferumque
> maluisti dici; Graece ergo praetor Athenis,
> id quod maluisti, te, cum ad me accedis, saluto.
> χαῖρε inquam, Τίτε. Lictor, turma omnis, cohorsque
> χαῖρε, Τίτε. Hinc hostis mi Albucius, hinc inimicus.

Albucius was indeed an Epicurean, Scaevola a Stoic; but
his antipathy for Albucius was not primarily philosophical.[2]
Nor was it due primarily to the preciosity of Albucius in public
speech. Though in one fragment Scaevola makes fun of this,[3]
Albucius' social greco-mania was apparently the main reason
for Scaevola's dislike: 'Graecum te . . . maluisti dici.'

Forty years later things had changed. T. Pomponius (to use
his original style) left Rome and Italy in 85, to obtain overseas
the dignity and security he could not foresee for himself in Rome.
He chose Athens for his new home, because, without neglecting
business, he could pursue cultural interests better there than
anywhere else; and he became as much a Greek as a Roman,
Atticus as much as T. Pomponius. He might have irritated a
conservative Roman a generation earlier. But the attitude was
different now—despite the recent offences of the Greek communities and of Athens. It may be that the social philhellene
was already as common as thirty years later, when Cicero,
justifying C. Rabirius' assumption of eastern robes as chancellor
to Ptolemy Auletes in Egypt, refers to the young noblemen and

---

[1] Cicero *Tusculans* v.108.
[2] See Marx' comments, op. cit. volume II p. 41.
[3] Lucilius II.84 f. (Marx) = volume I p. 8.

even senators seen in Greek dress on the streets of Neapolis.[1] Sulla—himself a social hellenizer[2]—was impressed by Atticus during his visit to Athens in 84 (perhaps especially by his advice on works of art for his collection), and was not angry when he failed to persuade him to join him in the return in arms to Italy.[3]

Though Atticus surpassed the *negotiatores* in his standing in the world and was distinguished from them by the special connections he maintained from Athens with Rome, his combination of business qualities with devotion to the interests of the Athenians, as their *patronus*, and to Greek culture, may suggest the character of the better element among the eastern *negotiatores*, especially those who assisted the communities where they settled. His attitude was benevolent, but realistic: as Cornelius Nepos wrote—

. . . saepe suis opibus inopiam eorum publicam levavit. Cum enim versuram facere publice necesse esset neque eius condicionem aequam haberent, semper se interposuit, atque ita, ut neque usuram unquam ab iis acceperit, neque longius, quam dictum esset, debere passus sit. quod utrumque erat iis salutare: nam neque indulgendo inveterascere eorum aes alienum patiebatur neque multiplicandis usuris crescere.[4]

Atticus lent money at compound interest to other Greek communities and in Italy, and a large part of his income certainly came from moneylending.[5] So it is hard to believe that he did not exact any interest, more credible that he lent on relatively easy terms of simple interest. This by itself would explain the esteem the Athenians had for him, since it was usual to exact rates of compound interest that now appear extortionate.

There were other Romans in Greece who treated their local communities with generosity, some in the matter of loans, others in different ways, and it is clear that the relationship of *negotiatores* and natives was not always that of oppressor and oppressed. A benefactor may indeed be a lover of popularity and public distinction, or one concerned mainly for returns in influence or

[1] *pro Rabirio Postumo* 26 f.   [2] Ibid., with Plutarch *Sulla* 26.5.
[3] Atticus' departure from Italy, Nepos *Atticus* 2.1–3; his demeanour in Athens, 3 f.; his relations with Sulla, 4.1 f.
[4] Nepos *Atticus* 2.4 f.
[5] R. Feger *P-W* Suppl. viii 'T. Pomponius Atticus' 516.

power. Likewise the beneficiary, in his expressions of gratitude, may be inspired by genuine recognition, or by corrupt motives productive of exaggeration and mendacity. Various forms of corruption flourished in Greek cities, and the lavish honours accorded to Romans must not all be taken at their face value. Cicero was not inept when he ridiculed Appuleius Decianus for citing the distinctions granted him by Pergamum as evidence of genuine respect for himself.[1] Yet, where inscriptions have something definite to say about the services of the benefactor, they may reasonably be considered here.

In old Greece the earliest known benefactors are the Apustii of Abdera, in business there as father and son. They are declared in two inscriptions to have done signal service to keep the city free and at peace. Though the date of these is uncertain and the text mutilated, this was presumably in the age of the Roman-Macedonian wars, and the words suggest some kind of political action, something the reverse of typical among the *negotiatores*.[2] Abderite appreciation of the character and conduct of another ʿΡωμαῖος, M. Vallius, is expressed in an honorific inscription, recording privileges granted to him; its words are the more convincing because less fulsome than often the case in such testimonials.[3]

The most persuasive document is the decree of Tenos (about 70 B.C.) recording the gratitude of the city to the Aufidii Bassi,[4] father and son, who saved it in a financial crisis caused by the repeated attacks of the pirate fleets. This banking family was resident on Delos in the second century, but may have moved to Tenos in the first century, with the decline of Delos.[5] Prolix as the decree is and preposterous in its order, the citation of the services of the Aufidii indicates long continued generosity, involving considerable financial sacrifice by father and son. L. Aufidius, having been a generous creditor to the Tenians, at his death left large claims on the city to his son. The son renounced two of these; on others he reduced the interest to 12 per cent; on others again he re-assessed the principal in a reasonable way and treated it as a fresh loan at 8 per cent only. Years passed and the

[1] *pro Flacco* 74 *ad fin.* f.
[2] Text edited by M. Holleaux, *B.H.* xxxviii.63 ff. For later improvements, see Rostovzeff 1509[28].
[3] *B.H.* xxxvii.124 ff.   [4] *I.G.* xii(5)860.
[5] Hatzfeld 84.

Tenians were unable to discharge these debts, being heavily pressed by less generous creditors. L. Aufidius then cancelled part of the total debt and made the rest interest-free, allowing eleven years for payment.[1] One might say that he was too intelligent to try to squeeze blood from a stone; but it is easy in such cases to be harsh, as the inscription says that other creditors were, in the hope of eventual success.

Gytheon in Laconia was an important port, but the town ran into financial difficulties c. 80–70 B.C. In these it was helped considerably by two resident Romans, the brothers Numerius and Marcus Cloatius. They appear from the honorific inscription attesting their benefactions to have stood to Gytheon almost as Atticus stood to Athens. First they remitted part of a considerable debt, although judgment had been given in their favour for payment in full. Then they gave hospitality in their home to certain important Roman personages (visiting the town on unspecified business), thus relieving the Gytheates of the necessarily heavy costs of entertaining them. Next, when Roman demands were made for corn and clothing, they saw that Gytheon was exempted. Finally, when M. Antonius Creticus required a money contribution, presumably for his war on the pirates, they stepped in and lent the money, subsequently halving the interest on the loan (which had been at the quite common rate, 48 per cent).[2]

The noble whom fate drove into exile (for emigration was an idea quite alien to his class) was sometimes able to make the best of it, enjoying, with the equanimity of philosophic reason, the intellectual delights that Athens or Rhodes or Mytilene could offer; even Metellus Numidicus, devoted to the life of war and politics, had the mental resources necessary.[3] Another sort of man, eaten up by impatience for recall, lost the philosophy he had once claimed, lapsed into the prayers and sacrifices he had dismissed as superstition, wallowed in the abject misery on which Lucretius poured his scorn.[4] In others, if there is anything typical in the conduct in exile of the poet's patron, Memmius, habitual arrogance, embittered by misfortune, took

---

[1] The main stages of the business are recorded in lines 19–45 of the inscription.

[2] *S.I.G.*[4] II.748; see Dittenberger's commentary on the persons and circumstances, with Rostovzeff II.952 and 969.

[3] Livy *per.* LXIX.   [4] Lucretius III.40–54, especially 49 ff.

the form of rude contempt even for those provincials most deserving of their regard. Memmius' quarrel with the Epicureans of Athens, when, for his own purposes, he wished to tear down Epicurus' house and the Epicureans appealed to Atticus and Cicero, need not be retold here.[1] Atticus' interest on behalf of the Epicureans carried weight with Cicero and shows him in a good light. In contrast, it is notable in what high-handed fashion Memmius behaves, what influence he has secured over the Areopagus to make them consent to his plan, how careful is Cicero's letter on behalf of Patro and the Epicureans, and how patronizingly, in his effort to conciliate the crudely self-interested Memmius, he pretends to regard Patro and his associates. This episode is in line with Memmius' high-handed treatment of the freedman of a Roman resident at Sicyon—the subject of another anxiously deprecating letter from Cicero.[2]

Obviously a noble exile, with adequate financial resources, could lord it in a provincial community. Some, if high-handed, were perhaps more constructive than Memmius. C. Antonius was forced into exile a few years after he had been Cicero's colleague in the consulate and lived more than a decade on Cephallenia. According to Strabo, 'he held the whole island subject to himself, as if it were his private estate'; but at least he began the building of a new town on Cephallenia, and was prevented from achieving the project only by his recall by Caesar in 47.[3]

ANATOLIA

129–88 B.C.

More clearly than in any province in any period, the name of Roman was hated in Asia at this time. It was long since the Greeks had been ruled by non-Greeks, by barbarians, and though the evidence is not detailed, one cannot but suppose much injustice and reckless disregard of provincial interests by the governors, and much in the behaviour of their subordinates, *amici*, and soldiers productive of bitter resentment.[4] Yet it is

---

[1] See Cicero *ad Fam.* XIII.1 *passim*.
[2] *ad Fam.* XIII.2, quoted below p. 197.
[3] Strabo 455 *ad fin.* Presumably Antonius' power on Cephallenia was based on estates there.
[4] Asia is unlikely to have had governors better than other provinces. In

probable that the extortions of the *publicani* caused deeper and more widespread anger, since the tax-farming system bore on whole communities, in every part of the province, and the demands made under it were seasonally recurrent, in the case of tithes, continuous throughout the year in the case of *portoria*. The moneylenders are heard of first after the war; but it may be taken as certain that they were already active in this period; and that the *publicani* were acting as moneylenders, temporarily remitting their demands if payment were promised with compound interest.

The opportunities for extortion provided by the tax-farming system required for their exploitation only the passive connivance of the provincial governor. There was no question, in this period, of a governor interfering with the system as such; injured communities had to go to law before his court for redress. Once it was clear that most governors were unlikely to decide for them, native communities were deterred from this step. Diodorus Siculus is certainly right in putting the main blame for the state of affairs on the *publicani*, with the equestrian juries at home, ready to countenance false charges against an ex-governor, and on C. Gracchus, author of the laws which set the train of abuses in motion.[1] For nearly three decades, it appears, individuals and communities either suffered passively or had their complaints dismissed, though redress in some few cases made it clear what a just and bold governor might do.[2] When Mucius Scaevola and Rutilius Rufus were sent out in 94, they became known as such men. Accumulated grievances were brought to court before them, and they decided many cases in favour of provincials, imposing punishments which were most

---

Spain, in the second century, good governors 'were famous chiefly for their contrast with the rest' (C. H. V. Sutherland *The Romans in Spain* 63). In Greece, the scandalous treatment of Chalcis before the provincial era (Livy XLIII.7.5 ff.), the maladministration of Iunius Silanus (Valerius Maximus v.8.3), and the ruthlessness of Rome against Corinth indicate how low standards could sink already in the very first period of Empire.

[1] Diodorus XXXV.25.1: Gracchus τῇ τῶν δημοσιώνων τόλμῃ καὶ πλεονεξίᾳ τὰς ἐπαρχίας ἀπορρίψας ἐσπάσατο παρὰ τῶν ὑποτεταγμένων δίκαιον μῖσος κατὰ τῆς ἡγεμονίας. . . .

[2] For these see Broughton *E.S.A.R.* IV.535 and Magie I.166. The most important cases are those in which C. Julius Caesar, father of the Dictator, vindicated the rights of Priene against the *publicani* (see Münzer *P-W* 'Iulius' no. 130 p. 186) and L. Caesar, the censor of 89, protected Ilium (Münzer ibid., no. 142 p. 468).

severe.[1] In addition Mucius' provincial edict appears to have modified the law of debt in such a way as to make recovery more difficult for creditors whose position might seem oppressive or dubious.[2] But there is no suggestion that they supervised or restricted the *publicani* in the actual course of their operations.

The honesty and success of Mucius and Rutilius were officially acknowledged by the Senate, in such a way that Mucius' edict could be cited as a precedent by later governors.[3] But, when Rutilius was prosecuted *de rebus repetundis* on his return to Rome and condemned by a jury made up of members of the financial class, this was a contemptuous demonstration to the provincials of disregard for their wrongs which must have greatly aggravated their resentment against the *publicani*. The main responsibility of these for the massacre appears from the glaring contrast between the Asian attitude towards Rutilius (when he returned in exile to the province, and throughout the war) and their general treatment of the ʿΡωμαῖοι in 88.[4]

88–85 B.C.

Appian alone gives a substantial account of the massacres of 88, but without answering some important questions. Mithridates, he says,[5] on entering Asia,

wrote secretly to all his satraps and governors of cities. His order was to wait for the thirtieth day from the date of the letter, and then to fall upon all the Romans and Italians in their districts, with their wives, children, and all freedmen born in Italy, kill them and throw out their bodies unburied; their property was then to be divided with himself. Punishment was threatened additionally for those burying the dead or hiding the living, and rewards offered for those revealing persons in hiding or killing them, slaves being promised freedom for the betrayal or death of their masters, debtors remission of half their debt for killing or revealing their creditors.

---

[1] See Diodorus xxxvii.5, with Livy *per.* lxx.
[2] This appears from Cicero *ad Att.* vi.1.15.
[3] Valerius Maximus viii.15.6, with Cicero *ad Att.* vi.1.15. The general nature of Mucius' and Rutilius' work in Asia is admirably discussed by E. Badian in *Athenaeum* xxxiv (1956) 112 ff. Badian thinks that they were sent out by the Senate on a special mission to settle a disturbed province; he vindicates the date 94 B.C.
[4] Rutilius' reception by the Greeks and his life in Asia throughout the war and after, Dio frg. 97.3 f. and Valerius Maximus ii.10.5.
[5] Appian *Mithridatica* 22, freely rendered.

As is obvious from the account which follows of the resulting atrocities in a number of cities, hatred of the ῾Ρωμαῖοι was intense and widespread; but Appian does not indicate whether or not it was universal. The local communities may have fallen *en masse* upon them. But equally Mithridates' agents may have found their instruments in a minority of fanatics, criminals, favour-seekers, and the like, whom the rest could not, or would not, stop. Certainly the triumph of Mithridates was resisted by some cities, Apollonis, Magnesia in Lydia, Stratoniceia and Tabae in Caria[1]—not to mention communities in Lycia and in Pamphylia, where pro-Roman feeling was not impaired by experience of actual rule by Rome. Even Ephesus adhered at first to Rome, permitting ῾Ρωμαῖοι to escape to Rhodes, though later fugitives were torn from the altars of Artemis and killed.[2] Whilst the orders of Mithridates were executed at Pergamum, Adramyttium, and elsewhere with savage glee, at Tralles the citizens were initially reluctant, and the Coans, according to tradition, protected local Romans and Roman refugees.[3] Chios, where ῾Ρωμαῖοι owned property,[4] had a pro-Roman party, and many Chians fled to the Romans.[5] Smyrna, pro-Roman since the Roman war against Antiochus and regarded with favour by Rome, does not appear in Appian's account of the massacre, and may have protected other Romans besides Rutilius;[6] in 86–5, when the tide had turned indeed, the city voluntarily helped Sulla.[7] These differences of attitude were recognized by Sulla, who rewarded the loyal communities at the end of the war.[8]

85–74 B.C.

The demand on Asia for 20,000 talents made by Sulla in 85 represented five years *arrears* of taxation and the estimated cost of the war to Rome; the cities had already had to meet the

---

[1] Apollonis, resistance inferred from Cicero *pro Flacco* 71; Magnesia in Lydia, Appian *Mithridatica* 21 (Magnesia on Maeander welcomed Mithridates, ibid.); Stratoniceia (ibid. and *O.G.I.* 441); Tabae, *O.G.I.* 442.

[2] Ephesus *S.I.G.*⁴ 742 lines 7, 10, with Dittenberger's note 1 to 742 and notes 22 f. to 741.

[3] Tralles, Appian *Mithridatica* 23; Cos, Tacitus *Annals* IV.14.

[4] Appian *Mithridatica* 47; cf. 46.   [5] Ibid., 46.

[6] For Rutilius at Smyrna, Cicero *pro Balbo* 28, Dio frg. 97.3, and Valerius Maximus II.10.5.

[7] Tacitus *Annals* IV.56.2.   [8] See Jones 62 f.

exactions of Mithridates, and their inhabitants had the normal *vectigalia* to pay.[1] The moneylending interests profited, for the communities, having inadequate funds, had immediate recourse to them, pledging whatever would be accepted—without attempting, it appears, to levy money from their own wealthier citizens.[2] Lucullus, responsible for getting the money under the system devised by Sulla, did what he could to humanize the collection,[3] inspired (it may be) by the standards of Scaevola and Rutilius. But he could not prevent the communities from borrowing (since little grace was allowed for payment) or moneylenders from charging exorbitant rates of compound interest; so, when he departed for Italy in 80, he left a situation bound to get worse. By 74 the Asian communities, having discharged the indemnity long since, had paid the moneylenders 40,000 talents (twice the indemnity) in returning loans at heavy compound interest, and owed a further 80,000 talents.[4] There seemed no hope that they would ever get out of the slough. Since many creditors resorted to extreme cruelties (sanctioned or condoned by the courts) against their debtors,[5] whilst the *publicani* were no more scrupulous than before the war, resentment against Rome and the local Romans again consumed the province. When in 74 Mithridates invaded Bithynia and Phrygia, many cities seemed at first likely to join him.[6]

Local events affect feeling as much as general conditions. At Lampsacus, if Cicero is believed, even after the war of 88–85, relations between the Romans and the Greeks were reasonably good, till Verres arrived on his *libera legatio* in 79.[7] When Verres, in the house of the Greek Philodamos and wholly against his wishes, tried to get his hands on his host's daughter, and his followers used violence, the indignation of the Lampsacenes fell on him and his accomplices, without redounding on the local Romans; the intervention of these to save Verres' life, in the riot on the day after the struggle in Philodamos' house, was not too badly taken; but eventually the character of the trial and

---

[1] For the facts see Plutarch *Sulla* 25.4, *Lucullus* 4.1, App. *Mithridatica* 62 *ad fin.*
[2] Appian *Mithridatica* 63.   [3] Plutarch *Lucullus* 4.1.
[4] Ibid., 20.4.   [5] Ibid., 20.1 f.   [6] Ibid., 7.5 f.
[7] Homines . . . Lampsaceni, cum summe in omnis civis Romanos officiosi, tum praeterea maxime sedati et quieti, prope praeter ceteros ad summum Graecorum otium potius quam ad ullam vim aut tumultum adcommodati': *Verrines* II.1.63.

condemnation of Philodamos and his son for the death of Verres'
lictor must have left much bitterness, not merely against Verres
and the provincial governor responsible for these judicial mur-
ders, but equally against the provincial Romans; for one of
these undertook the prosecution, on the understanding that he
would receive official help in collecting debts from the city, and
other Roman creditors sat on the jury, along with men sure to
vote as Verres wished.[1] How long, however, the bitterness may
have lasted one can only guess.

As has been seen, various cities, whose conduct during the
Mithridatic war Sulla approved, had their local autonomy confirmed in the post-war period. It would be interesting to see how
far their status was observed in practice in the following age,
and how far such autonomy affected relations between resident
Romans and the Greeks: most of all at Chios, where a senatorial
decree of 80 expressly ordained that the local Romans were to
be liable to the laws of the city. But there is no evidence, except
that under Augustus the status of Chios still stood in law and the
Chians thought it important to protect and maintain it.[2]

74–30 B.C.: general changes and their importance

In the *Verrines*, in 70 B.C., Cicero suggests that Roman
publicani and *negotiatores* were hated everywhere, except in
Sicily, among native provincials—hatred due, no doubt, first
and foremost to their behaviour, but certainly aggravated by
the conduct of the public representatives of Rome.[3] A great
change came about under Augustus' Principate in the attitude
of the East to the Roman state; as concerns the settlers there, it
appears that resentment lingered against them in some places,[4]
but not generally. The change was due in great measure to the
work of Augustus, following on that of Caesar. But there is
reason to think that the change of relationships may have

[1] The story as a whole, *Verrines* II.1.63–85. 'Accusator . . . adponitur civis
Romanus de creditoribus Lampsacenorum', 74; 'togati creditores Graecorum' on the jury, 73.

[2] The rescript of Augustus to the Chian appeal mentions the decree of
80 B.C.: *S.I.G.*⁴ 785. No other evidence.

[3] Cf. Cicero *de imperio Cn. Pompei* 37 f.

[4] Most notably at Cyrene (see above p. 145), but also at Cyzicus and
Rhodes, and in Lycia (see Bowersock *Augustus and the Greek World* 103 and
108; the context is a discussion of Greek opposition under Augustus and the
early Principate).

begun before Augustus, or even before Caesar; at least the relative standing in the world of the provincial Romans and of the Greeks, their relative ability to secure what they wanted, was already changing in the period 74–30 B.C. It cannot be said that by a certain date a *détente* is evident, a clear change of feeling. But changed circumstances may be noted which made it more difficult for the Romans to exploit the Greeks and, by putting them on more like equal terms, must have helped the coming of the eventual *détente*.

The changed circumstances were:

(1) Economic conditions in western Anatolia are likely to have been considerably improved by Lucullus' debt settlement of 71, his removal, by 70, of any immediate threat from Mithridates to the region, and Pompeius' suppression of the pirate fleets in 67.

(2) Pompeius' organization of Anatolia and Syria in 63–62, by fostering Greek city life, 'gave a new impulse to the diffusion of Hellenic civilization and prepared the way for the economic renaissance of the Near East'[1] (under the Principate). This remark is just, and it may be added that he probably conferred great benefits on Anatolia by extending the sphere of trade possible under the authority of Rome and thus promoting the connections of the region with distant lands.

(3) Though extortion by the *publicani* and oppression of debtors by moneylenders were still countenanced by bad or inadequate governors, the moneylenders of Asia and perhaps the *publicani* were put in their place for a time by Lucullus, and both classes were thenceforth liable to meet, not only punishment for illegalities committed, but, from some governors, restriction in their current operations.

(4) *Clientela*, as political tension and personal rivalry sharpened in Roman society, worked in a way bound to affect the relationship of the Greeks with the Romans living among them. With the increasing competition between Roman statesmen for influence in every part of the Mediterranean, the local notable could, in effect, sell the influence he had among his fellows, in such a way as to bring both himself and them, if he wished, up in the world.

(5) Influence for good may perhaps have come from Roman

[1] *C.A.H.* IX.396.

local benefactors, comparable with those attested in old Greece and the islands. None of the relevant honorific inscriptions can be assigned with certainty to the late Republic; but they will be worth discussion here.

Negotiatores, governors, and natives: I turn to point (3). It may well be that in the middle of the first century B.C. the majority of provincial governors were still either themselves extortionate, or prepared to countenance extortion by *publicani* or *negotiatores*. Such governors as Catiline in Africa, Valerius Flaccus in Asia (whose defence by Cicero consisted largely in ridicule of the witnesses) and Appius Claudius, the notorious predecessor of Cicero in Cilicia, were common; yet there are now more known attempts to check abuses than are found in any previous period.

Lucullus set the example. In 45 B.C. the permanence of his work in Roman Asia was noted by Cicero.[1] He not only saved it by his generalship, but was a great reformer as well, for 'in eodem tanta prudentia fuit in constituendis temperandisque civitatibus, tanta aequitas, ut hodie stet Asia Luculli institutis servandis et quasi vestigiis persequendis'. Lucullus, that is, established the lines on which Asia was to be governed, and even Caesar had not altogether departed from these. It is not known whether Lucullus' measures dealing with debt were closely connected with the rest, for Plutarch, who describes the debt settlement, says nothing of the wider programme to which Cicero alludes. But it seems likely that he looked at the state of the province generally, with an eye to its future contentment and loyalty.

Having borrowed from the moneylenders at heavy rates of compound interest to pay the Sullan indemnity, the Asian communities had come to owe them 120,000 talents (six times the indemnity), and had paid them 40,000 talents. The *publicani*, who must have found collection difficult, were behaving as badly as when Scaevola and Rutilius came to the province. Debtors, cities and individuals, were being used by them and the moneylenders with extreme cruelties, which may or not have been legal, but were certainly countenanced by authority. These things had brought Asia to the verge of revolt when Lucullus arrived in 74. Having little time and a military emergency to face, Lucullus could not, for the present, go beyond

[1] Cicero *Academica* II.3.

admonition of the offenders, but this, presumably made public, helped to check the movement of revolt, so that there was no threat to his rear when he turned against Mithridates.[1] When he returned to Roman Asia in 71 he took stronger action, by edict.

This was not the first time that moneylenders felt the hand of government in a province; Cato Maior had expelled many from Sardinia,[2] and in Cilicia, in 78–75 B.C., Servilius took the regulation of interest as one of his functions, though he was not severe.[3] But it was the first time that carefully thought out and elaborate measures had been taken, or the problem of debt seen clearly as affecting the security of the Empire. Lucullus' ordinances, if Plutarch is right, were largely successful, 'so that in less than four years all the debts were discharged and the properties made back to their owners free of mortgage';[4] his measures, though they did not run beyond his term and some communities again got involved in heavy debt, provided precedents (especially 12 per cent as the norm for interest) for governors concerned to protect provincials. Roman moneylenders and *publicani*, though the class had a considerable part in the ruin of Lucullus in 67,[5] were now to find some governors prepared to check them in their activities and a Senate not always favouring them against provincials.[6]

The first of these governors was Q. Cicero, ruler of Asia for the three years 61–59 B.C. His governorship is treated in two well known letters to him from Marcus, *ad Quintum fratrem* I, 1 and 2, of which the first is the more important. Written presumably soon after June 60,[7] it advises Quintus on his conduct,

---

[1] The scale of the debt, Plutarch *Lucullus* 20.4; cruelties in the exaction of debts, 20.1–3; Asia on the verge of revolt, Lucullus' admonition and its results, 7.6 f.

[2] Livy XXXII.27.3–4. 　　　　　　　[3] Cicero *ad Att.* VI.1.16.

[4] Plutarch *Lucullus* 20.3. 　　　　　[5] Ibid., 20.5.

[6] Apart from the attitude of the Senate to the Asian *societas* in 60 (below), note the decree which hindered Atticus from collecting money owed him by Sicyon (*ad Att.* 1.13.1 and 19.9, with II.21.6) and the attitude of the Senate in 50 B.C. (below).

[7] It was in June that the *societas* which overbid for the Asian *vectigalia* had its request for revision of the terms finally refused by the Senate (Cicero *ad Att.* II.1.8), and the apparent reference to this in our letter to Quintus suggests a date after June (*ad Q.f.* 1.33). But there is no reason to date it as late as the end of 60 simply because it informs Quintus of the prorogation of his office. The Senate may quite well have discussed this matter in the middle of the year or early autumn.

dealing with the perennial problem of the *publicani* and suggesting the proper attitude of mind in a governor towards both his native subjects and the Roman *provinciales viri*. There seems no reason to doubt its authenticity,[1] but, since Cicero had not been in Asia since his visit in 78, the picture emerging from it (as from the other letter) of the provincial Romans and of the Greeks derives, not mainly from Cicero's experience, but from reports to him by his brother and others, his inferences from these, and perhaps general talk.

Cicero opens the first letter by consoling Quintus for having to continue another year in a duty keeping him, so regrettably for them both, far from Rome. 'There is one good thing, however,' he continues, 'you are not exposed, as some governors are, to catastrophe beyond your control. On the contrary, the province can be governed without danger, if you are reasonably vigilant. The Greeks and the provincial Romans are both amenable to control. The Greeks are the most civilized subjects possible, and the Romans owe you special consideration and respect. For both *publicani* and *negotiatores* are under great obligations to me, and can discharge these only by showing particular regard to my brother.'[2]

On all this, especially as concerns the Romans, the letter itself is the best commentary. Quintus is supposed to object: however amenable these people may be to the governor's directions, '. . . inter hos ipsos exsistunt graves controversiae, multae nascuntur iniuriae, magnae contentiones consequuntur'.[3] 'Inter hos ipsos', whilst referring primarily to the clash of Greek and Roman interests, means also sectional disputes among the members of each race, as when, later in Quintus' governorship, Roman, no less than Greek, traders objected to the exaction by the *publicani* of the *portorium circumvectionis*. But the relations of the Roman moneylenders with the Greeks were clearly one of Quintus' main troubles. When Cicero tells him that he will have no difficulty in dealing with the impudence of *negotiatores*,[4] he probably has in mind their attempts to evade measures restricting interest on loans or intended to help indebted communities. Later in the letter he congratulates Quintus on his achievement to date in this field: 'nullum aes alienum novum contrahi

---

[1] As does Magie 1244[13].   [2] *ad Q.f.* 1.1.4–6.
[3] *ad Q.f.* 1.1.7.   [4] Ibid.

civitatibus, vetere autem magno et gravi multas abs te esse liberatas'.[1]

The letter goes on to the relations between the tax-farmers and the Greeks. The *publicani* will be the greatest obstacle to the success of his efforts at good government:

quibus si adversamur, ordinem de nobis optime meritum et per nos cum re publica coniunctum et a nobis et a re publica diiungemus; sin autem omnibus in rebus obsequemur, funditus eos perire patiemur quorum non modo saluti sed etiam commodis consulere debemus.[2]

But details are not given of these troubles. The *societas* farming the Asian *vectigalia*, having overreached itself in its bid in 61, presumably made thereafter profits well below those expected, since it did not secure the one-third remission requested till Caesar's consulship; its agents would try all the more to fleece provincials, if they were allowed.[3] There is no evidence that the *publicani* in Asia had administrative restrictions imposed on them by Quintus; but it appears from the letter that they were warned that illegalities would be punished.

The Greeks of Asia, for all the faults Cicero saw in them, are mentioned in this letter as reasonable people, who might be persuaded to be accommodating in their dealings with the *publicani* and consent 'non legem spectare censoriam sed potius commoditatem conficiendi negoti et liberationem molestiae'.[4] Indeed he makes lengthy, and somewhat naive, suggestions about the language Quintus might use to convince them that the taxes demanded were not unjust. As to the provincial Romans, on the other hand, no suggestion is made that they should be approached with sweet reason. Rather they ought to be handled most warily. Indeed there is dislike of them in Cicero's warning, markedly in contrast with the honorific language of his public utterances about provincial Romans:

how . . . among that class of men who, tempted by their greed for money, are ready to dispense with all the amenities from which *we* cannot tear ourselves, how, I ask, can you discover any who yet have a sincere affection for you, a mere stranger, and are not simply pretending to have it in order to gain their own ends? I think you

---

[1] *ad Q.f.* 1.1.25.   [2] *ad Q.f.* 1.1.32.
[3] Cicero expects just this: *ad Q.f.* 1.1.33.
[4] *ad Q.f.* 1.1.35. Cf. 6 'constat enim ea provincia . . . ex eo genere sociorum quod est ex hominum omni genere humanissimum'.

would find it extremely hard, especially when those same persons show affection for hardly anybody who is not in office, but are always at one in their affection for praetors. But if you happen to have found any member of the class to be fonder of you (and it might have occurred) than of your *position* at the moment, by all means gladly add him to the list of your friends; if however you are not quite certain about it, there is no class of man you will have to be more on your guard against in the matter of intimacy, for the simple reason that they are up to all the ways of making money, and stick at nothing to make it, and have no consideration for the good name of one with whom they are not going to spend their lives.[1]

Comments on the Greeks follow, less complimentary than the remark, early in the letter, about their *humanitas*.[2] Yet these are brief, and Cicero does not revel in them as he docs in his distaste for the provincial Romans. If this letter contains Cicero's real feelings about a class of men which he praised publicly, it is not surprising that others could not bring themselves to treat these people delicately.

Quintus' impatience with certain Romans in his province is reproved in a section of the second letter to him.[3] Whether or not Quintus was guilty of excessive severity in dealing with these men, or actual cruelty (as the letter suggests), he obviously hated people like the elder Catienus and the tax agents, Licinius and his son—'the old kidnapper and his vulture chick'. In matters of taxation the problems before him may have been more complicated than can now be seen. For the clash of economic interests, as has been noted, was not always between the Romans as a body on one side and the natives on the other; in 59 B.C. the excise tax known as *portorium circumvectionis*, an important revenue for the *publicani*, aroused great resentment among the provincial Romans, as well as among the Greeks.[4] But such division of the Romans and unity between Romans and Greeks, temporary though it was, probably helped to break down the diametrical opposition between natives and the immigrant minority.

The work of other governors was viewed by Cicero out of quite different feelings. Gabinius and Piso, as he saw it, betrayed him as the consuls of 58; resentment certainly coloured the

---

[1] *ad Q .f.* 1.1.15 (Loeb translation).
[2] Criticism, *ad Q .f.* 1.1.16; *humanitas* of the Greeks, 6.
[3] *ad Q .f.* 1.2.6.   [4] *ad Att.* 11.16.4.

view he took of Gabinius' government of Syria, when he spoke about it in 56, and his attitude to Piso, as governor of Macedonia, in that year and after Piso's return. It does not follow that truth lies in inverting Cicero's invectives—that each was a perfect model of justice and integrity. But it seems likely that they were not simply robbing the provincial Romans to fill their own pockets, but were trying to solve a difficult and pressing problem of provincial government.

Gabinius was already interested in the provinces in 67, when he sponsored legislation to restrict borrowing by provincials in Rome—and the law which gave Pompeius command against the pirates; his Syrian governorship started in 57, soon after his mortal offence to Cicero. In 56, Cicero, having submitted to the Triumvirs, was called upon to argue before the Senate for provincial dispositions serving the Triumviral purposes. Such dispositions demanded the recall, at once or soon, of Piso from Macedonia and Gabinius from Syria. Whatever Cicero may have felt about the Triumvirs and his own submission, he was not sorry to have the opportunity to attack the two men. The crucial part of the attack on Gabinius, in the speech *de provinciis consularibus*, runs:[1]

iam vero publicanos miseros (me etiam miserum illorum ita de me meritorum miseriis ac dolore!) tradidit in servitutem Iudaeis et Syris, nationibus natis servituti. Statuit ab initio et in eo perseveravit, ius publicano non dicere; pactiones sine ulla iniuria factas rescidit, custodias sustulit; vectigales multos ac stipendiarios liberavit; quo in oppido ipse esset aut quo veniret, ibi publicanum aut publicani servum esse vetuit. Quid multa? crudelis haberetur, si in hostes animo fuisset eo, quo fuit in cives Romanos, eius ordinis praesertim qui est semper pro dignitate sua benignitate magistratus sustentatus. Itaque, patres conscripti, videtis non temeritate redemptionis aut negotii gerendi inscitia, sed avaritia, superbia, crudelitate Gabini paene adflictos iam atque eversos publicanos.

The first sentence here is so absurdly hyperbolical that the rest must be taken with salt, most particularly the allegation that Gabinius refused to hear cases brought by the *publicani*. Yet, since it is plain that they were far from making their expected profits in his term,[2] it is likely that he took administrative action restricting their activities in a way without precedent

<hr />

[1] Op. cit. 10.   [2] *de provinciis consularibus* 11.

and perhaps illegal, and made a serious and at least partially successful attempt to bring them to order in the province. The attempt had serious consequences for him. For when Gabinius was replaced by Crassus and returned to Rome in 54, he was convicted on a charge of *res repetundae*. For this conviction the resentment of the *equites* was in part responsible. Yet it is not evidence of their power in the same sense as the conviction of Rutilius or the ruin of Lucullus; Gabinius would hardly have been convicted by the court had he not been recalled by the Triumvirs for their own reasons.[1]

Piso's measures in Macedonia (57–55) may have had wider scope than those of Gabinius. Again, it would be wrong simply to invert what Cicero has to say about a man he had come to detest. But Cicero's attack is not convincing, either in the *de provinciis consularibus* or the *in Pisonem* of 55. The latter is more important here, but only twelve of the surviving hundred sections are occupied with definite charges,[2] as distinct from wild denunciation, and none is substantiated with much detail. The indignation seems factitious, and the speech, if it is compared with the *Verrines*, makes an impression of silliness. People may have thought so at the time, for Piso, far from being ruined, was censor in 50, and at the opening of the civil war had sufficient confidence in his standing to make an attempt at conciliation. It is hard to see Piso as guilty of nefarious wrong in imposing a sales-tax and collecting it through his slaves instead of *publicani*, in collecting the taxes of Dyrrachium in the same sort of way, in protecting debtors against creditors, and other measures of this kind; rather he may be credited with a considered policy towards the *publicani* and moneylenders, if he was not always reasonable in the way he carried it out.[3]

Gabinius and Piso were attacked by Cicero because they treated the *publicani* and the *negotiatores*, not as a privileged class, but as provincial subjects. P. Lentulus Spinther, whom Cicero regarded as a benefactor, was doing likewise with the *publicani* in Cilicia in 56–54. Cicero, writing to him there in 54, makes a point, at the end of a long political apologia for himself, of praising his measures, though they had given offence among the

---

[1] The trial of Gabinius, *P-W* 'Gabinius' 429.   [2] Op. cit. 83 ff.
[3] Discussion of the charges by Rostovzeff II.987 ff. and, in close detail, by R. G. M. Nisbet in his *in Pisonem* 174 ff. (Appendix I).

equites.[1] He goes on to warn him that he may be storing up trouble for himself on his return. The warning is emphatic, and presumably he saw real danger threatening Spinther. Yet Spinther, like Piso, was not harmed: only when the Triumvirs allowed, could the *equites* now ruin a governor.

Appius Claudius succeeded Spinther in Cilicia. He was oppressive and extortionate, typical of the worst type of late Republican governor. His behaviour had caused much discontent, and there was also danger of Parthian invasion when Cicero arrived to succeed him. The risk, in this event, of revolts made it urgent to restore trust in Roman justice. Cicero, faced with this situation, was none the less reluctant to offend the *publicani* and *equites.* But he found action necessary. So he set the rate of interest on new loans at 12 per cent per annum, and, even in the case of tax demands which the *publicani* had deferred on the understanding that payment would be made with interest, he cut the rate to 12 per cent, provided the money was forthcoming on an appointed date. His influence with the *publicani* was such that they accepted these measures with good grace.[2] So he would have Atticus believe; and Cicero could indeed exercise tact and flattery with effect. But the outcome suggests that the *publicani* were not as sure of themselves as once they had been; some may even have seen the dangers of which Cicero was conscious.

With Cicero it is easy to suspect exaggeration and vanity. But apart from the praise which these measures earned from

---

[1] The passage (*ad Fam.* I.9.26) concludes the letter. It runs 'Scripta iam epistula superiore accepi tuas litteras de publicanis, in quibus aequitatem tuam non potui non probare; felicitate quadam vellem consequi potuisses, ne eius ordinis, quem semper ornasti, rem aut voluntatem offenderes. Equidem non desinam tua decreta defendere, sed nosti consuetudinem hominum; scis quam graviter inimici ipsi illi Q. Scaevolae fuerint. Tibi tamen sum auctor, ut, si quibus rebus possis, eum tibi ordinem aut reconcilies aut mitiges. Id etsi difficile est, tamen mihi videtur esse prudentiae tuae' ('quadam' for 'a quid' at opening of second sentence, Gronovius).

[2] For references to Cicero's activity in this sphere see Gelzer *P-W* 'M. Tullius Cicero' 983 *ad fin.* The important passage is *ad Att.* VI.I.16: 'de publicanis quid agam videris quaerere. Habeo in deliciis, obsequor, verbis laudo; efficio ne cui molesti sint. Τὸ παραδοξότατον usuras eorum quas pactionibus adscripserant servavit etiam Servilius. Ego sic. Diem statuo satis laxam, quam ante si solverint, dico me centesimas ducturum; si non solverint, ex pactione. Itaque et Graeci solvunt tolerabili faenore et publicanis res est gratissima, si illa habent pleno modio, verborum honorem, invitationem crebram. . . .'

Cato, his actions in the famous case of Cyprian Salamis seem to corroborate his sense of fairness and duty. His report of the matter to Atticus is convincing in its detail. Appius had permitted Brutus' agent, Scaptius, to use force against the Salaminians. When Cicero prohibited this and decreed a fair settlement in line with his edict, he was not only disregarding Brutus' interests, but also pressure from Atticus; and Atticus, in such a matter, represented the *equester ordo* generally.[1]

While Cicero was trying to repair the damage done by Appius in Cilicia, Bibulus was preparing the defence of Syria, a province even more exposed to the Parthians. He was no less conscious than Cicero what harm Roman injustice had done to the spirit of their subjects, and included in his edict provisions in restraint of tax-farming abuses;[2] but nothing is known of their detail, or of the measures which other governors may have taken at this time.

These episodes, from Lucullus on, seem not to be isolated and separate, but to reflect an increased interest in provincial administration, despite the depths to which bad governors often sank. This increased interest was common to the opposed political camps. Cato disciplined himself consistently when in the provinces, and demanded high standards from others, however mighty. It is not clear whether he was moved more by moral considerations or the needs of imperial security; but he evidently tried to influence provincial governors and the Senate. Whether or not he actually made a general appeal to governors about 51 (as a scholar has suggested), he may be presumed to have had a part in the senatorial decree of early 50, whereby the rate of interest in the provinces was limited to 12 per cent and the earlier edict of Cicero recognized and confirmed.[3]

Cicero, writing in 51, to the magistrates and Senate from Cilicia, says that discontent is such that no trust could be put in native levies, there or in Asia, in the event of Parthian invasion.

---

[1] Full account of the affair, with references, Gelzer *P-W* 'M. Tullius Cicero' 984.

[2] Bibulus' attitude, Cicero *ad Fam.* xv.1.5; his edict *ad Att.* vi.1.15.

[3] Cato's conduct in general, Plutarch *Cato* 9.5 f., with Miltner *P-W* 'M. Porcius Cato Uticensis' 169 *ad fin.* f.; the possible appeal to provincial governors, *c.* 51 B.C., Gelzer *P-W* 'M. Tullius Cicero' 982; the senatorial decree of 50 on rates of interest in the provinces, Cicero *ad Att.* v.21.13.

quam ob rem autem in hoc provinciali dilectu spem habeatis aliquam causa nulla est. Neque multi sunt et diffugiunt qui sunt metu oblato; et quod genus hoc militum sit, iudicavit vir fortissimus M. Bibulus in Asia, qui, cum vos ei permisissetis dilectum habere, noluerit. Nam sociorum auxilia propter acerbitatem atque iniurias imperi nostri aut ita imbecilla sunt ut non multum nos iuvare possint, aut ita alienata a nobis ut neque exspectandum ab iis neque committendum iis quicquam esse videatur.[1]

But, writing some time later, early in 50, he reported to Cato the success of his policy towards the Cilicians:[2]

his ego subsidiis [*aequitate et continentia*] ea sum consecutus, quae nullis legionibus consequi potuissem, ut ex alienissimis sociis amicissimos, ex infidelissimis firmissimos redderem animosque novarum rerum exspectatione suspensos ad veteris imperi benevolentiam traducerem.

There is no reason to give less credence to this than to his earlier report, and similar measures by governors elsewhere may have had good results; but steps taken by a particular governor were not necessarily adopted or imitated by his successor, and it does not seem that the various attempts to check the *publicani* and *negotiatores* had changed the basic situation at the outbreak of the civil war.

But the way for a radical attack on a problem is sometimes prepared by inadequate measures which do not succeed, or succeed only temporarily, yet show the need and sharpen the desire for thorough-going action; it may have been in this sort of way that Caesar was led to conclude, in 48, that he could secure the interest and loyalty of the eastern provinces only by completely changing the system of taxation in the region.

There was also a pressing reason in the results, in both Syria and Asia, of the recent conduct of the Pompeian governor of Asia and his associates, Caesar's account of which need not be wholly discounted because of the relish of the denunciation. In Syria Metellus Scipio and his staff had exacted large sums of money from communities and local rulers, compelling the tax-farmers meanwhile to pay the arrears to the state for two years and the return to be expected for the coming year. In Asia not only was the same demand made on the tax-farmers, but special

[1] *ad Fam.* xv.1.5. 'Multi' may refer to, or at any rate include, the provincial Romans,   [2] Ibid., xv.4.14.

taxes and monies were exacted both from the native communities and the provincial Romans; through this and much private extortion, indebtedness in the province was multiplied in two years, so that the situation in 48 was as pressing here as in Syria.[1]

Caesar abolished the system of collection by *societates* (as far as concerned the *decumae* and *scriptura*) throughout the region, and substituted collection by the cities, each being made liable for its portion of the total tax, which was reduced by a third.[2] Whether he was chiefly concerned with reform for its own sake or with the urgent necessity to have the eastern provinces contented and faithful, the effects of the measure must have been important. An important responsibility was acquired by the Greek cities, probably beneficial for them, though it is not known how they handled it. As to the *publicani*, there is no reason to suppose that many individual investors in the *societates*, in Italy or in the provinces, were ruined, since not only were other fields of state contracting (including the *portoria*) still open to them, but they could turn to many other forms of investment; but the *ordo publicanorum*, as a group with great influence and privileges, suffered a serious blow by the demonstration of its political impotence. It never recovered. Though the *societates* were still handling certain taxes under Tiberius and Nero, they did not regain their political importance, but came under even closer state control, till they were virtually taken into the machinery of empire.[3]

The influence of provincial Romans and of prominent Greeks compared: The *publicani* and *negotiatores* were able, over a period, to oppress the native communities of Anatolia and Syria, to bring successful pressure to bear on provincial governors, and to ruin those who offended them. But their collective influence, after helping to ruin Lucullus, was not such as in any way to restrain Caesar in 48 from his reform of the method of tax collection. Individually, in the political and military struggle of the

---

[1] Caesar *B.C.* III.31.4–32. 6 (Asia), 31.2 (Syria).

[2] Dio XLII.6.3; Appian *B.C.* v.4 (19); Plutarch *Caesar* 48; with the discussion of the possible details of the reform by Rostovzeff II.997 and III.1577 (note 99).

[3] For the particular changes in the system, Rostovzeff 'Geschichte der Staatspacht in der römischen Kaiserzeit', *Philologus* (Suppl.) IX.374 ff.; the collapse of the political influence of the *publicani*, ibid. 378 f., 381 ff.

revolutionary age, they failed to make their mark or were un-important next the ambitious Greeks and 'Levantines' whose names have come down in the records.

The important Greek or 'Levantine' had a usefulness which he could soon make apparent—to Pompeius or to Caesar, to Antonius or Augustus—because, as city notable or as ruling prince, he often influenced or controlled an entire community or region. The provincial Roman could hardly ever have com-parable influence over the community in which he lived, even if, by a sympathetic attitude or generous benefactions, he had broken down the resentment and the suspicion caused by the general behaviour of his class. When he had some influence, he may have been little inclined to use it politically, for his sort, even at home and in the final crisis of the Republic, were not politically minded, and in the provinces they would hope (some-times too optimistically) to escape the turmoil of Italy.[1] Thus it is natural that men so active in pursuit of their private inter-ests had no conspicuous part in the struggles leading to the civil wars, or in those wars; that they contributed money and neces-sities, served, willingly or unwillingly, in the armies, without any *negotiator* making a great name for himself.

Wherever Romans and Greeks lived side by side the contrast is striking, at Pergamum, at Mytilene, on Cos, and in other places. At Pergamum the Romans were numerous and occu-pied, by the early Principate, positions of civic dignity and honour; none became known in the wider world. The most im-portant Pergamene in the revolutionary age was a certain Mith-ridates—son of a citizen by a Galatian princess—who raised troops for Caesar in Anatolia and helped to rescue him in Alexandria in 47. This able and adventurous officer, rewarded by Caesar with a Galatian principality, was more useful to his régime than any Pergamene Roman.[2]

Mytilene in 88 gave friendly reception to Mithridates and did his will, revolted against Rome in 83, and held out for three years. The Senate, after ordering the destruction of its walls

[1] Like M'. Curius of Patrae (next chapter) and the men of Cales who went to Spain (above p. 34).

[2] 'Mithridates Pergamenus magnae nobilitatis domi scientiaeque in bello et virtutis, fidei, dignitatisque in amicitia Caesaris . . .', *Bell. Alex.* 26.1; other evidence, Rostovzeff 1527[98].

and Acropolis, may have considered razing the city.[1] Yet the influence of Theophanes on Pompeius, in the pirate and Mithridatic wars, was such that the latter was prepared to restore to the city the privileges it had before the beginning of the wars.[2] Later, in the delicate situation for Mytilene resulting from Pompeius' defeat, the rhetor Potamon, by skilful diplomacy, brought the city into favour with Caesar, and its position was henceforth assured. Potamon had a highly successful career under Augustus and Tiberius;[3] Theophanes, who soon made terms with the victor, had a son who became proconsul of Asia under Augustus and later descendants of importance.[4] By contrast, the only important fact known about the Romans in Mytilene is that Caesar, granting an appeal from the city in 45, declared against certain fiscal immunities which they had hitherto enjoyed as residents there.[5]

On Cos the Romans were substantial people, soon hellenized, and sharing in the public dignities of the community; but only one Coan, the romanized Greek, Curtius Nicias, tyrant of the city for eight years from 41, achieved a name in the wider world and a striking career.[6] From Cnidus, Theopompus became protégé of Caesar and a man of importance in the world to whom the city and the settlers there were under obligation.[7] Cilician Tarsus may be presumed to have had its Roman *negotiatores* under Augustus; but when Augustus wanted someone to keep an eye on this unruly city, he chose, not one of these, but his old tutor in philosophy, the Stoic Athenodorus, native of neighbouring Kana.[8]

These men, coming from places where Romans settled, are

---

[1] The vicissitudes of Mytilene, Herbst *P-W* 'Mytilene' 1415 *ad fin.* f., with references.

[2] Theophanes' success with Pompeius on behalf of Mytilene, Plutarch *Pompeius* 42.8, Strabo 617. Strabo's estimate (ibid.) of Theophanes as a man of the very first importance seems correct: ... Πομπηίῳ τῷ Μάγνῳ κατέστη φίλος ... καὶ πάσας συγκατώρθωσεν αὐτῷ τὰς πράξεις.

[3] The influence of Potamon with Caesar and his diplomacy, *I.G.* xii(2)35 col. (*b*); his career, Stegemann *P-W* 'Potamon' (3)1023 ff.

[4] Laqueur *P-W* 'Theophanes' (1)2099 f.

[5] *I.G.* xii(2)35 = *I.G.R.* iv.33.

[6] R. Herzog *Historische Zeitschrift* cxxv.189 ff., especially 206 ff., for his tyranny.

[7] Plutarch *Caesar* 48.1; *B.H.* xxxiv.425 no. 1, with *B.H.* xxxvi.667.

[8] See R. Syme *Tacitus* 507[4], referring to *P.I.R.*[2] A 1288.

only a few of the Greeks and 'Levantines' who made themselves a name in the late Republic or under Augustus.[1]

The eastern Romans do not rise much higher under the Principate. Their families achieve offices and dignities within particular cities, but in the cult of Rome and Augustus, ordered on a provincial basis, the higher positions go to Greeks or Orientals.[2] Their obscurity is underlined by the contrast between East and West. In the West, although the Balbi of Gades rise high before 'colonial' Romans even begin to make their mark, the latter eventually reach the top, in the persons of Trajan and Hadrian.[3] In the East, the Roman families were satisfied with local life, if not completely absorbed into that life. Granii of Puteoli established themselves on Delos and families of this name are found later scattered through the East. When Germanicus and Agrippina visited Lesbos in 18 A.D. and Agrippina became honorary gymnasiarch, M. Granius Carbo, living at Mytilene with his Greek wife, was ὑπογυμνασίαρχος to her; this hellenized Roman, who held other offices in Mytilene, is typical of the eastern Romans in the early Principate.[4]

Local benefactors: None of the inscriptions can be assigned with certainty to the Republican period; but the Cloatii of Gytheon and the Aufidii of Tenos may have had their counterparts in Anatolia even in that age.

On Chios, as has been seen, relations between Romans and natives were comparatively good even in the age of the first Mithridatic war. A decree in honour of L. Nassius and his family reveals considerable care on his part and on the part of the Chians for the precise fulfilment of his wishes as benefactor of the community; he had endowed the city with capital, the interest of which was to be used for a specific purpose (lost through mutilation of the inscription), and the decree carefully safeguards the money and its use.[5] This L. Nassius, obviously a

---

[1] For full discussion of these people, their individual careers and importance as a class of men, see Bowersock *Augustus and the Greek World*, more especially 7 ff. and 30 ff.

[2] Magie, appendix II, 'Provincial Dignitaries', 1601 ff.

[3] See R. Syme *Tacitus* 603 ff. (especially 604) for detailed genealogical investigations.

[4] *I.G.* XII(2)258.

[5] *I.G.R.* IV.1703. Text discussed and assigned to first century B.C. by Josef Keil *Jahreshefte des österr. arch. Instituts* xiv (1911) Beiblatt 54.

man of great local importance, was also a benefactor, as the inscription indicates, of the local Romans.

At Cyme near Phocaea L. Vaccius L. f. Aemilia Labeo was gymnasiarch to the city. During his term he restored the gymnasium, erected new baths for the young men, and endowed them, turning the revenues of an agricultural property to their upkeep. The Aeolic inscription attesting his benefactions is interesting not only for the lavish honours accorded the bene-factor, but because he rejects some as not suitable for a mortal man.[1] Insisting on this at some length, the inscription declares

τὰν . . . ὑπερβάρεα καὶ θέοισι καὶ τοῖς ἰσοθέοισι ἁρμόζοισαν, τὰς τε τῶ ναύω κατειρώσιος τὰς τε τῶ κτίστα προσωνυμασίας, τείμαν παρητήσατο, ἀρκέην νομίζων τὰν κρίσιν τῶ πλάθεος . . .

This was in the middle years of Augustus' Principate; well might Vaccius reject such honours!

In the same period C. Sextilius P. f. Pollio, a Roman resident at Ephesus, built an aqueduct for the Ephesians dedicating it to Ephesian Artemis, Augustus and Tiberius, and the city.[2] Sex-tilius' family may have been established some long time in Ephesus; his is one of these names found first on Delos and then in other parts of the Roman East—as is that of his wife, Ofellia.

A. Aemilius Zosimus came to Priene as a ξενὸς. He was made a Prienean, held the highest offices, and was a lavish benefactor of the community. When responsible for the young men's gymnasium, he reorganized its activities, made the baths free of charge, furnished oil from sunrise to nightfall, and increased the number of contests; as 'supervisor of the boys' education', he added to their sports contests in rhetoric and literature. Re-warded at the end of his career with extravagant honours, Zosimus may never have seen Italy, but have been a freedman of Greek or Greco-oriental origin.[3] Where this type of Roman citizen—for such Zosimus was—had a dominating position in local life, and where the Roman settlers sat at his lavish enter-

---

[1] *C.I.G.* II.3524.
[2] *C.I.L.* III.424, with 14194, a bilingual inscription.
[3] See *I. von P.* 112-14. The involved and prolix style unfortunately rules out quotation from these valuable documents; there is an excellent summary of Zosimus' activities in Magie I.256. He is styled Σέξτου, so it is not apparent whether he was a freedman or an *ingenuus*.

tainments alongside citizens of Priene and the various classes of foreign resident, the tone must have tended to break down aloofness between Romans and natives. Unfortunately this inscription cannot be dated closely.

There may then, already in the late Republic, have been four factors making for the reconciliation of the provincial Romans and the native inhabitants of the East: the efforts of certain governors to mitigate the exploitation of the Greeks by *publicani* and moneylenders, culminating in Caesar's measures of 48 B.C.; the rising status resulting for Greek communities and individuals from political competition for their support; the activities of local Roman benefactors; growing sympathy on the part of Roman settlers for Greek culture and ways of life, corresponding to the philhellenic trend in Italy itself. These are not likely to have been as important as the general reform of provincial government and treatment of provincials achieved by Augustus, but are likely to have made his work easier. The progress of reconciliation cannot indeed be traced through the years; but it is apparent in the early Principate that a great change has taken place. This is clear, on the side of the native provincials, from the strong interest they now take in acquiring Roman citizenship and in playing a part in the administration of the Empire; as concerns the settlers, it appears from their interest in local offices and local distinctions, and—equally important— from their penetration, in the early Principate, into regions where they had never settled before.

o

CHAPTER XIII

THE PROVINCIAL ROMANS AS SEEN BY OTHER ROMANS

SOME Romans with provincial affairs lived in Italy, but travelled frequently to attend to their business overseas. It will have been largely through these that the provincial Romans were kept in contact with their fellows at home. Such contacts are obvious and certain; but little appears about them in the authors. The rich provincial-Roman banker or merchant would find his language, in the social-moral sense, talked by his own kind in Rome or Puteoli or Brundisium. It is difficult to guess how he really appeared to the noble, whether the sort who, as a governor, would cynically serve his interests, or the sort who might try to check him; but it is notable that Cicero's public regard for the *equester ordo*—for which he had the strongest political reasons—does not rule his private feelings about the provincial element in that *ordo*.

In the speeches, when occasion arises, provincial Romans are mentioned with honour as a distinguished body of men of great importance to the country, and a point is made, whenever possible, of treating the *publicani* with much respect; many of the *litterae commendaticiae*[1] are on behalf of *negotiatores* overseas desiring his interest with governors or others in positions of authority, and might at first glance suggest that he found such men congenial. But these letters, when read in number, are depressingly stereotyped in their language (as Cicero was himself aware), and the reader finds a very different tone about the eastern provincial Romans in the private letter of advice to Quintus in 60 B.C.[2]

The passage has been quoted in full. The provincial Romans —Cicero could not be more emphatic—are men who 'pecuniae cupiditate adducti careant his rebus omnibus a quibus nos divulsi esse non possumus'; who 'omnes vias pecuniae norunt et omnia pecuniae causa faciunt'. They have no interest in anyone,

---

[1] *ad Fam.* XIII consists entirely of such letters.   [2] *ad Q.f.* I.I.15.

unless he can help them, and so hardly ever care a scrap for a private individual, but pretend the greatest affection for any provincial governor: '. . . privatum non fere quemquam, praetores semper omnes amant'. As they do not care a scrap for others, they are not interested in the good name of another: '. . . quicum victuri non sunt, eius existimationi consulere non curant'. If these strictures are fair to the majority of provincial Romans in the East, preoccupation with money and property will explain why they made little mark, individually or collectively, except in matters directly affecting their material interests.

But obviously not all provincial Romans were of this character. Those who made generous benefactions to Greek communities were presumably generous towards their fellow Roman residents. C. Rabirius Postumus, a typical great *negotiator* (though he did not settle in the East), did not hug his wealth to himself, if Cicero's words are to be believed in the speech in his defence:

multa gessit, multa contraxit, magnas partis habuit publicorum; credidit populis; in pluribus provinciis eius versata res est; . . . nec interea locupletare amicos umquam suos destitit, mittere in negotium, dare partis, augere re, fide sustentare.[1]

He was as generous as rich, and, whatever the motives of his generosity may have been, he was not one of the mere unprepossessing money-grubbers of Cicero's letter to Quintus. Equally remote from the strictures of that letter was the good friend of Cicero, M'. Curius, a well-to-do *negotiator* who removed from Rome to Patrae in Achaea at the outbreak of civil war so as not to get involved. The perfect host to Cicero, whenever he had need of his hospitality, devoted to his interests as to those of Atticus, full of solicitude for Tiro when he had to be left ill at Patrae during Cicero's homeward journey in 50, he was also a man of educated tastes, interested in Cicero's literary work, and himself, in Cicero's opinion, a wit whom Rome could ill spare.[2] It would seem that Curius' departure for Greece or something

---

[1] *pro Rabirio Postumo* 4.

[2] His hospitality to Cicero and his devotion to him and to Atticus, *ad Fam.* VII.30.1; XIII.17.1; 50.1. His care for Tiro, XVI.4.2; 5.1; 9.3 f.; 11.1. His interest in Cicero's work, VII.28.2. His wit, VII.31.2, 'veni igitur quaeso, ne tamen semen urbanitatis una cum republica intereat'.

in his conduct there made him *persona non grata* to Caesar, and that the letters of commendation written on his behalf by Cicero to Servius Sulpicius (governor of Greece in 46) saved him from serious trouble or calamity. His brief letter thanking Cicero is given at the end of this chapter; the only example of a letter from a provincial *negotiator*, it is interesting both for its liveliness, its easy, somewhat slangy expressions, and the way in which it combines an antithesis from stock Greek philosophizing with Roman business language.[1]

Perhaps of the same type as M'. Curius were T. Manlius of Thespiae, much liked by Cicero and a man of interests after his heart,[2] L. Saufeius, the Epicurean friend of Atticus who took up permanent residence at Athens,[3] and Curtius Mithres, freedman of Rabirius Postumus and host of Cicero at Ephesus, whom Cicero recommends to the provincial governor in a manner unusually convincing by its simplicity.[4] So it may be, despite the strictures of Cicero's letter to Quintus, that the better sort of provincial Romans had, in their way, something like Atticus' combination of qualities: prudence, business acumen, shrewd neutrality in politics, genuine culture, a limited and local, but not merely pretended, benevolence, and care for friends, present and absent.

The provincial Roman invoking Cicero's influence with a governor was usually anxious for a favourable decision in a law case, or tax-farming dispute or difficulty. But powerful help from Rome was needed sometimes in much graver matters. Thus M'. Curius had to use the influence of Cicero with the governor of Greece in some danger threatening his civil life and fortunes. L. Saufeius, who lived in Athens, but retained valuable possessions in Italy, would have lost all these in the proscriptions of the second Triumvirate, but for the prompt and energetic intervention of his friend, Atticus: '. . . Attici labore atque industria factum est ut eodem nuntio Saufeius fieret certior se patrimonium amisisse et recuperasse'.[5] Cicero's *clientela* included, as well as provincial *negotiatores*, their *clientes* and

---

[1] *ad Fam.* VII.29, to be read with 28.1 f. and 30.2.
[2] Ibid., XIII.22.1. 'T. Manlium, qui negotiatur Thespiis, vehementer diligo. Nam et semper me coluit diligentissimeque observavit, et a studiis nostris non abhorret'.
[3] See *P-W* 'Saufeius' (5) 256 f.   [4] *ad Fam.* XIII.69.
[5] Nepos *Atticus* 12.3.

freedmen. His relation with one of these men is of particular interest. M. Aemilius Avianius, settled in Sicyon, had an establishment there in which craftsmen produced sculpture for the market. He had another such in Athens, where his client, C. Avianius Evander, carried out, or directed, work in premises belonging to C. Memmius, who divided the years 53–48 between Athens and Mytilene. M. Aemilius Avianius, the head of the concern, was absent from Sicyon from 51 or earlier, staying at Carian Cibyra till 46.[1] He may already have left Sicyon, when in early 52 Memmius found it inconvenient that Evander should continue occupying the Athenian premises and gave his tenant harsh and abrupt notice, in a manner consonant with his attitude to Patro and the Epicureans of Athens. Cicero appealed to Memmius on behalf of Evander in a brief letter, which ran:[2]

C. Avianio Evandro, qui habitat in tuo sacrario, et ipso multum utor, et patrono eius M. Aemilio familiarissime. Peto igitur a te in maiorem modum, quod sine tua molestia fiat, ut ei de habitatione accommodes. Nam propter opera instituta multa multorum subitum est ei remigrare Kal. Quint. Impedior verecundia, ne te pluribus verbis rogem; neque tamen dubito, quin, si tua nihil aut non multum intersit, eo sis animo quo ego essem, si quid tu me rogares. Mihi certe gratissimum feceris.

Removal to new quarters, with many orders incomplete, was bound to cause Evander trouble and delay deliveries to customers. M. Aemilius Avianius, his patron, was perhaps a man of some provincial standing; yet he and Evander cut little ice with Memmius, and Cicero in his appeal is timid and tentative.

The case of M. Mindius of Elis and his wife, Oppia, suggests the way in which it might be useful to have a friend influential in the courts at Rome.[3] M. Mindius, who was a *negotiator*, died, and his half-brother, L. Mescinius, claimed his property, or the bulk of it, as lawful heir. The widow Oppia tried to secure part, and Mescinius, who had been Cicero's quaestor in Cilicia and was on close terms with him, told him (accurately or not) that she had 'fraudulently appropriated what did not belong to her'; he persuaded Cicero to intervene with Servius Sulpicius as provincial governor. Cicero wrote to Sulpicius, suggesting, in

[1] *ad Fam.* XIII.21.1.
[2] Ibid., XIII.2.
[3] Ibid., XIII.26 and 28.

suitable terms, that if Oppia and those associated with her were
reluctant to settle the matter out of court in a manner agreeable
to Mescinius, he should make it clear that he would send the case
for trial at Rome: this, Cicero was confident, would bring
Oppia to reason. The outcome is unknown; but it is again clear
that a provincial Roman was fortunate to have friends at Rome.

Note: Letter from M'. Curius of Patrae to Cicero, 45 B.C. (ad Fam.
VII.29)

S.v.b.; sum enim χρήσει μέν tuus, κτήσει δέ Attici nostri. Ergo
fructus est tuus, mancipium illius; quod quidem si inter senes coemp-
tionales venale proscripserit, egerit non multum. At illa nostra
praedicatio quanti est, nos, quod simus, quod habeamus, quod
homines existimemur, id omne abs te habere! Quare, Cicero mi,
persevera constanter nos conservare et Sulpici successori nos de
meliore nota commenda, quo facilius tuis praeceptis obtemperare
possimus, teque ad ver libentes videre et nostra refigere depor-
tareque tuto possimus. Sed, amice magne, noli hanc epistulam
Attico ostendere; sine eum errare et putare me virum bonum esse
nec solere duo parietes de eadem fidelia dealbare. Ergo, patrone mi,
bene vale, Tironemque meum saluta nostris verbis. Data a.d. III K.
Nov.[1]

[1] For comments on the language of this letter, Tyrrell and Purser *The*
Correspondence of Cicero v² p. 205 f.

INDEX

The incidence in the East of numerous names of typically Roman (as distinct from Italian) character is discussed in chapters VIII and X, p. 109f (Delos) and p. 152f (eastern provinces generally); mere inclusion of a particular name in the lists on those pages did not seem to call for its inclusion here. Italian (Oscan, etc.) names are fully indexed.